CW01151549

BACK TO EARTH

Rachel Sirtor,
July 99
7HB

BACK TO EARTH

South Africa's environmental challenges

James Clarke

SOUTHERN
BOOK PUBLISHERS

This book is dedicated to the memory of
Thomas Chalmers Robertson,
father of South African environmental journalism.

Copyright © 1991 by James Clarke

All rights reserved. No part of this publication may be reproduced or transmitted in any form or by any means without prior written permission from the publisher.

ISBN 1 86812 368 5

First edition, first impression 1991

Published by
Southern Book Publishers (Pty) Ltd
PO Box 3103, Halfway House, 1685

Cover design by Insight Graphics
Illustrations by Julie Clarke
Book design by IMPRESSUM, Cape
Set in 11$^{1}/_{2}$ on 13 pt Hanover
by Unifoto
Printed and bound by National Book Printers, Cape

Acknowledgements

Any book is the product of many people and it would certainly be impossible to thank everybody who helped and inspired me through this book. I can only record my indebtedness to *The Star* newspaper which, 20 years ago when John Jordi was editor, agreed to my request to embark on an environmental awareness campaign in South Africa. We launched CARE, a neat acronym which hid a rather clumsy battle cry: Cleaner Air Rivers and Environment. For most of the last 14 years Harvey Tyson, editor-in-chief until the end of 1990, encouraged my efforts and was one of the first editors in the world to see "environment" as hard news like politics and crime.

I owe a huge debt of thanks to scores of people outside the newspaper industry: there is Ian Player, a friend for 30 years, who kept me in touch with basic values which, as an urban man, I might have lost; Clem Sunter of Anglo American Corporation who helped bridge the gap between environmental concerns and economics; several civil engineers also taught me a great deal despite some heated differences – I think instantly of Eric Hall and Cliff Macmillan, but there were many more. In Government too, despite sometimes fierce differences, I owe a great deal to the forbearance of people such as Bill Visagie, Theuns van Rensburg, Dr Mike Cohen, and many others.

Among academics who, over the years, corrected me and helped mould my opinions are professors Phillip Tobias, the late Raymond Dart, Peter Tyson, Desmond Midgley, Nick Patricios, John Muller, Harold Annergarn, John Earle (who is always particularly helpful), John Skinner, Richard Fuggle, Andre Rabie, Roelf Botha, Revil Mason and John Hanks.

There were so many others ... my secretary, Jenny Webber, Dale Baker of the United States Information Service, Arend Hoogervorst, Geoff Craig, Japhta Lekgetho, Stan Verrier, Gys du Plessis, Clive Walker, Dr John Ledger, Jon Hobbs, Andre van Heerden, Gareth Singleton, Nigel Mandy and Dr Barry Senior. I am grateful to *The Star*'s librarians under Sheilagh Watt – particularly the ever-patient Shirley Oakes – and for the help received from the librarians of the

Argus (Cape Town) and *Daily News* (Durban). (Many of the drawings are based on photographs by staff photographers of these newspapers.) I thank, too, the Panos Institute in London, the Worldwatch Institute in Washington and the Urban Foundation in Johannesburg.

Inevitably the family became involved: I owe a great debt to Mary-Rose Nourse who rescued me more than once when my personal computer failed to behave as advertised; Vic Kabalin of Fish Hoek who introduced me to the delights of fishing in False Bay and to the tragedy now threatening south-western Cape; my own daughters, Jennifer and Julie, one a plant pathologist and the other a town planner – both enthusiasts. Julie did the drawings in this book. And then there is my wife, Lenka, who has grown used to my long, hermit-like retreats into my study.

I value the encouragement of Basil van Rooyen, an old friend, who now heads Southern, the firm which published this book, and Rita van Dyk (commissioning editor) and Catherine Murray for their professionalism and helpfulness.

Finally there was Thomas Chalmers Robertson to whose memory this book is dedicated. "TC", whose enormous humour and rolling phrases I greatly miss, introduced me to holism, something he had learned from the master himself – Jan Smuts. I am privileged to have known him.

James Clarke

Sandton 1991

Preface

When you are privileged to view the Earth from afar, when you can hold out your thumb and cover it with your thumbnail, you realise that we are really, all of us around the world, crew members on the space station Earth. Of all the accomplishments of technology, perhaps the most signficant one was the picture of the Earth over the lunar horizon. If nothing else, it should impress our fellow man with the absolute fact that our environment is bounded, that our resources are limited, and that our life support system is a closed cycle. And, of course, when this space station Earth is viewed from 240 000 miles away, only its beauty, its minuteness, and its isolation in the blackness of space, are apparent. A traveller from some far planet would not know that the size of the crew is already too large and threatening to expand, that the breathing system is rapidly becoming polluted, and that the water supply is in danger of contamination with everything from DDT to raw sewage. The only real recourse is for each of us to realise that the elements we have are not inexhaustible. We're all in the same spaceship.

Frank Borman
ASTRONAUT

Contents

Chapter 1	THE NATURE OF THE BEAST	1
	The overkill syndrome	3
	The tragedy of the commons	6
	The point of no return	8
Chapter 2	THE INSANE EXPERIMENT	15
	Good story, bad publicity	17
	The frog in the pot	21
	Ah, but I don't inhale	25
	The killer ingredient	26
	The tall stacks	32
	Is sulphur good for the soil?	38
	The Soweto dilemma	39
	Something in the air	41
	The sick building syndrome	42
	Asbestos fibres	44
Chapter 3	THE GREENHOUSE EFFECT	47
Chapter 4	THE HOLE IN THE OZONE	60
Chapter 5	TREES TO THE RESCUE	66
	The Faustian bargain	71
Chapter 6	A BILLION MOBILE CHEMICAL PLANTS	77
Chapter 7	WHO CARES FOR THE PUBLIC?	85
	The secret pollutants	91
	Playing for time	92
	An international law?	94
Chapter 8	FICKLE RIVERS	96
Chapter 9	THE BIG DRINKERS	104
	The Great Drought	108
Chapter 10	SQUEEZING THE SPONGE	113
	Second-hand water	120
	Dying lakes	128
	Paying through the hose	133
	Who should control water?	135
Chapter 11	THE LAST RESOURCE	136
	Freshwater fish	148
	Coastal development	148

Chapter 12	THE RED BLOOD OF THE EARTH	152
	Cities buried by sand 154	
Chapter 13	THE DEATH OF THE FORESTS	160
	The search for Supertree 170	
Chapter 14	THE TRAGEDY OF THE PLATTELAND	175
	The extent of the damage 186	
	Industry versus agriculture 197	
Chapter 15	SILENT SPRING 199	
	Fertilisers: getting more from less 210	
Chapter 16	VARIETY, THE SPICE OF LIFE 212	
	The big five and others 214	
	Endangered wildlife 215	
	State lottery 217	
	National parks 226	
	The flora 232	
	The threats 233	
	The future 236	
Chapter 17	POPULATION: THE WILD CARD 242	
	The population explosion 246	
	The urban contraceptive 251	
	The AIDS pandemic 256	
Chapter 18	THE BUILT ENVIRONMENT 260	
	Designing cities 263	
	Open spaces 270	
	The human scale 273	
	King Car 280	
	Noise pollution 287	
	Inside-out cities 290	
	The squatters 291	
Chapter 19	WASTE: SPACE AGE OR GARB-AGE 293	
	Dumps, tomorrow's mines 299	
	Recycling 302	
	Inexhaustible oil wells? 311	
Chapter 20	THE UNTROD YEARS 314	
	The Minister of Nothing 316	
	Back to Earth 321	

Further Reading   322

Index   325

1 The nature of the beast

Nature does not care whether the hunter slays the beast or the beast the hunter. She will make good compost of them both and her ends are prospered which ever succeeds.

John Burroughs

IT was fashionable in the 1960s and for much of the 70s to believe that man was born a killer and that, if not actually doomed to destroy himself, he was, at best, a hopeless case. It fitted the mood of the time. We had, in the first half of the twentieth century, fought two world wars and now the arsenals of the East and West contained enough nuclear arms to destroy the world many times over. There were, and still are, opposing fleets of nuclear submarines made up of vessels each capable of causing as much death and destruction as was caused during the six years of World War II.

Robert Ardrey, playwright turned anthropologist, with solid backing from Raymond Dart, the South African discoverer of the man apes, popularised the "born killer" theory in his *African Genesis* in 1961.

> *Not in innocence ... was mankind born. The home of our fathers was that African highland reaching north from the Cape to the lakes of the Nile. Here we came about - slowly, ever so slowly -on a sky-swept savannah glowing with menace ... Children of all animal kind, we inherited many a social nicety as well as the predator's way. But the most significant of all our gifts, as things turned out, was the legacy bequeathed us by the killer apes, our immediate forebears. Even in the first long days of our beginnings we held in our hand the weapon, an instrument somewhat older than ourselves.*

In 1977 Richard Leakey, the Kenyan fossil hunter, expressed the thought in his book, *Origins*, that man must have had a more basic instinct than a killer instinct. He suggested it was co-operation. That, surely, was it. After all, you could be the most dedicated killer in the world but try living naked in the veld and running down an antelope for dinner. No, humans survived because they learned to hunt as a team. Fangless and clawless though they were they were able to stand together on that savannah "glowing with menace".

Ironically, one of the greatest feats of co-operation is war itself. But one must note that the average man needs careful political conditioning by way of constant propaganda before he is prepared to fight other men to the death. Man is a hunter by instinct, not an aggressive killer. The act of hunting must never be confused with aggression. A lion does not kill an impala out of hate. A fox has nothing against chickens.

Co-operation is a fundamental instinct and it is this instinct which is helping us cope with the third great crisis of our existence. Humanity's first was when, as man apes, we were forced to abandon the retreating forests and compete with the great predators out on the plains. We had to learn to compete with the sabre-toothed tiger and run down fleet-footed plains animals and, by developing our co-operative instinct, we succeeded. Our second great crisis was when, as fully developed *Homo sapiens*, we began to live in organised settlements and grow our own food. This took a new order of co-operation. The third great crisis was the twentieth century. In this watershed century humankind moved away from being predominantly rural to becoming irrevocably metropolitan – the ultimate test of our talent for co-operation.

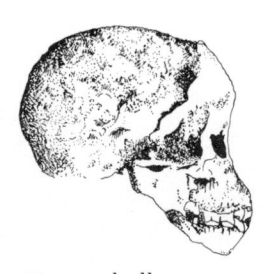

Taung skull

The overkill syndrome

My faithful old *New Imperial Dictionary*, being of 1950s vintage, doesn't list the word "overkill" but most post-60s dictionaries do: "Overkill – to obliterate with more nuclear force than required". One can though, use the word to describe the way South Africans kill snakes. They tend to take a large stick and flatten the animal until its remains are spread over a carpet-sized area. But right now I want to use the word "overkill" to describe a compulsion which drives most people to take far more than they need whenever they are faced with the opportunity. I believe, like all predators, we have an overkill compulsion.

A silly, but useful example of overkill is how people take peppermints when they leave a restaurant. Personally, I take just one. Offering peppermints, I recognise, is just a little gesture by restaurateurs and I'd hate to abuse it. But many seemingly nice people I know take a whole handful. They take a handful because the peppermints are free. The thought never occurs to them that maybe they will kill a good thing and that restaurants will one day withdraw the custom because people abuse it. You will also witness the overkill instinct during the Natal "sardine run" – a winter phenomenon when millions of sardines come swarming up the South African coast. Quite ordinary people appear to go berserk and rush into the breakers, women with shopping bags and men with beer crates, scooping up the fish and filling their car boots or simply dumping them on the beach. Afterwards, when the air grows foul with the smell of fish

Natal "sardine run"

dumped quietly in the night by people who caught far more than they needed, many wonder what possessed them.

The overkill instinct has had profound effects on the story of man, on natural history and on the planetary environment.

It is not peculiar to humans. Nor is it unnatural. Take a lion in the bush. It rushes out of hiding and kills a wildebeest. The survivors flee and the big cat begins to eat. It has no desire to kill more than one. What seems to happen is that when the others rush away, leaving the lion to throttle its victim, the lion's killer instinct switches off. There is nothing left to stimulate it. But put that same lion in a cattle kraal and it will try to kill every head of cattle in that kraal. A fox will do the same inside a chicken coop even though it cannot possibly eat all the chickens it kills. Yet under normal circumstances a fox will kill but one animal. It is simply that the chickens, or the cattle in the kraal, are unable to flee – so the fox's and the lion's killer instinct remains "on".

Professor Paul S Martin of the University of Arizona, in the 1960s, wrote of "the Pleistocene overkill". He suggested that when the first humans entered North America and found that the mastodons and mammoths, and the other large animals, did not run away at their approach – why should they run from such a puny little creature who hardly came above their kneecaps? – they wiped them out. They massacred not just individual species but whole groups of species. Whole genera were to disappear as man progressed down the length of the Americas. It was easy. Not quite as easy as taking peppermints but still easy. These little men were in fact highly skilled plains hunters and carried the most advanced weapon of the day – the fluted spear. When they crossed over the newly exposed Alaskan landbridge they caught the large beasts flat-footed. One can trace the extinctions all the way down the Americas and they keep step with the advance of *Homo sapiens.*

Dodo

Similarly, when Europeans began colonising islands across the world, the animals quickly succumbed. The dodo, the solitaire, the moa – nearly all the extinctions in recent history have been island species, each caught off guard by the sudden appearance of man. Each a victim of overkill.

Why did this tide of overkill not happen in Africa where *Homo* had been around for 2 million years? It was because the beasts of Africa had watched man emerge from the bipedal stone-thrower into a more and more efficient hunter. As man's weaponry improved so the animals learned to pull back. Each animal has its "flight distance", the distance at which it decides to flee when approached by a predator, and the animals of Africa simply increased their flight distance commensurate with the range of each new missile. The overkill in Africa did not come until the white man suddenly appeared carrying a long range gun. Only then did elephants become easy meat. Only then did the peppermint factor enter the picture.

Overkill has played such a central role in the history of man's handling of his environmental income and in his dealings with his animal contemporaries that it must be viewed as a force of considerable ecological significance. Yet, as I have said, man's obsessive overkill instinct does not make him unnatural. But it is something we have to understand and recognise, for it can become the death of us. We are creating an intensely urban environment for ourselves in which so many goods are being concentrated that our predatory instinct (our consumer desires) is being overstimulated. From childhood this instinct is constantly being excited by loud radio and television commercials designed by minds carefully trained in the psychology of marketing; as we walk down the street we see neon signs, posters, hoardings, skilfully dressed shop windows, all not merely begging us to buy, but convincing us that we *need* these things. The artificially stimulated consumer desires of the immature and of the unsophisticated cannot possibly be satisfied and thus urban society is riven by frustration. Look how an urban mob's first act is to loot shop windows.

The tragedy of the commons

Another natural flaw in man's behaviour pattern has been described by Garrett Hardin as "the tragedy of the commons". In an essay under that title, published in *Science* in (December 1968), Hardin wrote:

> *The tragedy of the commons develops in this way. Picture a pasture open to all. It is to be expected that each herdsman will try to keep as many cattle as possible on the commons. Such an arrangement will work reasonably satisfactorily for centuries because tribal wars, poaching, and disease keep the numbers of both man and beast well below the carrying capacity of the land. Finally, however, comes the day of reckoning, that is, the day when the long-desired goal of social stability becomes a reality. At this point, the inherent logic of the commons remorselessly generates tragedy.*

He goes on to describe how each herdsman is tempted to add one more head of his own cattle. "What difference does one more make?" he says to himself. All the other herders are, of course, doing the same thing. The common becomes overgrazed. "Each man," says Hardin, "is locked into a system that *compels* him to increase his herd without limit. Ruin is the destination to which all men rush." The emphasis on the word "compels" is mine for here is a manifestation of overkill. The commons are of value to everyone, and of value to nobody.

Hardin believes "freedom in the commons brings ruin to all." The costly failure of the Russian collective farm system seems to bear him out, as do the overgrazed, eroded, cattle-packed hillsides of Zululand. Hardin's herdsmen could well be industrialists. Left to their own devices they are quite likely to turn the tragedy of the commons into the tragedy of the atmosphere. So many industrialists perceive the air as a common dumping ground for pollutants. The individual industrialist has no intention of wrecking the atmosphere and, in fact, tends to derive comfort and justification from the fact that his contribution is only a minor one compared with the collective result. Yet another example of both the "tragedy" and overkill is the fishing industry which, because it is able to fish without much fear of surveillance, is notorious for its abuse of the marine common. As a result South Africa's fishing resources, as we shall see in a later chapter, have been appallingly damaged.

But Hardin is overly pessimistic because this type of situation, once it reaches a certain point, has been known to spur man's co-operative instinct and stimulate him into getting together with his fellow "herdsmen" and working out a set of agreements or laws, not simply to control greedy individuals but to control his own admitted weaknesses. The Law of the Sea is an example and so is the world moratorium on whaling and on trading ivory, and the Montreal protocol which set curbs on the use of CFC's (chlorofluorocarbons) in areosol containers and refrigerant gases. International laws ... now *there* is co-operation!

The point of no return

Laws are an urban invention. They boil down to a code of ethics which made sharing the restricted urban environment possible. It lays down the day to day rules which, essentially, try to curb the overkill instinct and protect the peppermints.

The pressures and new realities of urban life are forcing us to refine the rules by which civilisation can flourish. Urbanisation has many advantages. Two of the most important are that it relieves population pressure on farmland and it has a birth control effect. Urban populations do not explode because of higher birth rates, they grow because of influx. Few cities have grown much from their own fertility. Cities are better able to provide primary health care which reduces child death rates; this, in turn, induces parents to have fewer children. In fact, in the urban environment, large families can become a problem as far as accommodation is concerned (one cannot simply build another hut) and as far as cost is concerned.

"God made the country, and man made the town," wrote William Cowper. Jane Jacobs, in her fascinating book, *The*

It maybe hard to believe but man's basic instinct is probably to co-operate. The international Law of the Sea to conserve the oceans is a prime instance. Picture shows a "Floating Instrument Platform" (Flip), an ocean explorer which operates bows down. (Source: The Star)

Economy of Cities (1969), tends to question Cowper's neat axiom by arguing that towns made the countryside what it is. Cities, she avows, came before farms. She suggested that about 9 000 years ago a group of people, possibly on the Anatolian plateau of Turkey, learned how to fashion obsidian, a black glasslike substance found on some volcanoes, into knives and scrapers. This would have represented a great leap in technology. The group settled in a particular spot and began to trade their artefacts for meat, grain and other vegetable matter. After a while, the toolmakers, who in time would probably have been joined by basket and bag-makers, would have demanded live meat and would quickly have learned that some animals were more easily subdued than others and could be kept for long periods in pens where they would become settled enough to breed. This type of settlement, "New Obsidian" as Jacobs called her imaginary first town, would also help to explain how grain cultivation was such a sudden event. New Obsidian would have received its wild grain from all points of the compass, and from all kinds of grass species. The baskets would have spilled over and, in a short time, produced some useful fat-grained hybrids which the New Obsidianites would have scattered just beyond the settlement and, perhaps, used children and the less skilled to chase away the birds, and eventually harvest the crop. The first farms were born – an invention of the city.

The pattern of urban initiative in agriculture persists to this day. The tractor was the invention, not of a farmer, but of urban man. So was the next most important appliance in food production, the refrigerator. Today the most agriculturally advanced countries are the most industrialised. The countries least able to feed themselves are the essentially rural ones.

Although cities may date back 9 000 years they were never really big. Jericho and the other great cities of the Bible were only a few hectares. Jericho itself was 5 hectares and accommodated 30 000 people at most. Today's huge megalopolises are a very recent phenomenon.

At the beginning of this century there were only 1,5 billion people on Earth. By 1991 there were 5,3 billion. At the beginning of the century 80 per cent of Europe lived in villages or small market towns. Today 80 per cent live in metropolitan areas.

In 1980 South Africa reached a critical point in its development – its population became 50 per cent urbanised. We discuss in a later chapter Professor Wilfred Mallows's theory that in every developed country's history this 50 per cent threshold is the point of no return and that, inevitably, as a nation tips over into becoming an urbanised state its population growth begins levelling off. There seems to be a ceiling to urbanisation which is somewhere above 85 per cent. West

Germany is 85 per cent urbanised, while Sweden and Belgium are 87 and The Netherlands 89. Britain is 91 per cent. Each of these countries has reached zero population growth.

It is a popular view that metropolitan man is an aberration, that we were not meant to live this way. Yet, when you consider it, totally urbanised man – the sort who lives in an air-conditioned apartment on the fifth floor and who microwaves prepared foods and communicates by fax – is a perfectly natural animal just like a mouse ... or a lion if you prefer.

One must also accept that no matter how our cities look, they too are natural. After all, they evolved along straightforward lines to fulfil natural needs. Apartment blocks are found in nature as anybody who has seen the multichambered nest of the sociable weavers will testify. Termites invented highrise and air-conditioning millions of years before man was around; bats had sonar long before the SA Navy, and the water-squirting archer fish had ground-to-air missiles, and the fat, sluggish tick had cottoned on to intercontinental air travel by riding on the backs of migrating swallows.

Man's destiny is to live largely in metropolitan environments. It is inevitable. Cities have evolved as a natural course of man's home-making drive – yesterday a group of grasshuts, today Mexico City. Despite imperfections which need to be urgently addressed, metropolitan living is a logical and sustainable conclusion for a creature which is not only highly gregarious but is intelligent enough to find a million ways of making itself comfortable. Highrise apartment areas are agglomerations of nests made of nothing more unnatural than minerals from the earth. The family car, or even the turbo-assisted Porsche 959, is a natural progression of man's desire to get about. Bulldozers are natural too, being just super-shovels to augment the scooping capacity of our hands. The lifting capacity of a big tower crane helps us move 10 ton girders without grunting. When you analyse it, even the supersonic, multi-nuclear-headed intercontinental ballistic missile which can vaporise cities is but a super spear – with a touch of overkill about it.

What then has happened to urban man? Why does he pollute? Why is he so complacent about the rape of the Earth, the collapse of soils, the plundering of the seas? Are we perhaps going through a hiatus caused by the bewilderingly rapid growth of metropolitan areas? Have we lost touch with the reality of what lies beyond the urban edge – the fields upon which we are so utterly dependent? Alvin Toffler put it best in *Future Shock* (1970): we are unable to cope with the rapidity of change, he said. We are in abrupt collision with the future. We are suffering from "future shock". Our reaction is to leave things to the politicians, but now we can see the politicians are equally bewildered and few have the courage, or mental capacity, to think beyond the next election.

Education should be helping but educationists too have been caught unprepared. Look only at how shallowly most schools teach children about nature. Young people come away knowing all about stamens and pistils and the alimentary system of the frog, but totally unaware that their own survival depends on nature and on nothing else. The Natal conservationist, Ian Player, once said: "The study of nature should be the study of survival."

From the dawn of Jane Jacobs's New Obsidian until the dawn of this century, cities were human scale. Jericho, Mohenjo Daro, Sofala ... all of their citizens would have been able to smell when a drought gripped the land, just as they would have been able to appreciate the aroma of wet earth and of harvest time. All knew where their food came from. All were in touch with the reality of nature. Only in the last 50 or 60 years have there been children who grew up not knowing milk came from cows.

I have often wondered why the New Testament ignores nature conservation. Somebody suggested it was because the New Testament was directed at urban people living in Jericho-sized cities and they did not need to be told the obvious. After all, sheep and cattle wandered through town and, just beyond the city walls, were the fields. There was lots of environmental wisdom in the Old Testament anyway. The explanation is unsatisfactory. At the time of the New Testament the land of the Bible was steadily being wrecked by poor farming methods and the greed of despots. The period marked the beginning of the end for the cradle of agriculture. Today many of the cities of the Old Testament lie buried by desert sand. Where Babylon reaped two wheat crops a year there is now a wasteland.

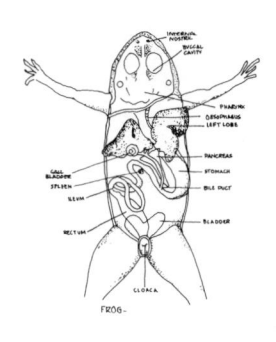

Lynn White Jnr, in his classical essay *The Historical Roots of Our Ecological Crisis*, wrote of how the Judaeo-Christian tradition had, by taking the Bible so literally, caused enormous destruction. It saw the Book of Genesis as giving humanity an open hunting licence. Did it not say we must "subdue" the Earth and "have dominion over all the fish of the sea, and over the fowl of the air, and over every living thing"? Too late the church authorities changed the words from reading "have dominion" to "have stewardship". Too late, because the missionaries had already done their work and their work, as they saw it, was to crush the pagan belief in nature and replace it with the Christian's view that nature is there for man's sake. White wrote:

> In antiquity every tree, every spring, every stream, every hill had its own genius loci, its guardian spirit. These spirits were accessible to men, but were very unlike men; centaurs, fauns and mermaids show their ambivalence. Before one cut a tree, mined a mountain, or dammed a brook it was important to placate the spirit in charge of that particular institution, and to keep it placated. By destroying pagan animism, Christianity made it possible to exploit nature in a mood of indifference.

Chief Seathl, in a letter to the US Government in 1855, spoke for millions of aboriginal people who believe that to worship nature is to worship God:

> One thing we know which the whiteman may one day discover. Our God is the same God . . .

The chief is also credited with the following:

> I have seen a thousand rotting buffaloes on the prairies, left by the whiteman who shot them from a passing train. I am a savage and I do not understand how the smoking iron horse can become more important than the buffalo that we kill only to stay alive. What is man without the beasts? If all the beasts were gone, men would die from great loneliness of spirit, for whatever happens to the beasts also happens to man. All things are connected. Whatever befalls the earth befalls the sons of the earth.

The Judaeo-Christian world must now adjust its view and understand that for all our turbo-assisted speed, for all our bulldozer strength and for all our nuclear spears, when stripped down to our soft skins, we are peculiarly defenceless animals. We were fashioned as a part of nature. We cannot repeal its laws.

We are animals. And whether it was yesterday, when we ran unexpectedly into a sabre-toothed tiger, or today when we may suddenly be confronted by a mugger, we still react like other mammals: the vestigial hairs on our back and neck become erect in a pathetic attempt to make us look bigger and fiercer; the palms of our hands and soles of our feet immediately begin to sweat to give us purchase should we opt for fleeing (the sweaty palms will help us swing to safety into the nearest municipal tree); the blood drains from our body surface making us go pale but at least saving us from losing too much blood should we sustain a flesh wound; and we may, involuntarily, dump the contents of our bladder and bowels to shed some weight – again to assist our flight from the scene.

Make no mistake, we are animals, and whatever we have invented to increase our stature, whatever we have done to rearrange the global scenery, nature still claims us in the end, with a terrible indifference. She will, as John Burroughs wrote, "make good compost of us all". And (as I wrote in *Our Fragile Land* in 1974) should our species one day fail entirely, nature would, without pause or sentiment, wrap up her elaborate *Homo sapiens* experiment. Her fishmoths would move in to eat our great works of art and our literature and all our grand philosophies; her white ants would swallow our woodwork and the wind and rain would, in nature's own time, erase our monuments. After the passage of a few million years the concrete vestiges of man's brief sojourn would be like the coral under the sea, a lifeless series of structures which speak of great energy expended merely to help nature achieve her mysterious ends.

One of the riddles about modern man is that we have retained the survival instincts – the animal instincts – of our pre-human past, and yet we have picked up some behavioural patterns which seem inimical to our survival as a species. We appear to be bent on destroying the natural world on which we are totally dependent. We have become so mechanically powerful, so practised at clear-felling forests, damming rivers and bulldozing landscapes that we now treat nature as if it were a bowl of steakhouse peppermints.

Industry has been allowed to change the very nature of the atmosphere; civilised nations have plundered the seas; governments have allowed whole regions to be turned into desert; commerce, its killer instinct locked into the "on" position, is aggressively greedy.

It is not all doom though. There is an unmistakable global trend towards what is needed most – an *attitudinal* change by leaders and educated people, regarding the planet's damaged environment. The Greens movement is very pervasive. Ours is the first generation to seriously worry about what impact its actions might have on generations unborn.

A problem is that the momentum of man's overkill is such that we must expect even more grievous losses regarding air and water quality, soils, forests and species diversity in the near future. It is as if we are aboard a speeding supertanker whose captain, forewarned and now thoroughly alarmed about the danger ahead, has called for "full astern" knowing the ship's momentum will carry it forward another five kilometres before it can stop.

In a way, this book is about the next five kilometres.

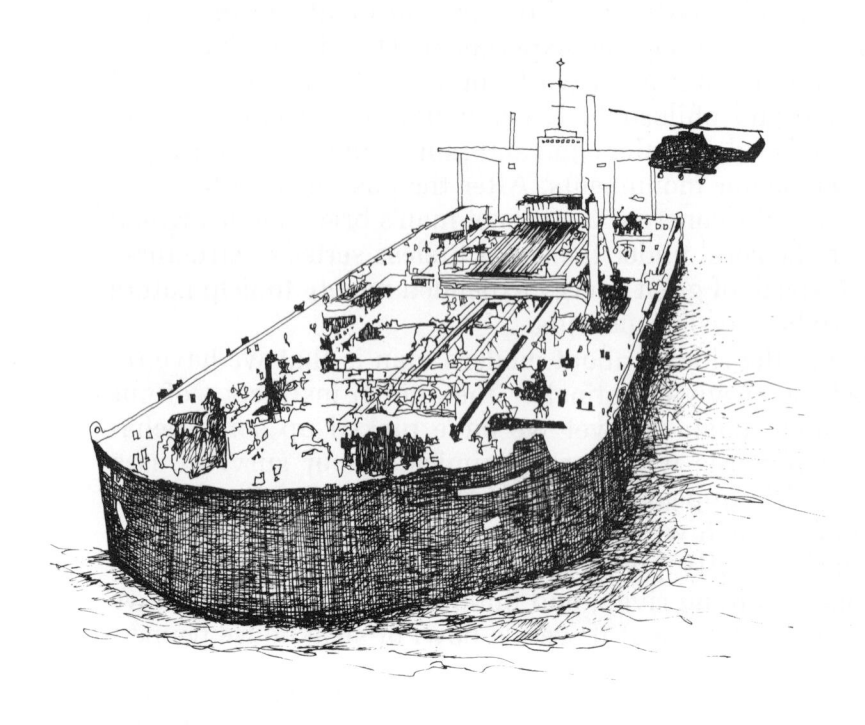

2 The insane experiment

> ... this most excellent canopy, the air, look you, this brave o'erhanging firmament, this majestic roof fretted with golden fire, why, it appears, no other things to me than a foul and pestilent congregation of vapours?
>
> William Shakespeare

IN June 1990 the satellite, Voyager I, sent back an image of planet Earth taken from 6 000 million kilometres away as the spacecraft travelled deeper into space beyond our solar system. And there we were! A tiny bright blue speck in the eternal silence, encased in a shimmering but diaphanous membrane of life-supporting air and water. We looked very lonely. As Carl Sagan said, if there is indeed intelligent life out there in the cosmos then that is an awesome thought. On the other hand, if there is no one else out there, if we are truly alone, then that is even more awesome. The only truth we have to go by for the foreseeable future is that there is only one Earth.

Yet we have allowed this planet's life-support system – its finely tuned arrangement of air, water and soil – to become seriously damaged. Governments, the world over, have allowed industry and other interests to conduct a massive and wild experiment on the chemistry of Earth's atmosphere without the faintest idea of what it might be doing.

FS Rowland and ISA Isaksen in their introduction to a book on the Berlin Dahlem Workshop on the atmosphere (*The Changing Atmosphere* 1988) described how, in the "dynamic turmoil" of the air, a seemingly insignificant gas can create profound changes. The authors point out how "current atmospheric descriptions now include an array of quite reactive chemicals usually in very small but potent concentrations." Many of these chemicals have only just been introduced. One of them, as we shall see, is active only in sunlit hours and has a concentration, near the Earth's surface, of only about one part in 100 000 billion – yet it is proving to be a frighteningly powerful agent for changing the character of the planet's protective and life-giving atmospheric skin.

The Earth's atmosphere comprises 78 per cent nitrogen (78,09) and 21 per cent (20,94) oxygen. The less than one per cent that is left comprises several gases, the most important of which is CO_2 – carbon dioxide – which amounts to a mere 0,03 per cent. It is, in a sense, the tiny linchpin of the whole living system. Plants absorb CO_2 in order to convert sunlight (by a process known as photosynthesis) into food. In doing so plants give off a waste gas called oxygen. Mammals, such as human beings, cannot survive without oxygen. In using oxygen we, in turn, give off a waste gas called CO_2 which plants absorb. It all adds up to a very agreeable arrangement

Good story, bad publicity

Cleopatra's Needle, the 180-ton, 21 metre high, red sandstone obelisk which stands on the Thames Embankment in London, stood for 35 centuries outside Cairo. It was one of a pair erected in front of the Great Temple at Heliopolis and its chiselled hieroglyphics reveal that it had no connection with history's *femme fatale*, Cleopatra. The Needle was 1 500 years old when she was born. The Government of Egypt presented one of the obelisks to Britain a century ago. Today you can hardly read the hieroglyphics, not because of the obelisk's 3 500 years in the desert but because of the few decades it has spent in London. The stone, being calcium carbonate, has been reacting with airborne pollutants such as sulphur dioxide and oxides of nitrogen, and, like an Alka Seltzer tablet, has been fizzing away for almost 100 years. (The second "Cleopatra's Needle" was presented to New York and has suffered similarly.)

Statues, great architecture and other works of art have similarly suffered throughout the world. Venice's elegant cityscape is rotting from air pollution; the Parthenon above

The east and west faces of New York's Cleopatra Needle

The Parthenon, Athens

Iron Age spear from the University of Witwatersrand collection

Athens, built in the fifth century BC, is suddenly decaying; the 4 500 year old pyramids in Egypt are crumbling and so is the Sphynx whose great head is in danger of falling off; the Taj Mahal in India, and the Statue of Liberty in New York – all victims of a steady corrosive fall out. The picture emerging from Eastern Europe is even more horrific: statues and buildings of great cultural value have rotted in the acid rain. In Poland some look as if they have been burned by fire. Throughout Europe a third to one half of natural forests are now damaged and large forest areas in Czechoslovakia, Germany and Switzerland are dead.

South Africa has not escaped damage. There is an example of the rapidity with which acid rain damage can appear at the University of the Witwatersrand: Iron Age artefacts which had lain in the veld for centuries before being consigned to the university's archaeological collection, are now corroding rapidly in the city air. South Africa's uniquely beautiful and very ancient petroglyphs – those mysterious, age-old stone engravings of animals found on loose boulders scattered across the veld – are also being eaten away by the very air we breathe. Johannesburg city buildings have to be washed down every five or six years these days – each cleaning removing yet another layer of decayed stonework and concrete. Rain gutter firms are doing a roaring trade because gutters last only half the time they used to last. The first signs of acid rain damage are now appearing in the Eastern Transvaal where pine needles are changing from a healthy dark green to a sickly mottled beige.

Yet we are told by industrialists, health officials and by politicians that there is nothing to worry about. They will assure us that, thus far, nobody has found irrefutable evidence that our chemical-laden air is unhealthy. Not in South Africa. The evidence does not exist for one very good reason: nobody has conscientiously researched it. Even in Soweto, where researchers found the air was "two-and-a-half times worse than the Eastern Transvaal Highveld" (whose pollution levels are notorious), no attempts to gauge health effects were made until, in June 1990, a 10-year-long "Birth to 10" programme to monitor the development of children in the Johannesburg-Soweto region was started by the Medical Research Council. Dr Yasmin von Schirnding of the MRC told The Star (26 August 1990) that next to gastro-enteritis, respiratory diseases were the next biggest killer of children under five. She added: "We also found that acute respiratory problems in children may possibly lead to chronic lung ailments in adulthood."

A month before, Czechslovakia's Minister of Economics, ecologist and Civic Forum leader, Josef Varousek, estimated air pollution in Czechoslovakia - a notoriously polluted country - shortened life expectancy by between five and seven years (compared with the West).

There have been only two attempts to assess the impact of air pollution on public health in South Africa. Both were rudimentary, both were alarming, and both were underplayed by all concerned.

The two surveys revealed that boys born in polluted Highveld towns such as the coal-mining town of Witbank in the Transvaal and the petrochemical centre of Sasolburg in the Orange Free State, are generally 2 centimetres shorter than boys in clean rural towns. There is also evidence that their breathing is affected by air pollution. One of the researchers, Professor A M Coetzee of Pretoria University, in 1984, compared the physical development and lung functions of 335 Standard 3 schoolchildren in Sasolburg using, as "controls", 147 children in the relatively unpolluted rural towns of Heilbron, Frankfort and Parys. He found boys in Sasolburg were 2 centimetres shorter and showed impaired lung functions.

The press published Coetzee's findings and this caused great dismay in the town council and among local industrialists - not because of the findings but because of the bad publicity. Two years later (28 October 1986) the council, local industry and Government health officials met to discuss the problem. Judging from an *aide mémoire* on this meeting, held under the auspices of the National Petroleum Refiners - the memorandum was signed by NPR's managing director, H J Lombard - it is clear that all parties were angered by the fact that the press had "extracted from the report what they considered a good story irrespective of the bad publicity on the town and industries." The Government's chief air pollution officer (Capco), Martin Lloyd, who was present, according to Lombard's *aide mémoire*, "apologised for the fact that the industries were not officially informed (about the health checks) and indicated that a more effective attack on the press would be for the industries to collaborate with the municipality to prepare a press release and to support it with statistics of pollution levels measured in the area."

Coetzee's survey, apparently done on a shoe-string budget, was obviously far too skimpy to be of much scientific value but it should have immediately alerted the Government to conduct another, more comprehensive survey. Yet it was not until 1988 that anybody did so. That year, this time using a sample of 2 000 children, Professor Saul Zwi of the University of the Witwatersrand compared the development and lung functions of children aged six to 10 in industrial towns such as Witbank, Springs and Welkom with those of children living in "clean" towns such as Nylstroom in the northern Transvaal and Wolmaransstad in the western Transvaal. Professor Zwi, under the auspices of the Council for Scientific and Industrial Research (CSIR), found boys in the polluted towns were appreciably shorter than those in country towns. Although their lung functions did not appear to be affected the boys were far more prone to early morning coughing, wheezing and asthma than were the boys in the rural towns.

The fact that only boys appeared to suffer did not surprise Professor J C A "Tony" Davies of the Department of National Health who, when he spoke about the two surveys at a National Association for Clean Air pollution workshop in Soweto in June 1990, pointed out that "girls are tougher than boys." He said in most childhood diseases the death rate was higher among boys. He also mentioned that not a single health survey, apart from the two mentioned, had been carried out before or since. This was an extraordinary admission considering the levels of air pollution on the Highveld and the enigma posed by the two reports.

There is no "cancer atlas" to show where in South Africa different kinds of cancers may be clustering, or where respiratory complaints are most common. In the United States and Europe, even where pollution appears to be less heavy than in South Africa, medical research and epedemiological studies have come up with worrying but vital information. A cancer atlas in the United States not only pin-pointed areas where the health authorities had expected certain cancers to be clustered – Los Angeles for instance where, because of photochemical smogs lung cancer is more common than in most other places – but it usefully revealed one lonely spot high up in the scenic north. An investigation showed that a copper mine, unable to sell its arsenate of lead, a by-product of its process, had been dumping it in the atmosphere by sending it up its stack. The death rate from cancer on the plant and in the mining community was way above the national average and the plant was closed immediately. The company had been dumping the arsenate of lead ever since Canada, which used to buy it, had declared it too carcinogenic (cancer-producing) to handle. The episode demonstrated how, even in this enlightened age, industrialists sometimes reveal a callousness that is chilling.

In Britain a similar study revealed a cluster of leukaemia cases around Sellafield nuclear power station in north-western England. At first a power station leak was suspected; then radon, a gas which exudes from granite beneath people's homes. Now the theory is that nuclear workers, contaminated by non-clinical doses of radiation at work, may have induced leukaemia in their children at conception. Whatever the final answer at Sellafield it reveals how a national cancer atlas is a good indicator of pollution trouble spots.

In 1989, at Phalaborwa in the north-eastern Transvaal, farmer Antoon Lombard lost 45 cattle from copper poisoning after they had eaten grass heavily contaminated by copper. Their livers contained three to nine times the lethal dose. The local copper mining company threatened to sue a reporter of *The Star*, the Johannesburg daily, should she try to connect the copper refinery to the incident. It was later ascertained that the company's pollution control equipment had been out of commission for some months. The Department of National Health's Industrial Hygiene Division defended the plant saying: "This (contamination) is to be expected in the vicinity of such a large mining complex". The government official then reminded the reporter that the town of Phalaborwa depended on the mine for its economic existence. Time and time again one comes across this attitude, that a town's economics override health considerations.

South Africa's reluctance to delve too deeply into the health effects of air pollution is not unique.

The frog in the pot

The British science journal, *New Scientist*, in an editorial in

1989, suggested people were like frogs: put a frog in a pot of hot water and it will spring out. Put it in a pot of cold water, and slowly bring it to the boil, and it will sit there until it boils to death.

This is really what happened in London. I was born there but spent much of my youth living on the edge of England's "Black Country". This is in the Midlands and the region earned its name from the black grime which discoloured buildings and even trees.

As children we were unconcerned by all this. In fact at school we were taught to be proud of Britain's dirty skies – they were, our teachers assured us, a sign of Britain's industrial might. Britain, like Phalaborwa and Sasolburg, believed air pollution was an inevitable by-product of economic progress.

In the 1940s when German bombers were busy providing us city children with lots of open space, and well into the 1950s, England experienced smogs which were so bad that, if one were to descend today, people would flee in terror. The word "smog" is made up from the words "smoke" and "fog". Fog, of course, is just a thick mist and is a quite natural and harmless winter phenomenon. I recall the smogs vividly. There would be no discernible dawn and one would wake to a silent world, even in what was one of the biggest, and certainly the busiest cities in the world. There was silence because, first of all road, rail, and air traffic were at a standstill and, second, the smog smothered any sound there might have been.

I do not recall resenting the smogs as a child. I think we actually enjoyed them, like we enjoyed the bombing. The realities of both evaded us. It would take us an inordinately long time to walk the few kilometres to school and we would make much mischief on the way and then simply disappear into the silent gloom.

The stonework of the school to which I went was continually sloughing its outer skin. The granite could be peeled away layer by layer, a process we were anxious to hasten. We had no idea what was actually eating our school but, whatever it was, we were on its side. At morning assembly the older children were allowed to stand right at the back of the hall and, in a very heavy smog, would not be able to see the stage from where the headmaster led the hymn singing:

*And did the Countenance Divine
Shine forth upon our clouded hills?
And was Jerusalem builded here
Among these dark Satanic mills?*

London, in mid-twentieth century, had given up its fight against smog. As early as the twelfth century its city fathers had recognised that the smog was unhealthy. They banned the burning of "sea coal" (soft coal shipped down from Newcastle) and the penalty for a first offence was "a verie greate fyne". For a second offence one's premises were demolished. A third offence met with hanging. But the ultimate in pollution laws patently did not work.

In the mid-nineteenth century Charles Dickens wrote:

Fog everywhere. Fog up the river, where it flows among the green aits and meadows; fog down the river, where it rolls defiled among the tiers of shipping and the waterside pollutions of a great (and dirty) city. Fog in the Essex marshes, fog on the Kentish heights. Fog lying out on the yards and hovering on the rigs of great ships ... Fog in the eyes and throats of ancient Greenwich pensioners, wheezing by the fireside.

A commission of inquiry in the 1930s found that as the smoke was from industry, and as industry was a mainstay of London's economy, nothing could be done – the Phalaborwa philosophy. The complacency ended in 1952 when a 10-day smog caused London's death rate to rise by at least 4 000. It was labelled the Killer Smog. R E Waller, of the British Medical Council, speaking at an international air pollution conference in Pretoria in 1979, described how the staff of St Bartholomew's Hospital in London watched helplessly as people died coughing and gasping in hospital beds. The hospital requisitioned World War I muslin gas masks, to no avail. Another person who witnessed it was Professor Tony Davies, now Director of the National Centre for Occupational Health in Johannesburg. He was working at Guys Hospital in London and recalls how somebody opened a window "and the smog flowed in until visibility was considerably reduced. We could not get the stuff out of the wards. There were no oxygen tents available in London in those days and although we tried all sorts of masks we were forced to watch people lying there, fighting for breath and dying. It was absolutely frightening."

Within four years of the Killer Smog Britain passed an effective Clean Air Act which, in essence, relied on industry's co-operation and which applied a kind of means test for factories in that they had to take "the best practicable means" to abate pollution. If taking measures threatened an industry's profitability then this was sometimes taken into account. The "best practicable means" criterion was often abused by industry. In South Africa, which enacted similar legislation in 1965 (the Atmospheric Pollution Prevention Act) some plants have become masters at using this clause to their advantage and the public's disadvantage. In Britain a degree of coercion was necessary from the authorities but most of the coercion came from the public and the media. Some factories, when they suffered a breakdown in their clean air equipment would buy space in newspapers to apologise for creating smoke and to explain the nature of their problem.

In the British capital today there are vestiges of Dickens's London - rows of dreary little houses, all joined together and bristling with yellow ceramic chimney pots, but there is not a wisp of smoke. The Clean Air Act has worked well as far as particulate matter is concerned. Londoners are forbidden to sell, buy or burn ordinary coal. They are obliged by law to buy only smokeless fuel. Local authorities subsidised the compulsory change over from open fires to combustion stoves which burned only smokeless fuel. The availability of North Sea gas has also helped cut visible pollutants. London's average year-round visibility, which was about 1 kilometre in the 1950s, is now 10 kilometres.

What is significant about London's smog, and for that matter the appalling conditions in West Germany's Ruhr Valley, and in Los Angeles and Tokyo and Mexico City, is that people are prepared to tolerate smog as it gets worse and worse - like a frog in a pot. The human being's adaptability can sometimes be our undoing. According to a Worldwatch Institute report (No 91 of 20 January 1990) a fifth of humanity inhales unhealthy air. In greater Athens deaths "rise sixfold on heavily polluted days". In the United States "air pollution causes as many 50 000 deaths a year." In economic terms this represents a loss of $40 billion a year through lost productivity.

Ah, but I don't inhale
The average person inhales about 15 000 litres of air a day, which in weight is many times more than the food we eat. A labourer or athlete might take in five times as much. The oxygen from the air is absorbed into the bloodstream via the walls of the alveoli, bunches of tiny air cells whose collective surface area would cover a tennis court. All things considered the lungs are tough organs capable of taking considerable abuse.

There is empirical evidence that maybe man can adapt to a fair amount of smoke inhalation. Some years ago, the now retired pathologist, Professor Ian Webster of the National Centre for Occupational Health in Johannesburg, called for fresh lung tissue – that of some healthy person who had been killed – so that he could compare it with lung tissue from miners. (When a miner dies in South Africa his lungs are examined to see if his alveoli walls are thicker than normal – a sign of pneumoconiosis or miners' phthisis caused by dust inhalation. His dependants are paid compensation relative to the thickness of the walls). In due course Professor Webster received the lungs from the body of a young man killed in a road accident. The victim had been in prime health and had never smoked or worked down a mine, and he had, daily, cycled several kilometres to his job on a farm in the Orange Free State. To the Professor's surprise the youth's alveoli walls were so thick he would have recommended high compensation for miner's phthisis. The professor's puzzling find was written up in the *British Medical Journal* and about a year later two Australian doctors responded saying they had witnessed similar alveoli damage among Papua-New Guinean mountain porters – tough people capable of carrying 30 kilogram head-loads up steep mountain paths despite their apparent lung impairment.

The common factor turned out to be that these people, as children, slept around open fires in unventilated huts. The fires were made from wood or dried cow dung. In the Drakensberg mountains one sees thatched huts in winter with smoke pouring through the roof. Visibility inside is minimal and if you are not used to it you'll go into a spasm of coughing and your eyes will stream as soon as you enter. For as long as man has known how to light a hearth fire – maybe 1,5 million years ago – even in developed countries

Unventilated huts

people have been sleeping in smoke-filled spaces until very recently. The chimney is a relatively modern invention.

Man must surely have become adapted to inhaling carbon, the chief ingredient in wood and coal smoke. I believe this is why so many people enjoy smoking – it is possibly an atavistic thing. For 40 000 generations the comforting tang of wood and leaf smoke signified to our hunter/gatherer ancestors, as they trudged back to their caves and encampments, the neareness of home and companionship and the security of the fireside. In the recesses of our minds there are buried many such inherited memories. It is the *nature* of smoke that has changed. Inhaling industrial air is quite different from inhaling the smoke of a camp fire. It is impregnated with chemicals, compounds and particulates, many of which were unknown in nature until this century. We are physiologically ill-equipped to cope with them. Somebody once pointed out that air pollution is the worst sort of pollution: when water is polluted you do not have to drink it, but when it comes to the witch's brew of chemicals that sometimes passes for air, we have no choice but to inhale it.

Lloyd Timberlake and Laura Thomas in their book *When the Bough Breaks* (1990) which looks at the way deteriorating environments are affecting child health, say that children are particularly sensitive to air pollution. They say a three year old takes in twice as much air (per kilogram of body weight) as an adult, thus exposing the child to twice the potential damage.

Children are extremely vulnerable to air pollution

The killer ingredient

The killer ingredient in London's infamous smogs (the last of which was in 1962 when the death rate rose 600 above average) was sulphur dioxide.

Sulphur dioxide (SO_2) is released mainly from burning coal and it converts to sulphur trioxide (SO_3) which is a powerful acid. The acidity of the water droplets in London's smogs probably had a pH factor of 1,7. The term "pH" is used to indicate acidity and alkalinity. Liquid that is neither acid nor alkaline has a pH of seven. Anything over pH7 is alkaline (like caustic soda) and anything under seven would be acid. Milk, for example, is slightly acid because it contains lactic acid. It has a pH of just under seven. Vinegar has a pH of three. Battery acid has a pH of one. If battery acid were to land on your skin it would burn. In Cape Town, in the smoggy days before Koeberg nuclear power plant led to the closing of the city's coal and oil-fired power stations, atmospheric acidity sometimes caused women's stockings to dissolve on their legs.

Athlone power station visible above the early morning inversion, Cape

According to Webster, when he addressed the International Conference on Air Pollution at the CSIR in 1979, airborne particles of a critical size help sulphur get into the lungs. Most airborne particles are trapped in the nose hairs or are caught before they reach into the lungs and coughed up, and sulphur dioxide itself is soluble in nasal and throat fluids. In London's mustard-coloured smogs these tinier particles slipped through the lung's defences and allowed sulphur to come into contact with the lung tissues, upon which the sulphur dioxide became akin to battery acid. By the time I was 21 I had a scar on my lungs from years of inhaling industrial air. I was told by my doctor: "It's a badge. Anybody who X-rays you in future will know whence you came. Wear it with pride!" A perfectly stupid statement when you consider our limited supply of lungs.

In January 1989, Professor Peter Tyson, climatologist at the University of the Witwatersrand, and others, produced for the CSIR a report which revealed the extent of industrial air pollution over the eastern Transvaal Highveld (ETH). The report commented: "the emission densities are between five and just under 10 times greater than those found in West Germany and the United States, and approximate the worst conditions found anywhere." The authors included comparative figures from the USA, Canada, East and West Germany and Britain.

The report revealed a sorry picture: the ETH suplhur dioxide emissions were 31,25 tons a square kilometre a year. East Germany, notoriously dirty because of the quality of its coal and the way it burns it, emits 30 tons. One of the United States's biggest industrial regions, Ohio, emits 19,8 tons a square kilometre a year. Britain emits 14,3 and West Germany, where years of sulphur pollution, resulting in acid rain, is now killing its forests and eating its statues, emits only a quarter of the ETH's volume.

The Tyson report, by the authors' own admission, is cautious. At the time this report was made public, a second report, privately commissioned by manufacturers of electrostatic precipitators and other clean air equipment, was published by *The Star*. It held that the ETH sulphur emissions density was not 31,25 tons but 57,5 tons – almost twice as high as East Germany's. A subsequent CSIR figure suggested it could be even 60 to 80 tons a square kilometre. The Department of National Health pointed out that it is unfair to compare the ETH region (30 000 square kilometres) with a whole nation such as East Germany (108 000 square kilometres), or even with Ohio, which is about the size of East Germany. In fact taking South Africa as a whole (all 1,2 million square kilometres) its average national sulphur emissions, according to Tyson's report, amount to a mere 0,8 tons a square kilometre a year. It is true that most of South Africa, most of the year, has beautifully clear blue skies but it is equally true that sulphur emissions are concentrated in the region which is the most heavily populated – the southern half of the Transvaal.

According to Gerhard Held of the CSIR, in the triangle formed by the giant power stations at Matla, Duvha and Arnot, just south of Middelburg, sulphur emissions rival those of the Ruhr Valley – around 860 tons a square kilometre a year.

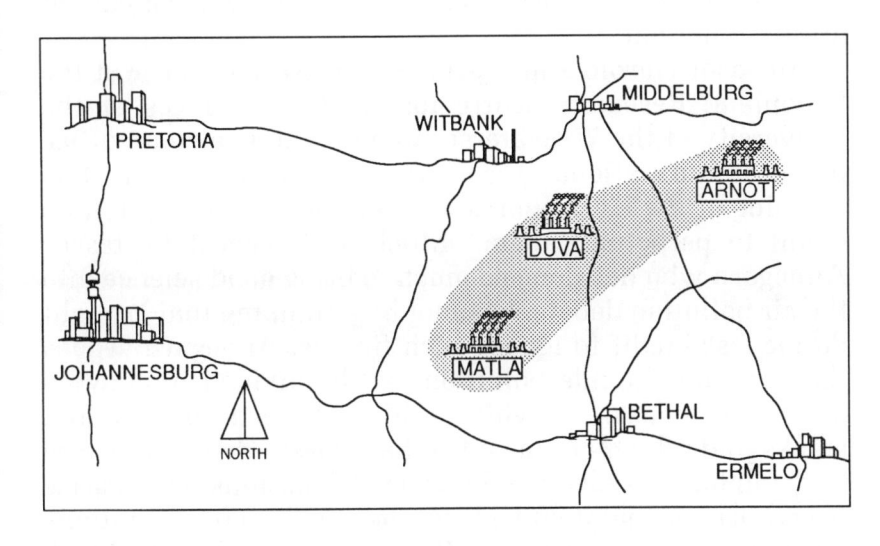

South Africa's worst pollution belt

Even this last figure was still way below some of the readings coming from Poland and Czechoslovakia, where conditions in 1990 were so smoggy that cars had to switch their lights on at midday. People were being evacuated from four villages in Silesia, Poland, where cancer was up 50 per cent on the Polish average and lung complaints up 30 per cent. Poland, a third of the size of South Africa, was dumping almost twice as much sulphur in the air. In Czechoslovakia emissions were 20 times the European

The effects of acid rain

average. Minister Josef Vavrousek said that more than two-thirds of Czechoslovakia's forests were affected by acid rain and that half of the country's surface water was biologically dead.

The trouble in South Africa is that industrialists, as well as the Department of National Health, tend to take comfort from such comparisons. They do not consider the situation in South Africa critical enough to warrant serious action. Professor Andre Rabie, a brilliant environment law academic at the University of Stellenbosch, speaking from the floor at South Africa's first International Air Pollution Conference in 1971, asked a Department of Health official why Tom Burke (a tiny town in the northern Transvaal) had not been declared a smokeless zone. The official, clearly puzzled by the question, said: "Because Tom Burke does not have a pollution problem." Rabie said: "That's the problem with government policy – it demands we wait until problems develop before we take action. We cannot afford to do that."

Professor Harold Annegarn, chief research officer at the Schonland Research Centre for Nuclear Sciences at the University of the Witwatersrand and who is also an office bearer in the National Association for Clean Air (Naca), is scathing of the ETH figures. He told me: "It will do you no credit to perpetuate them." Much as I respect Professor Annegarn who has done so much to bring good science into the air pollution debate, I cannot help thinking that it might do me less credit to ignore such figures. Annegarn argues that sulphur dioxide pollution can be divided into two – high level emissions which are discharged through tall stacks and which are meant to harmlessly disperse before they fall back to earth; and low level emissions which arise from burning coal dumps, from the smaller power stations with low stacks, from small industries and from black residential areas which mostly have to burn coal because they have no access to electricity. Annegarn insists that the only worthwhile statistics are those relating to ground level sulphur quantities.

But what goes up must come down, somewhere. One does not have to be a scientist to know that pumping a million tons of sulphur a day into the air above a highly populated region, and into an atmosphere which is stagnant for the four months of winter, is, to say the least, a non-therapeutic practice. The ETH also happens to be the most important agricultural region in South Africa.

The industrialised Transvaal Highveld region is 1 600 to 2 000 metres above sea level, which means there is a fifth less oxygen than at the coast. This makes the efficient combustion of practically anything difficult. A diesel vehicle which runs cleanly in Durban may emit volumes of black exhaust once it climbs onto the Highveld. Lighting a braaivleis fire is always easier at the coast while on the Highveld it tends to smoke for a long time before the coals are hot enough to consume all the ascending smoky volatiles. Smoke is unburned coal – or, if you like, it is somebody's money going up in smoke.

The Highveld has a second handicap: its temperature inversions. These are particularly pronounced in winter when warm layers of air trap cold air below. A typical winter's dawn sees a layer of cold air trapped at ground level under an inpenetrable roof of warm air. In industrial areas the rising of the sun reveals a solid-looking brown wall of pollution.

Fumes trapped by the early morning inversion near the Klip power station

The tall stacks
On the one hand South Africa is fortunate in having an abundance of coal – enough to last it 300 years at current rates of extraction. On the other hand it is unfortunate in that these coal supplies are on the Highveld, a climatic zone unsuitable for coal combustion. Giant power stations, with dedicated coal mines, dominate the ETH's undulating savannah. The coal, mostly of fairly poor quality, is crushed to a fine powder before it is poured into the furnace to make steam. Considering the complicated and useful chemical composition of coal the day will surely come when we will view such a crude use of coal as sheer extravagance.

In 1990 Eskom (Electricity Supply Commission) commissioned a 3 400 MW coal-fired power station – Lethabo – on the Highveld near Vereeniging. Lethabo power station burns 15 million tons of coal a year. This power station, just to give some idea of its output, could supply the state of Israel with all its electricity needs, and still have one of its six turbines off. The Transvaal has eight of these enormous power plants. The fuel quality at Lethabo is so poor that engineers jokingly refer to it as topsoil. About half the coal's content is ash. The power station dumps its waste gases straight into the atmosphere – an annual 30 million tons of carbon dioxide (the major gas in the greenhouse effect) and 250 000 tons of sulphur dioxide (the major ingredient in acid rain). The laws of thermodynamics are such that power stations which convert steam energy into electricity, are only 35 per cent efficient, at best. A survey in Britain showed half the energy was lost by the energy industry and another half was lost by energy-users (*New Scientist* Letters, 14 July 1990). I doubt it is much different in South Africa.

Even more power is wasted by consumers. All round coal-fired power stations are becoming anachronisms and the sooner the world finds an alternative fuel the better.

Waste is a big factor. Professor Desmond Midgley, the retired Witwatersrand University hydrologist, said at a Cape Town conference on climatic change in 1989 that twice the output of the power station complex on the Transvaal coalfields takes the form of waste heat. "By the year 2000 the heat release to the atmosphere from the Transvaal coalfields will probably be at the rate of about

100 000 MW and that, apart from the accompanying sulphur dioxide, is bound to be environmentally significant."

Eskom, which produces two-thirds of the African continent's electricity, and which also supplies some of South Africa's neighbouring states, has a current capacity of 34 000 MW and is completing installations which will bring its capacity up to 43 000 MW. It also has 5 000 MW available in the Tugela River where a series of modest dams could be built to produce, mostly, pumped storage energy. Admittedly, to store energy (the methods are explained later) one has to expend energy. All this, yet the highest demand on record was 21 800 MW in 1989. It is true that generation companies have to be optimistic: in depressed times they must prepare for economically good times because it takes eight or nine years to construct a big power plant, and booms cannot wait for power utilities to catch up. But in view of the huge over-capacity in 1990 and the virtually unexplored possibilities of conserving power, one seriously wonders if South Africa needs to build another coal-fired station.

Eighty five per cent of South Africa's electricity is derived from coal and four-fifths of the country's electricity is generated on the ETH. In the midst of the ETH's cluster of power stations are plants such as Secunda, Sasol's huge oil-from-coal complex which processes 43 million tons of coal a year, and several metallurgical industries – all having sprouted from the coalfields and all helping to put into the air about 1,2 million tons of sulphur dioxide annually.

The Department of National Health's policy, until 1990, was to allow industry to use high stacks, some reaching 300 metres, the idea being to disperse the gases and particulates as widely as possible. In other words to use fresh air to dilute bad air. The tall stacks tended not to solve the problem so much as to spread it across the sky. Even then one wonders how effective dispersal really is. For instance before Sasol corrected the problem, its Secunda plant, 120 kilometres east of Johannesburg, used to release extremely smelly hydrogen sulphide from its two 300 metre stacks. Under certain weather conditions, this invisible gas used to descend directly on the Witwatersrand, focused like a torch beam. One wonders what odourless and therefore undetected, but possibly dangerous gases are being focused on this densely populated area.

Dispersal of gases and solids, even at 300 metres, is no permanent answer, especially on the Highveld with its stagnant air. One sees demonstrations of this quite frequently when fly ash from Eskom power stations meets up against an inversion "roof" 500 metres above the ground and spreads out like a giant umbrella from which it filters down, day and night. Although Eskom's electrostatic precipitators are usually 98 per cent efficient it still means each stack, *daily*, pushes into the air 2 000 tons of fly ash. One occasionally sees, when precipitators break down, huge quantities of thick smoke and dust literally tumbling out of the stacks and dropping directly to earth. The average fly ash fallout is at least 1 400 tons a day, going by official figures, which tend to be optimistic.

Nevertheless, the Department of National Health and Eskom insist that the annual average of air pollution levels is way below where health might be affected. The annual pollution average is one thing, but what about winter peaks? Again, Eskom assures us, the daily peaks and even hourly peaks are way below critical levels. This cannot be true of the whole ETH and there must certainly be areas where the levels are way above the danger threshold. Eskom has a sulphur monitoring network which Annegarn says is quite dense – "certainly more comprehensive than anything in the USA." But it is hardly a satisfactory arrangement as far as the public is concerned and reflects a certain dereliction of duty on the part of the Department of Health. The public would breathe easier if an independent agency, whose first commitment was unarguably to public health rather than industry, was responsible for monitoring the air and was obliged to report annually on progress or otherwise.

As far as the smoky and sprawling sub-city of Soweto is concerned smoke emissions frequently exceed recommended health levels suggested by such bodies as the United States's Environmental Protection Agency (EPA) whose standards seem to have been accepted by South Africa's Department of National Health. Nevertheless, until June 1990, when the SA Medical Research Council began its "Birth to 10" survey in Greater Johannesburg, the Department had conducted no meaningful studies on public

The insane experiment 35

Township and industrial smoke drift across Johannesburg on a winter morning before it became a smokeless zone

health on the Highveld. The departments of Agriculture and Forestry seemed more concerned - they had at least begun to survey the effects of sulphur fallout on crops and timber plantations.

Acid rain damage was, by the late 1980s, becoming apparent in the eastern Transvaal's extensive pine forests. At about the time the CSIR reported possible acid rain damage to trees, the Dutch State Forestry Service, having completed a study of 1 500 stands of trees, reported that every one of them was at least "lightly damaged". Trees, being in the ground longer than food crops, tend to accumulate acid effects, but as the Transvaal's soil acidity is increased by the continued sulphur fall-out so one must also expect crop damage to begin manifesting itself.

A cyclist makes a point in Johannesburg traffic

The Tyson report mentioned that the pH of rain tested in the Highveld occasionally drops to 2,8 - like vinegar - and that the worst area for acid rain was in the southern Transvaal around Standerton which is an important maize and dairy district. The report predicted that acid rain would increase by another 25 per cent once Eskom had all its turbines spinning. What then? Eskom does not envisage a clean up of power station gases although it has announced that in future all new power stations will be designed with desulphurisation equipment.

Car exhausts also add to acid rain. When nitrogen oxides and unburned hydrocarbons from car exhaust pipes react with sulphur dioxide from coal-fired boilers the result is a particularly acidic brew. Acid pollution from cars is partly, and in some areas, largely, responsible for destroying aquatic life and forests in Europe, North America and the Far East. Most of the acid damage in Athens and Rome, for instance, is from car exhausts rather than industry. In Britain 30 per cent of acid rain is from nitric acid (from cars mostly) and 70 per cent from sulphuric acid. In the last two or three years scientists have become more and more concerned about what are called "nox gases" - oxides of nitrogen which come from car exhausts and coal-fired power stations. They are now being linked with lung cancer and asthma by the American Lung Association and the British Lung Foundation. The latter believes nox is worse than sulphur dioxide.

Most of South Africa's acid rain is in the form of a dry fallout. This is even true of a wet country such as Britain where dry fallout is characteristic of urban areas and power station concentrations such as one finds along the River Trent, and in Yorkshire. According to the UK Review Group on Acid Rain whose findings were reported in *New Scientist* (12 January 1984) dry deposition does more damage than "real" acid rain.

It is just a matter of time before crop damage from acid fallout begins to appear in the Transvaal and Free State. Half of South Africa's high production cropland - mostly comprising maize lands - is in the ETH itself according to Brian Huntley who, with Roy Siegfried and Clem Sunter wrote *South African Environments into the 21st Century*. According to a special report by the World Wide Fund for Nature - *Acid Rain and Air Pollution* (1988) - if the annual average sulphur dioxide level exceeds 30 micrograms per cubic metre (30 parts per million) it will eventually result in "a decline in the productivity of crops". This figure is exceeded in most of the eastern Transvaal Highveld.

Is sulphur good for the soil?

Discussing sulphur fall-out at a conference at Megawatt Park, Sandton a few years ago an Eskom scientist suggested that sulphur fall-out was good for agriculture and said farmers in the Transvaal actually added even more sulphur to their land. While this is true, it is true only in some cases. It does not make sense to spread fertilizer over town and country, over lakes and swamps and forests and over sulphur-sensitive crops just because some farmers do not mind. Farmer Paul Reynolds of Val, on the western edge of the eastern Transvaal Highveld, said: "Because sulphur is one up on the periodic scale to selenium, the grass on my farm is not taking up the latter and, as a result, conception among my cows has markedly declined. This means milk yields are down unless I inject my cows with both selenium and vitamin C".

The Central Electricity Generating Board of Great Britain is funding experiments to find out whether sulphur dioxide is good for the land. It points out that airborne sulphur dioxide is a good fungicide. Indeed, until the 1960s London's rose growers never complained about "black spot", a fungal disease, simply because air pollution killed it. Unfortunately air pollution killed people too. Sulphur, like many pollutants, is useful in certain doses but it can also reduce a plant's resistance to cold and can cause certain diseases and aphids (a serious pest) to increase.

Acid rain from sulphur pollution has devastated 500 000 hectares of Czechoslovakia. The Canadians claim acid rain, mainly caused by industrial sulphur from the United States, is responsible for the disappearance of fish from 15 000 lakes and threatens 300 000 more. Eight per cent of Finland's lakes have been sterilised and three-quarters of Norway's lakes are acidic. Great swathes of forests – in some countries up to a third of their forests – are ruined. Most of the damage is far from industry's high stacks and it demonstrates how unacceptable the tall stack policy is as a solution to anything. Nearly all of Scandinavia's damage is from pollution from Britain and the industrial heartland of Europe. Scandinavia, a region which relies mostly on clean power (nuclear and hydro) has the misfortune to be at the end of sky sewers coming in the shape of jet streams from the south.

Eskom in 1990 stated it would cost R500 million to retrofit the two end boilers in each giant "six pack" power plant to remove sulphur. The "six pack" title stems from the fact that they each have six turbines, each with a boiler. The boilers are placed in a row in such a way that the middle ones cannot be retrofitted with desulphurisation equipment because there is no space. In other words, to reduce sulphur dioxide emissions by only one third would cost, for all the big power stations, R4 000 million and would increase electricity tariffs between 20 and 30 per cent. That was the prediction early in 1990. But by June that year Eskom was talking of R1 000 million to retrofit each power station and within a month of that, at an Eskom workshop, I heard the figure R1 200 million. One can be forgiven for thinking Eskom is guessing. Frankly, I believe the figures are being inflated to scare the public off from demanding pollution controls. Many industries, not just in South Africa, use this ploy, usually ending with the warning, "and it will be the consumer who will pay in the end."

Suggestions from fuel expert Professor David Horsfall of the University of the Witwatersrand that Eskom should study the possibilities of partly desulphurising coal by washing it were greeted with scepticism by Eskom. The fact is that South Africa partly desulphurises export coal before shipping it off to Japan. Horsfall is optimistic that cleaning coal before it is burned would not only ensure a reduction in sulphur emissions from all of a power station's boilers (instead of just the end two) but would be considerably cheaper than the conventional method.

Bearing in mind the very high cost of desulphurisation equipment, clean coal-fired power stations may soon be costing more than nuclear plants. Coal plants cost less to build but their running costs, because of the enormous amount of coal which has to be mined and transported, is, in the medium term, greater than nuclear plants.

The Soweto dilemma

Ian McRae, Eskom's chief executive, confirming Eskom's

reluctance to plunge into a desulphurisation programme, argued that as far as air pollution was concerned there can only be one priority: "Seventy per cent of South Africans do not have access to electricity in their homes," he said in a broadcast in May 1990. In Taiwan, he said, 99 per cent of the people had electricity and in Japan almost 100 per cent. Western Europe would be close to 99 per cent. "We have to get electricity, as quickly as possible, to black urban areas such as Soweto," said McRae. He saw this move as costing R6 000 million and said it would have more impact on improving the quality of life for more people – millions upon millions of people – than cleaning up power stations. In any event, he said, Soweto was "two and a half times more polluted than the ETH". By 1990 Eskom had, in the space of three or four years, brought electricity in Soweto homes up from 25 per cent to 90 per cent. McRae was right about the urgency of bringing electricity to black areas. Nobody would argue about that. But he was wrong if he thought it would solve Soweto's smoke pollution.

A British delegate at a Soweto workshop on air pollution in June 1990, Bill Muirhead of Falkirk, said:

> *Stoves don't smoke. It's coal that smokes. So, clean the coal! Whatever you do don't oblige poor people to chuck out perfectly good coal-burning stoves and have to replace them with expensive electric stoves.*

The point was reinforced at the same conference by Mike Harris of Richlab, a coal technology research centre in Johannesburg, who pointed out how an electric stove was no substitute for a coal stove. An electric stove merely cooked meals, he said. But a cast iron coal stove not only cooked meals and kept stews simmering for hours while everybody was at work, but it also heated all the household water, kept the house warm, kept the kettle boiling, boiled the washing and dried it overnight, and was great to sit around with the family.

Muirhead said that when, soon after London's Killer Smog, England brought in smokeless zone laws it did not ban the coal stove. "There would have been riots if they'd tried." He said that even today coal stoves are favoured over electric stoves by large households as well as many middle-class homes in Britain.

Britain's dramatic atmospheric cleanup was achieved not via smokeless stoves but via smokeless fuel, and only when the option was open to all to buy smokeless fuel were smokeless zones declared. That, according to some, is the direction in which South Africa should be moving. South Africa is one of the very few places where smokeless stoves are still being made. While there's no export market for smokeless stoves there would be a huge export market for smokeless fuel.

But until South Africa puts a realistic price on coal and electricity there is little likelihood of money being left over for much needed coal research. In 1990 there was not one meaningful coal research project being conducted in South Africa. This was hardly surprising. The 1990 price for average quality coal was around R42 a ton at the pithead – just about the cheapest in the world. In view of the country's pollution problem, a resource economist might wonder at the sanity of this. The worst and smokiest kind of coal was, in 1990, selling at R11 – about R2,30 less than it had been selling at in 1985.

The Worldwatch Institute suggests that an electricity conservation programme – something Eskom has never tried beyond advising householders that fluorescent lights use less electricity than ordinary bulbs – can mean the difference between building and not building a power station. If South Africa cut its demand and so saved building another megawattage-station, which in 1990 terms would cost (with desulphurisation equipment) R12 billion, then the saving would at least pay for a significant reduction of sulphur dioxide in existing power stations.

Something in the air

Uranium 235 (from which nuclear fuel is made) has a halflife of 700 million years, which indicates it is only a little radioactive. It means that a kilogram of uranium 235 from a Witwatersrand gold mine, let's say, will weigh 500 grams in 700 million years' time. Something with a shorter halflife would indicate its nuclei are burning up more furiously, thus raising the level of radioactivity but burning out sooner. A long-lived isotope is, in effect, merely smouldering harmlessly away. Uranium then, as it is mined, is not dangerous. But as uranium decays it releases various isotopes including a gas called radon. Radon has a halflife of less than four days. It exudes from rocks, granites in particular. Many South Africans inhale radon daily but it is harmlessly exhaled. But radon has "daughters", solid, fiercely radioactive particles, capable of becoming trapped in the lungs and causing cancer. These daughter particles have halflives which can be measured in seconds.

Radon gas can build up in enclosed environments, even in badly ventilated homes or offices standing on granite domes. The area between Johannesburg's inner northern suburbs to Pretoria actually sits on a granite dome. There was a minor flurry of concern in South Africa in 1989 and 1990 regarding radon after British researchers, at the University of Bristol, found, in 15 countries, a close correlation between radon and certain types of cancer - mainly leukaemia, cancers of the kidneys, liver, lungs and skin. There was a particularly high incidence in Britain where radon gas is believed to kill 2 500 people a year through lung cancer.

The South African Medical Research Council sent an investigation team to Britain and the United States, afterwards one of the doctors told *The Star* she felt the problem was probably too small to be detected in South Africa because homes built on granite were not closed up for weeks on end, as happened in colder countries, thus radon would not build up to dangerous levels.

One feels uneasy about the finding. Air-conditioned buildings on the Rand can live off recirculated air for weeks during winter because, with the price of electricity, their owners are loathe to let out warm air and then have to reheat fresh air every day. The MRC was, of course, giving an off-the-cuff opinion and continues to investigate.

The sick building syndrome

New data regarding radon might emerge now that some interest is being taken in what is nowadays called the sick building syndrome(SBS). For years office workers the world over have felt that if one person gets influenza, everybody will get it, because the virus will be passed around by the air conditioning system. In fact viruses probably cannot be circulated, but lots of other things can. The air inside an air-conditioned central city office building is usually more polluted than the outside air.

Twenty-nine-year-old Wits Technikon graduate Richard Truter of the Johannesburg health department, one of the most knowledgeable men on SBS in South Africa, said that as people spend more time indoors than outdoors the health effects of polluted office air are very relevant. He explained how polluted air from the street is sucked into a building by air conditioners and even by the lifts going up and down acting like pumps. The outside pollutants were now mixed with those which originated inside – car exhaust gases from the basement (but found on the highest floors); tobacco smoke; toxic off-gases (to use SBS jargon) from copying machines; chemicals from treated furnishings and even the glue fumes from carpets – fumes that may remain circulating for weeks and even months on end. Formaldehyde, a gas which even in low concentration makes the eyes smart, is common in office air. It comes from chip board, glues and other products.

Unless a building is flushed out daily workers sit in a cauldron of reacting chemicals and compounds and begin to show all sorts of symptoms.

Sealed buildings became a widespread phenomenon after the 1974 oil crisis. Building managers, having run up a considerable bill heating up a building in winter, became loathe to flush out the warm air. The same after cooling a building in summer. The problem is more serious in extreme climates.

Humidifier water is known to breed "humidifier fever" and even lethal legionaire's disease and pass them into public air. An investigation of 450 sick buildings in the US showed that in 52 per cent poor ventilation was the direct cause of discomfort and dissatisfaction. Seventeen per cent were traced to toxic gases from office machinery. Eleven per cent came from outside sources (drawn in by the air ducts); 5 per cent were microbial; in 3 per cent of cases workers were suffering effects from inhaling gases given off from building fabrics, carpet shampoos and so on – and 12 per cent were unknown.

Hysteria can be a factor in the 12 per cent, says Truter. "Somebody complains of feeling ill and then it ripples through the office. But the fact remains that staff dissatisfaction is more prevalent in a sealed building than in an old fashioned ventilated one. So are blocked noses, dry throat, headaches, lethargy, sore, burning eyes and dry skin."

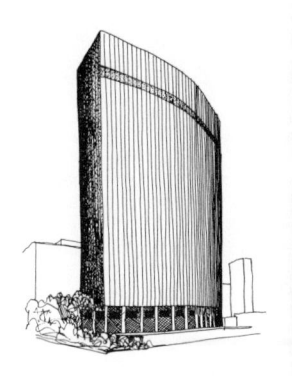

Asbestos fibres
Although airborne fibres were also a factor, Truter said that so far, after three years of investigating, neither he nor his colleagues had come across even remotely serious levels of asbestos.

Asbestos was a serious problem in South Africa up until the 1980s, especially in the asbestos mining areas where, when the mining companies pulled out they left asbestos dumps uncovered. The fibres of asbestos, if inhaled, can cause ARDs (asbestos related diseases). Constant exposure, usually experienced only by asbestos workers, can cause asbestosis which has a 10 per cent fatality rate. Another disease is mesothelioma, which can be induced by inhaling just one fibre of critical length and which takes up to 40 years to manifest itself, when death is fairly swift.

Pretoria toxicologist, Professor Douw Steyn, at the second International Air Pollution Conference in Pretoria (1979) angered South African delegates by showing pictures of asbestos workers with their hair white with fibres. Embarrassed South African delegates argued that the pictures were 15 years out of date. Yet, while the manufacturing industry had cleaned up its act long before, the asbestos mining industry had not. Even then, in 1979 it continued to perpetrate a lethal situation. Here, again, the Government's Health Department saw its first loyalty as being with industry. When public complaints were voiced in 1969 about a criminal situation in asbestos mining areas, the Minister of Health, Carel de Wet, spoke of the "so called dangerous effects" of asbestos and had told protestors that they lacked knowledge and were reacting to sensational reports.

Even by 1984 the situation was still appalling. *The Star* exposed how, on a farm at Penge in Lebowa in the north-eastern Transvaal women, babies strapped to their backs, continued to scavenge rubbish tips at which the mines had dumped asbestos waste. Children were playing on the dump while dust rose into the air. The wind had contaminated the area with fibres. Eddie Koch of the Johannesburg *Daily Mail*, in June 1989 described how, in the same area, the dust rose from the dirt roads which had been surfaced from waste from the dump, and how there were still bare mounds around the Mmafafe school. At least the locals had stopped making building bricks from asbestos. In the northern Cape near Kuruman, South Africa's only other asbestos mining area, there have been several cases of ARDs because of poor housekeeping by the mines.

The asbestos industry itself seems unlikely to reach its former peak, experienced in 1977, even though its products are nowadays both safer to manufacture and to handle. Ninety three per cent of its production used to be exported but so nervous has the overseas public become about asbestos products that they are difficult to sell. Everite, the major manufacturer in South Africa, did a survey (published in 1987) showing that of the 25 000 workers employed in the industry since 1942, 178 contracted ARDs (0,07 per cent) and 21 had died. A further 32 ARDs cases were recorded by a firm it had recently acquired. But one wonders how conscientiously the industry kept track of former casual workers who died in retirement. Asbestos is a slow killer. Nowadays Everite has a policy of medically checking employees for 50 years after they leave the industry. Not being involved in mining they did not include, in their statistics, the casual workers who had been employed at places such as Penge.

The new South African limit to airborne asbestos is one fibre to the millilitre (1 f/ml) and, even then, masks must be worn. When West Germany adopted a similar limit, its Health Minister commented:

> *Basing all relevant calculations on very conservative suppositions and calculations, the cancer risk incurred with a permanent (24 hours) and life-long exposure to 1 f/ml is in the same order as smoking two cigarettes a year.*

Tests of the air in Soweto, where a number of homes have asbestos roofs, show a level of 0,001 f/ml. This is in fact about the background level one is likely to find in pristine nature. At Penge, where Gencor took over in 1981, the airborne fibre count dropped from 62 f/ml in the 1960s, to 45 f/ml in 1977 and to 1,2 f/ml in 1989. The current figure is well inside internationally accepted limits. There were no published counts of ARDs until Gencor took over. In 1984 90 new cases were recorded. By 1987 the incidence had halved and since then only one or two more have been added. Nevertheless, although asbestos products are now safe and the mining industry, at last, appears to have its house in order, many hundreds of people are suffering and will go on suffering well into the next century. The clean up, it should be noted, has been achieved not through Government initiative but through pressure from the public and its press.

Most of the dangerous stuff in the air is invisible, and a lot of it is being dumped clandestinely by factory managers to save money and so make their balance sheets look more attractive to head office. Not much of the dangerous stuff is emitted by accident. Polluters know what they are doing and, sadly, a lot of them are protected by legalised secrecy and only the Government knows what they are up to.

It is easy, of course, to become neurotic about it all. Look how, in California, women's hair spray annually puts 27 tons of compounds into the atmosphere. Is that dangerous? There are no data. Is it healthy then? If not, should it be banned? If hair spray were to be banned what else should be put on the list for banning? There is an answer: all manufacturers should be compelled to prove that the environmental impact of their product is acceptable from a public health point of view. Until they can it must not be sold. Such a law is difficult. But it is easier than having to restore the Earth's atmosphere to its original healthy composition.

3 The greenhouse effect

> The primrose way to the everlasting bonfire.
>
> William Shakespeare

ON 23 June 1988, James Hansen of the Goddard Institute of Space Studies appeared before a US Senate Committee which was looking into the prospect of a changing atmosphere. Hansen had spent years studying the greenhouse effect and, as John Gribbin puts it in his *Hothouse Earth*, he had a "reputation for caution". Hansen said:

> The Earth is warmer this year than at any time in the history of instrumental measurements. Global warming is now sufficiently large that we can ascribe with a high degree of confidence a cause and effect relationship to the greenhouse effect. The effect (has begun) to affect the probability of the occurrence of extreme events ... the evidence is pretty strong that the greenhouse effect is here.

While sulphur dioxide (SO_2) is the major agent in the world for acid rain, carbon dioxide (CO_2) is the major agent for the greenhouse effect. The astonishing thing about carbon dioxide is that although it is vital to life on Earth, it constitutes by volume only 0,03 per cent of the planet's atmosphere. The air we breathe is almost four-fifths nitrogen and one-fifth oxygen with several trace gases. It has maintained this balance of gases for a considerable time and the familiar living world around us is programmed for these proportions and it makes no sense haphazardly experimenting with new proportions. But that is what we are doing.

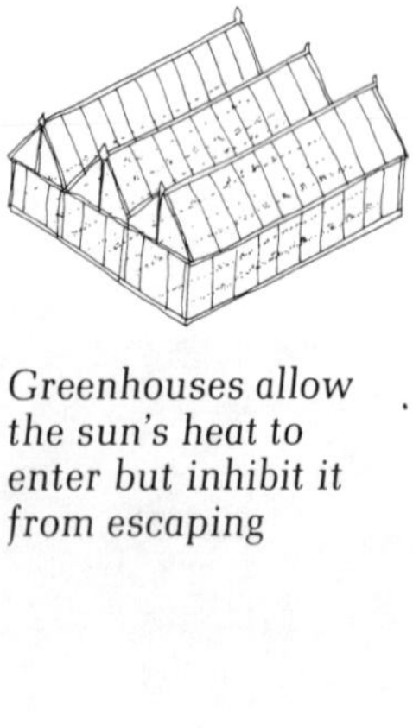

Greenhouses allow the sun's heat to enter but inhibit it from escaping

The build up of CO_2 was first noticed in the International Geophysical Year of 1957-58 at the observatory on Mauna Loa, Hawaii which had been testing the seasonal fluctuations in CO_2. It found a very slight dip every summer – seven parts per million (7ppm) – as the growing season absorbed CO_2. The fluctuation was against a CO_2 baseline of 315 ppm (by volume). Thirty years later the baseline had moved up to 350 ppm – an average increase of 3,5 per cent a decade.

Plants, which absorb CO_2 in order to grow, are, according to some theories, no longer able to cope with the amounts man is pumping into the atmosphere.

Excessive CO_2 in the atmosphere is having an effect similar to glass in a hothouse – it lets the sun's rays through to warm up the Earth's surface but then it traps a lot of it stopping it from radiating back into space. So the Earth is getting warmer and warmer. Despite some industrialists arguing that the case is not proven there is no doubt in the minds of most scientists that the greenhouse effect is real. The United Nations International Panel on Climate Change (IPCC) confirmed in a 1990 report that "sudden and unpredictable" climatic changes were likely unless carbon dioxide emissions were cut. John Houghton, director of Britain's Meteorological Service, commented that of the 200 scientists in the IPCC only 10 were uncertain.

Nearly all of South Africa's man-induced CO_2 comes from coal. In the United States power stations contribute 33 per cent; industry 25 per cent, transportation 31 per cent and homes and offices 11 per cent. Every ton of coal burned produces two tons of airborne carbon dioxide. If one accepts that South Africa, once all of its 1991 industrial infrastructure (including that which has been mothballed and that which is being constructed) is on stream, would be burning around 200 million tons of coal a year, then we will be emitting 400 million tons of CO_2 a year. That's about 10 tons for every person in the country – almost 10 times the world average. South Africa, when compared with the rest of the world, is probably one of the bigger contributors of CO_2. The United States (according to a Worldwatch Report) releases 22 per cent of the world's total industrial CO_2 emissions, Russia almost 19 per cent and Japan (third biggest contributor) 4,4 per cent. South Africa, not listed by Worldwatch, releases about 1,6 per cent.

The IPCC believes that the developed countries are producing half the world's carbon emissions. But, by 2025, the industrial world will be producing only a third. This is not so much because the rich countries will be cutting CO_2 emissions but because the developing nations will be increasing their output.

The world's CO_2 emissions add up to about 18 000 million tons a year according to the Worldwatch Institute. Carbon emissions are estimated at 5 700 tons. The *Scientific American* (May 1990) carried an estimate that nature absorbs 4 000 million tons, of which 3 000 million tons are absorbed by landplants and the rest by algae in the sea.

The summer of 1988 brought record temperatures and droughts to the United States. The USA's five hottest years on record were all in the 1980s. Britain also recorded its four hottest years in that decade. By 1990 an anxious

Europe appeared willing to make large economic sacrifices to reduce greenhouse gases but the United States began to have doubts. President George Bush questioned the data and said the US would not spend money until there was sounder evidence that it was necessary. "What if we spend billions," he said, "to combat something that might never

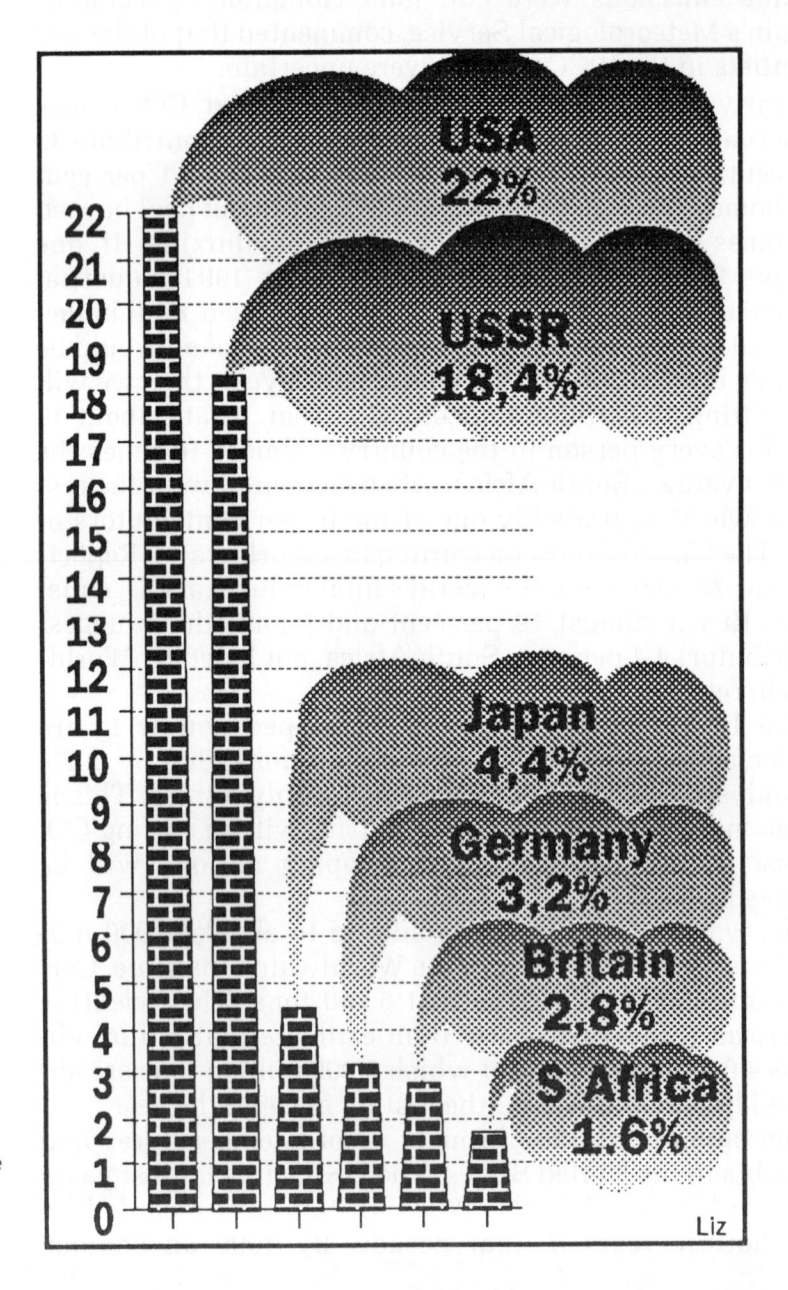

This is how South Africa compares with the world's five biggest contributors to globally carbon dioxide pollution.

USA 22%
USSR 18,4%
Japan 4,4%
Germany 3,2%
Britain 2,8%
S Africa 1,6%

happen?" West Germany's attitude was that the world could not afford to wait. Its Minister for the Environment, Klaus Topfer, said there may be gaps in world knowledge but the risks were too great to wait and see what might or might not happen. He proposed a 25 per cent reduction in emissions of CO_2 by 2005. Since then 15 nations and the entire European Community have agreed to either freeze or cut CO_2 emissions, and that means drastically reducing their use of oil and coal.

The Worldwatch Institute (December 1990), believing that the risks are indeed far too dangerous, proposes that the global carbon budget for 2030 be set at 2 500 million tons - a cut of roughly 55 per cent from now. That would mean cutting coal consumption 90 per cent. It points out that a world producing only 2 500 million tons will be far different from a world producing 6 000 million tons - a figure US industrialists are prepared to risk. More accurately, the industrialists are prepared to gamble their children's world.

Kenneth Mellanby, former director of Monks Wood Experimental Station and now editor of *Environmental Pollution*, writing in *New Scientist* (23 June 1990) wrote of the inexorably rising CO_2 level:

> *What the results on our climate will be no one knows, though many have opinions. Complex and expensive computer models suggest figures for global warming of between 1 and 9 degrees by the year 2050; this scatter of results reinforces my view that, while these exercises may be fun, there is so little firm data that back-of-the-envelope calculations would be more sensible. Nevertheless, a substantial number of responsible scientists believe that there is a serious possibility that these rises in greenhouse gases will produce disasters on a scale that mankind has never faced before. The warming of the oceans and the melting of Antarctic and Greenland ice, could cause the ocean levels to rise, drowning much of the low-lying and densely inhabited land throughout the world. Climatic changes could make the grain belt of America too dry to grow cereals. Global food shortages, with increasing world population, could be horrific.*

As the turn of the century draws near we can anticipate some sort of international Law of the Atmosphere and

The melting of the polar regions will raise the sea level

nations which do begin the costly process of reducing greenhouse gases may well boycott those who avoid doing so. They would argue that "dirty" countries are wrecking the global atmosphere, and, by avoiding a carbon cleanup, those countries would gain an unfair price advantage for their goods in the international market place.

Carbon dioxide in the atmosphere has increased in volume by almost a fifth (19 per cent) since the start of the Industrial Revolution. Scientists know this from sampling old air trapped for centuries in bubbles in the Antarctic's icecap. Nitrogen dioxide (NO_2), mainly resulting from industrial activity and car exhausts, is up by a quarter. Efforts to curb this gas have been ineffective and not even half-hearted.

Then there is methane, a trace gas but, molecule by molecule, 20 times more efficient as a greenhouse gas than carbon dioxide. Since industrialisation methane has doubled in volume. Enormous quantities are put into the atmosphere by biological decomposition. Curiously, termite activity (termites have their own compost heaps underground) are responsible for hundreds of millions of tons. As the world's farmlands become degraded so termites, and their methane contribution, increase. Thus one can say poor farming methods add to the greenhouse effect. Methane also comes from manure and compost and stomach gases. A human being produces 50 grams of methane gas a year, a cow produces 50 kilograms.

Jim Lovelock, the man who postulated that Earth may be a living organism (Gaia, he called it) capable of resisting infection and even running a temperature - as it appears to be doing right now - suggests that a little after life on Earth began there was a sudden drop in temperature. This was because the first form of life - waterborne bacteria - in photosynthesising, used up a critical amount of carbon dioxide. He says temperatures suddenly fell from a pleasant 28 degrees to a chilly 15. But what lives must also die: vast quantities of bacteria began decomposing in marshlands which now gave off methane. Thus nature made herself a greenhouse and the chilling was countered.

To gain some idea of the thinness of the Earth's atmospheric "skin" it would be 1 millimetre thick in proportion to a desktop globe of the world. It comprises only 0,7 parts per million methane and this appears to have remained constant since the Earth began to warm up after the last Ice Age, 10 000 years ago. But in the last 300 years industry and intensive farming have increased the amount alarmingly. Methane is now increasing by 1 per cent a year says John Gribbin who estimates that for every gram of methane produced by nature, another gram is produced by agriculture, sewage works, municipal landfills and other man-related sources.

There are four natural greenhouse gases - carbon dioxide, nitrous oxide (nox), ozone and methane. All are on the increase. There is a fifth, an unnatural contributor, made up of chlorofluorocarbons (CFCs), which we will discuss later.

As Mellanby observed, there is a great deal of controversy about just how much the world will warm up. There is even a school of thought which says it will not warm up at all. Others argue the greenhouse effect will cancel itself out by creating more evaporation and, therefore, more cloud cover and rain; the clouds will then reflect the sun's rays back into space and thus cause a cooling. A few postulate an acceleration of the next ice age which is round about due. Another argument is that the cloud cover will enhance the greenhouse effect by a factor of three. The disturbing thing about the controversy is that here we have two major groupings of scientists, working with the same facts,

Termites are responsible for hundreds of millions of tons of methane

coming to diametrically opposed conclusions. We could laugh it off and go back to bed except for one thing: they both predict radical change resulting in climatic chaos.

There is at least one contrary point of view that is worth noting. Sherwood B Idso, research scientist with the US Water Conservation Laboratory, Department of Agriculture in Phoenix delivered a paper in April 1989 which threw some light, and some heat, on the subject. He feels the CO_2 build up is a good thing and suggests that plant life, at the moment, "is actually starved for carbon dioxide." Idso says:

> We know this to be true because of the results of literally hundreds of experiments where plants have been grown in CO_2-enriched atmospheres characteristic of the times of Earth's past history when they developed their basic physiological properties and to which the plants of today are still better adapted. In general the experiments suggest that a 300 to 600 parts per million doubling of the air's CO_2 content increases the overall growth of all plants by about one third and that a 300 to 900 ppm CO_2 tripling boosts productivity by two thirds.

Idso says that a CO_2 increase would alter plants physiologically so that they lose less water. "Thus grasslands will flourish where deserts now lie barren; shrubs will grow where only grasses grew before; and forests will make a dramatic comeback." Ultimately he sees a global warming of fully 8 degrees Celsius.

He decries the "doom and gloom" lobby's prediction of melting polar caps and increasingly ferocious hurricanes – "they are trying to convince us to forsake the primary energy sources which sustain our industries and which form the basis of our civilisation." (I find it difficult to accept that coal and oil form the basis of our civilisation. Of our technology, yes. But civilisation is something else.) He talks of how the CO_2 content of the air was as high as 70 000 ppm in the planet's very young days and that life on our planet "existed in an equitable thermal environment for at least 3,8 billion years." This is only partly true. For the first many hundreds of millions of years there were only waterborne bacteria and for 3,4 billion of those 3,8 billion years life could be sustained only under the sea. A fish might call that equitable.

Nevertheless Idso underlines some interesting uncertainties. He even suggests that the drop in CO_2 from the primordial 70 000 ppm to as low as 180 (in the last ice age) reveals that in recent times plant life came perilously near to dying out through lacking CO_2. He questions current computer models of how the atmosphere, and life itself, will respond to more CO_2. The complexities are, he says, way beyond present computer capacities. But this brings us back to the point that we are idly playing with the atmosphere without knowing what might happen.

Idso does not defend pollution *per se* and he is certainly not alone in believing the greenhouse effect will postpone the next ice age. But what is the layman to make of it all? He cannot put his trust in science, not on this score. He can only urge politicians to take the West German line – curb this "mad professor" experiment on the Earth's atmosphere.

The majority of scientists agree that the Earth is warming up and that the effects will be negative for some countries. The question is, by how much? John Gribbin says that when all the feedbacks are put into a computer model, and assuming carbon dioxide levels double (which they will, in 70 years, if present trends continue) then the Earth is likely to heat up by between 3 and 5 degrees. The effects would be profound. Many already hot areas in the world, including in South Africa (one thinks of the northern Cape and parts of the Karoo) would become uninhabitable in summer. There is a general consensus that South Africa will receive less rain and experience more evaporation. At the National Conference on Geosphere/Biosphere Change in Southern Africa in Cape Town in 1989, Desmond Midgley warned that South Africa could dry out in 30 to 50 years' time and become hotter than it has ever been.

As a result of that conference Peter Tyson wrote to the Government, on behalf of delegates, drawing attention to the seriousness of the global warming threat:

> The Government and private sector must give high priority and generous financial support to research into global change and its effect on South Africa ... the future of millions of people in the country will be critically dependent on how the negative effects of global change are predicted and managed.

In various recent reports by the Worldwatch Institute in Washington there seems to be a growing consensus among those who support the greenhouse theory that it will be the inland regions, in the middle to high latitudes (the high ones being closest to the Poles) which will warm up most. South Africa can then expect a drying out of its Maize Triangle which covers the northern Orange Free State and much of the Transvaal Highveld. The Karoo, which already covers one-third of South Africa and which has been creeping northwards and eastwards for years, will accelerate its advance. In the general drying up of the interior we may well lose animal, bird and plant species. Across the world many traditional food-growing areas such as the North American Prairies would be affected and some croplands would have to be relegated to rangeland. A few areas may score: Canada and Russia may find that marginal grain areas will become warmer and therefore less marginal.

The global warming would cause a melting of the Antarctic's ice and of glacial ice. The seas, in consequence, would rise. (The melting of the northern polar cap would not in itself increase sea levels because most of that ice is floating and, therefore, its disappearance would actually lower the sea's level. The melting of Greenland's ice cap, lying as it does on land, would increase levels.) By the end of the 1980s the seas were already rising – but this was more the result of heat expansion and not a polar thaw.

The worst case scenario is that the seas will rise to such an extent that they will inundate low-lying areas – a fifth of Holland, reclaimed from the sea by engineers, could be inundated. A vast crop-growing area of Bangladesh would be lost and all the Maldive Islands in the Indian Ocean where 30 000 people inhabit 200 islands, would be submerged. All cities at sea level will be severely damaged and some would become impossible to maintain as cellars remain perpetually flooded and as every spring and neap tide inundates central streets. London would frequently be inundated as the tidal Thames rises to unprecedented heights.

Closer to home: spring and neap tides would become more dangerous, frequently washing into seaside towns. Durban would have to build a high sea wall to stop the sea rolling across Marine Parade and into hotel lobbies. Even in a more optimistic scenario Durban stands to lose its beaches entirely, as would most resorts. Cape Town's

Seafront defences will have to be reinforced as sea levels rise

Foreshore would be threatened. The economies of coastal areas would be devastated.

It is also widely forecast by climatologists that climatic events such as cyclones, hurricanes, blizzards, heatwaves and so on are likely to increase in frequency and severity.

When it comes to action regarding the greenhouse effect we are seeing the rare phenomenon of politicians springing to their feet a little ahead of the general public. Certainly this was so as far as the "ozone holes" discovered above the polar regions were concerned. It is because of this mood, and because of the mounting evidence of radical change, that I believe the world will have an international convention to protect the atmosphere within this decade.

In October 1989, Christopher Flavin, vice-president of the Worldwatch Institute in Washington, in his "Slowing Global Warming: a Worldwide Strategy" (*Worldwatch Paper 91*), said:

> International treaties on global warming will be far more complex than the ozone agreements. While ozone depletion is caused mainly by a particular class of industrial chemicals, many of which can be replaced, global warming is caused by gases that are central to the activities of modern societies. In addition, there is greater scientific uncertainty about the impacts of the greenhouse effects,

which provides ammunition to those seeking to slow the process. On the other hand, awareness and concern about climate change, are much deeper today than was the case with ozone depletion in the mid-eighties.

Flavin felt that it was important to set ambitious goals for cleaning up carbon and for the industrial nations to set about achieving them immediately. Such steps might include a halt to the building of more coal-fired power stations, far greater efficiency in industrial energy use and more intelligence in the design of domestic and commercial buildings. Transport would be revolutionised. Mellanby says three quarters of today's car journeys could be made by electric cars. It will mean huge shifts in the balance of business power – oil companies would be curbed as would the car manufacturing multinationals which have stymied attempts to break with the petrol engine.

The first step towards global action was taken in September 1987 when several industrialised nations met in Montreal to discuss the ozone phenomenon and voted for collective action. Eight months later, in May 1988, in Toronto, the Canadian government hosted a world conference on "The Changing Atmosphere". Forty-eight nations

This scene on Cape Town's Foreshore will become commonplace under the greenhouse effect

sent political and scientific representatives. Also present were 15 international agencies and 47 non-government organisations. The more conservative scenario which arose from this conference was that the average global temperature will rise 4 degrees over 40 years and that sea levels will rise 140 centimetres. The conference resolved to request the industrialised world to reduce CO_2 by 20 per cent by 2005.

In October 1990 prime ministers, cabinet ministers and officials from 139 countries met in Geneva for the second conference on the World's Changing Climate and agreed to formulate an international law to reduce greenhouse gases – but the law would have to wait until the UN Environment and Development Congress in Rio de Janeiro in January 1992. The delay was disappointing. Europe, Canada, Australia and Japan wanted immediate action to peg CO_2 at present levels, and then start reducing them. The United States, Russia and Saudi Arabia – all big oil producers – wanted more time.

Some say the cost will cripple industry. But that's just one way of looking at it. The cost of getting to the moon appeared crippling, and even non-productive, but it created a host of new technologies from transistors to non-stick frying pans, as well as new industries and many thousands of jobs. Similarly, the elimination of CO_2 will create new opportunities and new technologies and new jobs. The "crippling cost" of curbing the greenhouse effect will almost certainly be less than the cost of being crippled by an unpredictable climate.

Thus far South Africa has no plans at all for curbing CO_2 nor does it have standards or targets. CO_2 is not mentioned in the Department of Health's Draft Air Pollution Control Policy (1990).

4 The hole in the ozone

We do it wrong, being so majestical,
To offer it the show of violence;
For it is, as the air, invulnerable,
And our vain blows malicious
mockery

William Shakespeare

THE Montreal meeting in 1987 resulted in the Montreal Protocol calling for a world-wide curb on chlorofluorocarbons (CFCs) which, only months before had been identified as the cause of the holes in the ozone layer above the polar regions. Twenty-four nations signed an international action plan immediately and several signed later, including South Africa (in January 1990). South Africa has undertaken to freeze CFC production at 1986 levels and to cut 20 per cent by 1992 and a further 30 per cent by 1998. But the country's only manufacturer of CFCs, the big chemical and explosives company, AECI, later stated it would cut production 50 per cent by 1992 (aerosols use 50 per cent of their production and were rapidly disappearing from shops by 1990) and that it hopes to eliminate CFCs entirely by the end of the century. South Africa is responsible for 1 per cent of the world's CFCs, Britain for 3 per cent and the United States for 25.

In 20 years of mounting anxiety over the deterioration of the human habitat nothing has scared the world's politicians more than the sudden discovery that there was a gaping hole in the ozone above the Antarctic. The extent of it shook scientists too, especially as such an event had not been predicted in any of their computer models. A similar phenomenon occurs over the Arctic in the northern Spring. It is not so pronounced but as it swings over relatively highly populated areas in northern Eurasia its potential to affect health is greater. In 1990, a comprehensive publication by a joint team of trade unions and science institutions in Sweden sponsored by the Federation of Industries said that ozone was disappearing on a worldwide scale. But following the second revision of the Montreal Protocol at the 1990 London negotiations, which ended in an international agreement signed on 29 June, it became clear that the volume of chlorine in the atmosphere, being released from CFCs, should peak before the end of this century. This was 50 years earlier than scientists had feared. India and China, potentially huge consumers of CFCs now that their economies are picking up, said they would be prepared to sign in 1992. Nevertheless the damage already done will exist for decades unless there is a third revision of the international agreement aimed at actually *repairing* the damage.

Ozone is a form of oxygen but, unlike the oxygen

Sunbathing is becoming increasingly hazardous

Antarctic

molecule which has two atoms (hence its symbol O_2), ozone has three (O_3). Ninety per cent of the ozone in the atmosphere is high up in the stratosphere and for aeons molecules of ozone, whose lifespan is weeks, have undergone a process of destruction and regeneration while maintaining a balance. If all the ozone were compressed into a layer at sea level it would be only 3 millimetres thick. So there isn't much. But there is enough to absorb a critical amount of the sun's ultraviolet rays which, if the ozone shield did not exist, would lethally irradiate life on the Earth. One of the effects of thinning of the ozone shield is that it will cause an increase in skin cancer, but a bigger threat is that it will aggravate global warming.

The hole above the Antarctic was discovered by British Antarctic scientist Joe Farman in 1982. Up until then some scientists, finding their readings on ozone levels were no longer making sense, blamed it on faulty instruments. And because nobody was really interested in ozone they simply stopped collecting the data. When, in the spring of 1987, the hole was found to be 8 kilometres deep and as big as America, everybody began jumping.

Professor Malcolm Scourfield, aerologist at the University of Natal (Durban), says that each spring, as the Antarctic's ozone hole appears, ozone is drained from above South Africa. "Any change in Antarctica directly affects South Africa."

Joe Farman, quoted in the London *Sunday Times* in 1989, revealed that "in one layer of the atmosphere (over Antarctica) we actually lost 95 percent of the ozone in six weeks." Science writer, Fred Pearce, in the same article, commented: "Now the evidence is growing that the ozone layer is thinning right across the northern and southern hemispheres. The guess is that this thinning is a dilution effect, brought on by the ozone destruction over the poles."

In 1987, scientists aboard two Nasa aircraft, flew through the hole and found "at an altitude 18 kilometres above the ground, more than half the ozone above Antarctica was destroyed. And changes in the amount of chlorine oxide present marched precisely in step with changes in the amount of ozone. When chlorine oxide went up ozone went down." As John Gribbin (*The Hole in the Ozone* 1989) wrote: "The smoking gun had been found." Chlorine atoms in the stratosphere were changing ozone into oxygen – O_3

was becoming O_2 – and thus ozone's ability to shield the earth from ultraviolet rays was being neutralised.

Finding the smoking gun was one thing, but who was holding it? The culprit was a group of very stable man-made compounds, chlorofluorocarbons, with widespread, everyday uses, which were ascending into the atmosphere, perhaps taking 25 or more years to reach the stratosphere, where the sun then freed their chlorine which then attacked the ozone. In the polar spring the first rays of the sun after the long sunless winter trigger this reaction. Afterwards the hole repairs itself. But just how big might this hole get? And just how much damage can this layer tolerate before it becomes irreparable? *Nature* in September 1990 revealed that the 1989 Airborne Arctic Stratospheric Expedition found 35 per cent of the ozone above the Arctic may have been destroyed during the winter of 1988/1989. Ozone from adjacent areas was flowing in to the area where the ozone had been thinned out. There was no hole but it seemed likely one would appear sooner or later. Even if we immediately stop using CFCs, the damage is going to continue because of the years it takes for CFCs to climb through the atmosphere.

The growing hole in the ozone layer

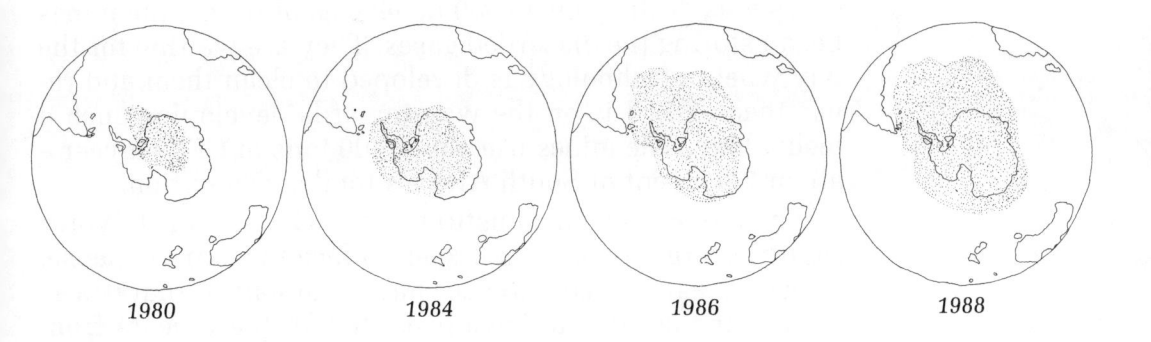

1980   1984   1986   1988

There is another kind of ultraviolet radiation which never reaches the ground, called UV-C, but some authorities believe UV-C might penetrate if the holes deepen. UV-C, in a laboratory, has been found to destroy nucleic acids (RNA and DNA) and protein – the basic molecules of life. The UV rays which concern us at present (UV-B) are known to affect soya beans – a 25 per cent increase in UV-B reduces soya bean yields by the same percentage.

CFCs were invented in the late 1920s and today have many applications: in South Africa almost 50 per cent are used in aerosol spray cans, about 20 per cent in refrigerators and air conditioning units as coolant gases, and nearly 30 per cent to create foam plastic for such things as fast food packaging and polystyrene cups. A small amount is used in cleaning solvents in the computer industry but the industry is a substantial user overseas.

Replacing CFCs in aerosols presents no great problem. And as far as solvents for the computer industry are concerned that should be no great problem either. Interestingly for South Africa, Du Pont in the United States is hopeful about a substitute solvent made from orange peel.

Foam plastic is already being banned in some countries, mainly because it is light, bulky and non-biodegradable, and thus very expensive to dispose of in the waste stream. The biggest problem is finding a reasonably priced substitute for CFCs as coolants. In South Africa, until 1989, the gold mines, who have the biggest refrigerators on Earth – they need them to cool the air deep below ground where the rockface is actually hot to the touch – vented tons of CFCs at a time when they overhauled their systems. Once it became clear that each molecule of chlorine from these CFCs was destroying 10 000 molecules of ozone, the mines began storing the discarded gases. They are waiting for the day when a technology is developed to clean them and re-use them. AECI is on the way towards developing such a technology. The mines use about 400 tons of CFCs a year – about 7 per cent of South Africa's total consumption.

When it comes to substitutes for CFCs, Third World countries are obviously not keen to face the extra expense. Their delegates at conferences have complained that it was unfair for the West to have benefited all these years from using cheap CFCs – they cost in South Africa about R5 500 a ton – and to now expect the Third World to forsake them. The West will probably subsidise CFC substitutes for the Third World.

Two stopgap coolants will be hydrochlorofluorocarbons (HCFCs) and hydrofluorocarbons (HFCs), the latter containing no chlorine at all. But both will still be destroying ozone, though at a reduced rate. They will be six to 15 times more expensive than CFCs. There are less harmful substitutes and these are belatedly being researched. There is talk, meanwhile, of replenishing ozone by attaching tanks of ozone to airliners for release at high cruising altitudes.

From a health point of view Scourfield says: "What is frightening is that for every 1 per cent ozone depletion it is predicted there will be a correlating 2 per cent increase in skin cancers." Two years ago the World Health Organisation predicted that a 10 per cent depletion in ozone would result in a 3 percent increase in ordinary skin cancers and a 1 per cent increase in melanoma, the malignant kind of skin cancer. Already, according to the South African Medical Research Council, 60 per cent of all whites over 60 suffer skin cancer, mostly of the benign type. People with black skins do not suffer as much from exposure to ultraviolet light. What is not known is what extra ultraviolet light will do to surface fish and plankton of the southern oceans from where massive amounts of protein come and what it might do to light-skinned livestock.

Ironically, despite fears regarding the seasonal thinning of high altitude ozone, the other fear is that low level ozone – which is an eye-smarting poison – is *increasing* over the middle latitudes of the northern hemisphere, because of industrialisation. Gribbin estimates that ozone – produced when vehicle and factory fumes cook in the sun – is thickening over industrial regions by between 0,5 and 4 per cent (in parts per billion) depending on the area. He says that at the beginning of the Industrial Revolution there was probably a quarter of the ground level zone that exists now, and by 2030 we can expect today's level to double. Again nobody can predict what precisely will happen. Gribbin says low altitude ozone, as an agent in the greenhouse effect, is a far bigger problem than either nitrous oxide or methane.

5 Trees to the rescue

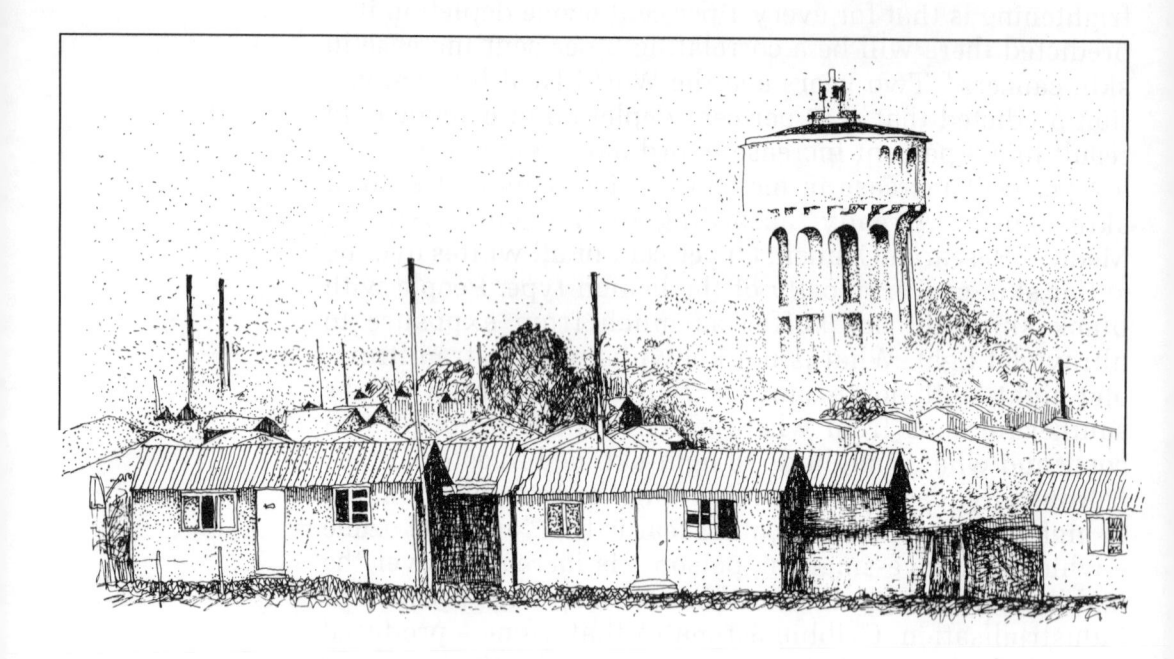

Woodman, spare that tree!
Touch not a single bough!
In youth it sheltered me,
And I'll protect it now.

George Pope Morris

A 1991 radio item said that an American authority had suggested that scrap iron should be thrown into the sea as this would have the effect of feeding marine algae which would then become a floating mass capable of asborbing CO_2. My immediate reaction was anger: having damaged the air we are now about to damage the sea just to see what happens. The idea does not seem too bright... but there is no doubt that growing more plants, especially trees, will absorb millions of tons of CO_2.

There is a current timber shortage in the world, both of hardwoods and pulp wood, and most countries are clearing forests. Although Canadians and Americans are criticising Brazil for its destruction of the Amazon, those two countries are reducing their own forest cover. In fact the Brazilian picture is not quite as bad as is sometimes made out. I met the rather elusive Professor Philip Fearnside in his Amazon Forest Research Centre in Manaus in 1988. On my way to see him my plane was held up at Cuiaba airport for hours because of smoke from forest burning. Smoke had blanketed much of Brazil that September. But Fearnside was reassuring: he told me that only 5 per cent of the Amazon forest has so far been destroyed. Most of the fires I had seen involved secondary growth – the areas having been burned before and partly regrown. All the same, there were forces at work, especially mining interests, which were threatening unprecedented destruction to this vital CO_2 sink.

There is no doubt that if the existing great forests can be preserved, or rather conserved (for there is no reason why they should not be utilised on a managed basis), and if every country established a vast tree growing programme, we could mop up a significant proportion of the excess CO_2. Australia has already announced it will plant a billion trees during the 1990s. That's enough trees to absorb 50 million tons of CO_2, somewhat less than 1 per cent of worldwide industrial output. South Africa, through the Jewish National Fund, is planting 5 million – not nearly enough for a country which is dumping so much carbon in the air. The 5 million trees would absorb 250 000 tons of CO_2 – about as much as South African industry puts into the air every 6 hours.

Trees slow up in their absorption rates once they mature, which, in South Africa's climate, is at 20 to 30 years old (in the case of plantation trees such as pine and eucalyptus). But then they can be cut down and used as fuel in place of oil and coal and thus less CO_2 would be released. Some could be used for building. To absorb the equivalent of all the CO_2 put out by a single big Transvaal "six pack" coal-fired power station one would have to plant a forest 90 kilometres in diameter.

While tree planting definitely helps, there are more practical options for reducing carbon pollution:

1. Building no more coal-fired power stations (unless some technological solution is found to trap CO_2). California has already barred coal-burning throughout the state.
2. Using more hydro power, although even this form of power is becoming unpopular because of its environmental effects. The Indian government has met with massive public opposition over proposed new dams. The fact remains that technically, as opposed to politically, Southern Africa need never build another thermal power station. The Zaire River (formerly the Congo River) has, in just one section, a latent energy yield of 120 000 MW - enough to supply more than double Africa's present needs. Certainly it is all that Southern Africa will probably ever need. The Zaire has a second site capable of yielding as much as South Africa will be generating in 10 years' time. Eskom's attitude is that it is prepared to help Zaire exploit this but it would never rely on any foreign country for more than 12 per cent of South Africa's needs because a breakdown in political stability in that country, or in a country traversed by supply lines, could disrupt the supply.
3. South Africa has two successful pumped-storage hydro schemes. It has a relatively small one on the Palmiet River near Cape Town and the other, the Tuva scheme (for Tugela/Vaal) is a 1 000 MW plant in the Natal Drakensberg near Bergville. Water is pumped from the Tugela into a holding dam at the bottom of an escarpment and, when the peak electricity demand period ends each day and power stations have surplus power, coal-fired power is used to pump the water to the top of the escarpment. When the next peak period comes the water is let down the escarpment to drive turbines at the bottom. (Some of the water remains at the top to run into

the Sterkfontein Dam which supplies back-up water for the Vaal Dam.) South Africa could use its ultra deep gold mines, as they become exhausted, as pumped storage schemes. These mines have shafts up to 4 kilometres deep and the water would be evaporation free underground. The Tugela River can provide an additional 5 000 MW reserve, mostly via pumped storage schemes, but environmental impact studies have yet to be done.

4. Another way to curb CO_2 is to conserve power – something which South Africa has never tried. The fact that buildings are extremely wasteful of energy and that no university teaches its architects the energy conservative approach to building design reveals just how under-priced electricity is. At the University of the Witwatersrand architects do not receive lectures at the building sciences department where great attention is paid to energy conservation techniques and materials.

It is commonplace in north-facing offices in Johannesburg for people to open the windows in winter because the sun shines directly through, while at the south end of the floor people sit with electric fires. Modern buildings are sometimes even less efficient, especially some which are sheathed in glass – like greenhouses. A new Government building in Pretoria accommodates 2 600 people but uses the same amount of power as a town of 23 000. Johannesburg's tallest building, the Carlton Centre, uses as much electricity as the city of Kimberley. Tall buildings, apart from the enormous quantities of power needed for air conditioning, also use a lot for their internal public transport – lifts – which mostly carry one person at a time.

Victorian "airconditioner"

Richard Liversidge, director of the McGregor Museum in Kimberley demonstrated, rather dramatically, how twentieth century technological man might have lost sight of fundamental wisdom. Liversidge bought a quaint, corrugated iron roofed house in suburbia which dated back to the 1890s. In summer, when temperatures in Kimberley reached into the 40s, the house became unbearably hot. He wondered how Victorians tolerated such discomfort, until he noticed that Victorian homes which had not been modernised had on their roofs small turrets with slatted sides which looked a bit like

Solar-panelled house

beehives. He found one on a scrap heap and cut a hole in his roof to accommodate it. Even as his hacksaw cut the hole the hot air from inside began to woosh out in a hot blast. The perfect air-conditioner! No electricity, no maintenance – and it sucks the hot air out, causing the cool air from under the shady veranda, which sensibly surrounds most old homes in Africa, to blow like a soft breeze down the passages.

There are various alternative ways of harnessing energy. Solar power is one. According to the Worldwatch Institute Cyprus, Israel and Jordan heat between 25 and 65 per cent of their domestic water by using solar panels. Two-thirds of Israel's homes have solar panels which provide hot water and stored power for lights at night. The technology is grossly ignored in South Africa. Eskom no more than dabbles in it and research is starved of funds. The world is fortunate in having the United States with its free-swinging style when it comes to technology. That country has several dozen solar power plants, each one more sophisticated and more promising than its predecessor. In California an 80 MW plant is operating and in the near future one of 450 MW should go into operation. California is leading because it has, in several areas, many hours of guaranteed sunshine. So does South Africa. In fact Kruger National Park's new camps use solar-powered batteries for lighting and the railway system uses it for signals in remote areas, as does the freeway system to power emergency telephones.

A major reason why South African households do not utilise the country's abundant sunshine to at least heat their water is that the financial incentive is low. Coal-fired electricity is relatively cheap (just see how we waste it) and the cost of solar panels, because of the small demand, is relatively expensive. By the time a household is about to recoup its costs for solar power, the panels need replacing. If the Government were to give tax rebates on solar power it would be a different story. Eskom has said it will not save much electricity because domestic users consume so little compared with industry and commerce. But that attitude reveals a certain chauvinism on the part of Eskom. From a householder's point of view, using solar panels to heat just domestic water would save one-third of the household bill – and

collectively householders could reduce the national pollution load by a significant 1 or 2 per cent.
6. Wind power has also been studiously ignored even though the eastern Cape which uses only about 600 MW of Eskom electricity (its needs can be supplied by just one of the six turbines in Eskom's newest power station) could be self-sufficient if it harnessed wind power because it has ideal sites. Sweden, in 1990, announced it was building a giant windmill off the coast. If it came up to expectations it would erect 60 of them and replace the entire production of its nuclear power stations. The coal lobby points out that wind power costs are prohibitive. This was true 10 years ago. Then we would have been talking of almost 75 cents a kilowatt hour (interpreting US figures). Now it is down to 20 cents and by the end of the nineties it should be down to 12 cents. California receives 20 per cent of its power via windmills.
7. Then there is biomass. This is already the primary source of fuel for half the world's population – through wood-burning and the burning of cattle dung. In sub-Saharan Africa three-quarters of energy needs are provided by biomass and new generation wood stoves are three times more efficient than conventional wood burners.

Wind turbine

There has been talk of producing ethanol from sugar cane in South Africa (and indeed in other parts of Africa) but there is something obscene about using cropland and precious irrigation water in malnourished regions to grow petrol for cars. Using sugar cane residues is a different matter. Eric Larson and others, in a paper delivered at the Energy from Biomass and Wastes conference at Lake Buena Vista, Florida in February 1990 said sub-Saharan Africa could generate "some 50 000 MW" from such residues.

The Faustian bargain

There is another way of supplementing energy. It was invented by a New Zealander and it uses neither coal nor oil. It has been successfully tested in South Africa with incredibly impressive results – and not a wisp of smoke. Even better, the fuel is so plentiful in South Africa that we could even export it. This carefully guarded plant, on a stretch of arid Cape coast, noiselessly generates 1 800 MW – enough to supply greater Johannesburg. The plant, astonishingly small and clinically clean, and with no rail sidings, feedstock dumps, fuel conveyor belts or ash dumps, nevertheless has ordinary steam boilers and conventional turbines. The whole thing has run without a hitch for six years and has another 20 or more years of life.

The source of heat? Uranium. For this is Koeberg nuclear power plant in the south-western Cape. South Africa is likely to have more such "nukes" before today's toddlers are in middle age, depending on public acceptance.

Nuclear power stations are expensive to construct, but once up they are cheaper to run than coal-fired power stations. The latter have to be fed with coal. Koeberg would have consumed 50 million tons of coal by now and put out 100 million tons of greenhouse gases and 500 000 tons of sulphur dioxide.

(It can be argued that in the case of Koeberg the energy-environmental-impact equation is not quite as simple as I have made out. Because South Africa was denied imported enriched uranium fuel, the country was forced to either abandon Koeberg or enrich its own uranium at Valindaba near Hartbeespoort Dam in the central Transvaal. It chose the latter and, although the figures are secret, it must have taken an awful lot of electrical energy – from coal – to run the enrichment plant which makes Koeberg's fuel. Naturally, the more "Koebergs" South Africa builds the more economic nuclear power will become.)

Dr C J H Hartnady, director of the Precambrian Research Unit at the University of Cape Town, suggested at an Earthlife Africa symposium at Hermanus in 1990 that Eskom should consider developing what he called "a nuclear corridor" down the west coast from Rössing uranium mine in Namibia down to Vaalputs where Eskom now dumps its low level radioactive wastes. This desolate stretch of coast has, for years, been out of bounds to the public because this is where De Beers digs diamonds from the beach sand. When the diamonds run out the land could be transferred from De Beers to Eskom. He sees a potential for the complete cycle – uranium ore to enriched fuel, to power generation to waste dumping – all in a confined, uninhabited and geologically stable area. The potential is 10 000 MW – more than enough to enable Eskom to close down some of its more offensive coal-fired plants on the Transvaal Highveld.

Ironically it was the Three Mile Island incident, on 28 March 1979, that won a lot of formerly anti-nuke lobbyists over to supporting nuclear power. Yet here was, potentially, the worst type of nuclear accident – a loss of coolant, and the threat of a meltdown of the reactor core. Over a period of three days a combination of misunderstandings, poor communication on the plant and outside, and overlapping authority led to near public panic. At one point engineers, watching the cores' temperatures rise when they assumed they should have started to drop, tried to overrule the computer. They failed, but they succeeded in writing off a reactor and, economically speaking, greatly damaging their industry as a whole.

The TMI affair was an economic disaster, not a human one. It hurt nobody except the industry which badly needed to be humiliated. For years it had scoffed at the public's distrust of nuclear fission. Yet who could blame the public for its fear? Nuclear fission had been introduced to the public in a sudden and violent way, with a flash "brighter than a thousand suns" which incinerated a city with its people. Who of us who recall those days can forget the photograph of a person's shadow left on the pavement of Hiroshima? The more peaceful application of nuclear fission following World War II was secretive in the extreme, which led to further distrust. The burgeoning nuclear priesthood began speaking a language designed not to bridge the gap between it and the public but to widen it. And totally overshadowing the undoubted success of the first commercial nuclear power stations which sprung up from the 1950s onwards, was the sinister battle of wits as East and West built up enormous stockpiles of nuclear weapons.

Nuclear explosion

Scientists were clearly unable to control the power that they had unleashed and politicians were, patently, not to be trusted with it.

The accident at Three Mile Island was a landmark in the nuclear industry's public relations. Suddenly nuclear scientists and technicians had to talk in a language and produce diagrams that the public understood. Months later polls showed that many people were reassured by TMI. Their nightmare – the "China syndrome" in which an out-of-control core is supposed to go on and on reacting until it burns its way through the power station floor all the way to

China – had, at least as far as many people were concerned, almost come true. Yet nobody had been hurt.

All the same the nuclear industry was stopped in its tracks in most parts of the world. Perhaps the global economic downturn and the stabilisation of population growth and its associated levelling off of energy demand affected the picture. To this day there are multi-billion nuclear power stations which have never been commissioned. France did not lose her confidence in nuclear power and now produces two-thirds of her electricity from uranium. Switzerland, which has vowed never to build another nuclear station, is happy to buy off France. Germany too does not want to build another but it does have natural gas and it is following the conservation option.

About a fifth of the world's electrical power comes from nuclear reactors.

As Three Mile Island gradually passed to the back of the public mind and as the world grew more concerned about the effects of pollution from coal and oil, so came Chernobyl. In 1986 the disintegration of a reactor at Chernobyl near Kiev in Russia provided a stunning demonstration that some countries which opted for nuclear power had neither the knowledge nor the skills. Chernobyl, like Koeberg, is a pressurised water reactor, except Russia, not having the technology to make a large enough pressure vessel, improvised by making smaller, separate, pipe-like vessels. One of them was faulty. The reactor virtually had no container building (the lead-lined, superstrong steel and concrete shell which encapsulates all western reactors) and when the pressure vessel blew, the blast lifted the 2 500 ton roof off the reactor building and flipped it into the air. Four years afterwards, Britain, having spent R50 million compensating farmers whose farms were contaminated by fallout from Chernobyl (2 200 kilometres away) was still confining 600 000 animals from 700 farms because of the risk of their meat or milk spreading radioactivity.

Thirty one workers died in the Chernobyl tragedy. But that was a lot fewer than the 432 who died in 1960 fuelling up coal-fired Highveld and Taaibos power stations near Vereeniging – they were buried alive when the mine caved in at Coalbrook. But, of course, Chernobyl's radioactive fallout will shorten the lives of 28 000 people. But the figure is misleading. The majority of those premature deaths involve people whose dose of radiation has been about the equivalent (or less) of somebody moving from Durban to the Transvaal Highveld where, because of the altitude, there is more solar radiation. Nearly all those 28 000 will live to a ripe old age and if they do die prematurely it will be days not years.

On the subject of risks, Professor Michael Golan of the Massachusetts Institute of Technology worked out in 1977 that an average coal-fired power station will cause the deaths of seven to 10 people a year from emphysema. By that reckoning Koeberg, if it were burning coal, would so far have cost 15 to 18 lives from foul air alone. An interesting and not entirely irrelevant fact is that a coal-fired plant emits so much radiation from the coal itself that it would set off Koeberg's alarms.

The biggest problem with nuclear power remains the problem of what to do with the waste. There isn't much – 200 kilograms a year for Koeberg. The low level waste is buried in trenches at Vaalputs in the northern Cape, but the high level stuff (spent fuel rods, etc) is at present lying in a specially constructed "swimming pool" at Koeberg, cooling off. At some stage it will have to be moved and buried. Hartnady is critical of the Government and the Atomic Energy Council, which actually runs the Vaalputs site, for failing to realise the urgency of the situation and for being slow to put down deep boreholes to test the geology as far as its suitability for burying waste is concerned. The nuclear industry, worldwide, has yet to bury one gram of nuclear waste.

Koeberg

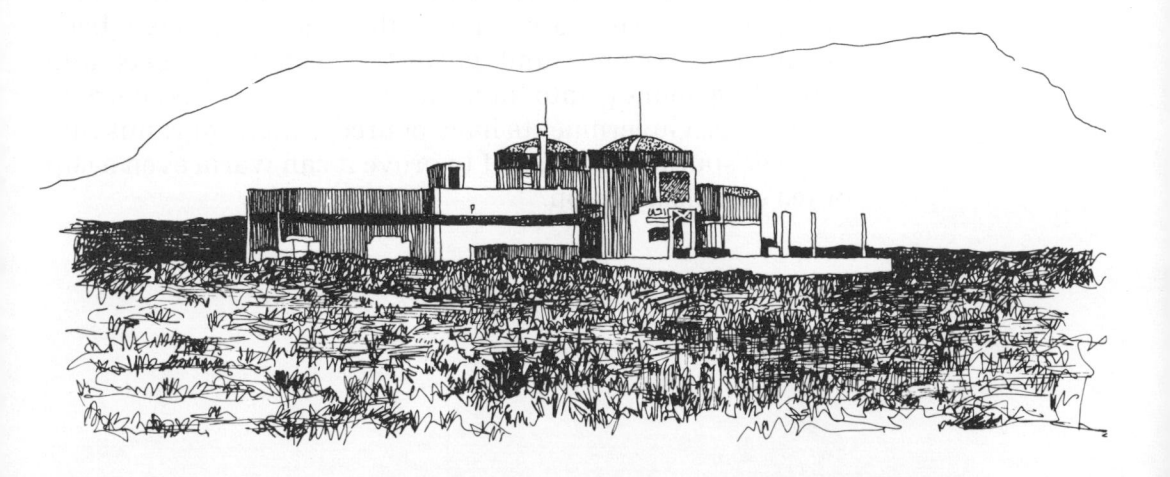

High level waste needs to be isolated from people. It needs to be stored, preferably underground, in a formation which will be undisturbed for, to be absolutely safe, 300 000 years. (This is assuming we will never find another use for all this waste heat, which assuredly we will.) Plutonium, the most dangerous by-product, has a half life of 24 000 years. In other words 200 kilograms of plutonium reduces to 100 after 24 000 years. It is generally accepted that 10 half lives – 240 000 years – will be needed before plutonium will decay to a relatively safe level. Here South Africa is fortunate because it sits on the most stable of all the world's geological plates – the Africa Shield. South Africa's geological structure is characterised by formations which have remained intact for 2 400 *million* years. The site at Vaalputs possibly rates as the safest on Earth.

Storing dangerous radioactive waste for tens of thousands of years in some surface facility is not satisfactory. After all, only 10 000 years ago the northern hemisphere was overlain by a thick ice cap which had scraped it clean. If the ice age comes back, and it will within a few thousand years (unless the greenhouse effect stops it), it will scrape even cities away. Speaking of short-term surface changes, 18 000 years ago the world's sea level was 100 metres lower than now. So geomorphologically lots of things can happen.

For all I have said here, power from nuclear fission may be something of a Faustian bargain. But it is much less environmentally risky than today's finest coal-fired plants.

The ideal power source will be something which is self renewing, environmentally benign, leaves no waste and which poses no undue risks to those working with it. This is where governments have failed us: they have been beguiled by science and powerful vested interests into shovelling money into nuclear power at the expense of better bets. Governments have poured billions of rands into a power source that has yet to prove it can warm even a cup of tea – nuclear fusion.

6 A billion mobile chemical plants

> It is nevertheless apparent that the principle of the motor car has a great future before it, especially in a country troubled with such specialities as horse sickness and Rinderpest.
>
> Leading article, *The Star*, 20 December 1896

SECOND only to coal as a major threat to planet Earth's atmosphere is the motor vehicle. Or, more specifically, the petrol and diesel fuel on which it runs. The world's 1,3 billion petrol-driven motor vehicles contribute a very significant proportion of the more serious atmospheric pollutants. Every car is a mobile chemical factory discharging its toxins right where people live. Every year another 45 million cars are born.

Just as Henry Ford is supposed to have said "You can have any colour car you want as long as it is black" so tomorrow's ministers of health will be saying we can have any colour car we like as long as it is "green". I doubt the petrol-driven engine will be taking us very far into the future. Indeed, Los Angeles has announced it will phase out petrol engines entirely within 15 years. I believe most cities will. Britain's Department of Environment initiated new research in February 1991 aimed at improving planning controls to discourage driving in urban areas. A White Paper spoke of the need to reduce the need for car journeys and the distances driven and to "allow people to choose more energy-efficient transport such as public transport, bicycles and walking." Surprisingly the Department of Transport, notorious for its policy of encouraging more highways and, therefore, more cars, agreed to co-operate.

Scientists at the University of Los Angeles (Davis), say that petrol and diesel fumes cause up to 30 000 premature deaths a year. In 1986, according to the Worldwatch Institute, 75 million Americans (almost one in three) lived in metropolitan regions where carbon monoxide, particles and ground level ozone from car exhaust gases failed to meet air quality standards. In industrialised countries cars contribute three-quarters of carbon monoxide emissions, half the nitrogen oxides, just less than half the hydrocarbons and about one-eighth of the particulates in the air.

The traffic-generated smogs for which places such as Los Angeles are notorious are not of the same nature as London's "pea soup" smogs. Actual visibility in a Los Angeles-type smog is about 30 metres, while London's smogs were down to 3 metres. In fact these photochemical smogs are not really smogs in the strict sense because they contain no natural fog and occur in dry air. The components of California's lung-tickling, eye-smarting smogs are entirely man-made, being formed mostly from car exhaust gases suspended in stagnant air where they cook in the sun to become a highly reactive brew. Johannesburg and Pretoria experience similar but less severe photochemical smogs and Rand Airport, on the east side of greater Johannesburg, has several times been closed to light aircraft because of the photochemical haze which is often thickened by industrial smoke.

Cars also contribute at least a fifth of man-made carbon dioxide, the major greenhouse gas.

Traffic smogs are not only dangerous to human health, but they corrode metal and stonework and have done considerable damage to works of art and structures such as the Parthenon in Athens and the elegant structures of Ancient Rome. Both of these cities have announced severe curbs on cars in recent years and have banned them from some streets, but the cultural cost of the car has been tragic. It was a great invention, surely man's most generally useful invention, but what a pity it was never improved beyond the primitive. Even a Rolls Royce is primitive in terms of energy efficiency and pollution emissions.

It is unrealistic to believe the car can be ruled out of our lives but it is just a matter of time before it changes in a fundamental way. The "town car" as well as buses of 2020 will almost certainly be silent and electrical. Cars will be smaller and certainly no faster than today's vehicles. They will probably be less powerful and only the police and, possibly, emergency vehicles will be physically able to travel at speeds over 130 kilometres an hour. Maybe we will have town cars as well as long distance "touring cars", the latter being larger and more powerful. But in the cities traffic will be so quiet that drivers will be able to talk to each other in traffic jams (there will surely be traffic jams).

At present, progress towards developing a truly advanced car is being hampered by a powerful lobby with a huge stake in the *status quo*. A friend who is developing a revolutionary battery-driven bus was asked by a combi manufacturer: "What are you trying to do to us? What will happen to all the people working in spark plug plants or carburettor factories?" Imagine if Victorian horse traders tried to stop the emergence of the horseless carriage on the grounds that farriers and smithies would be jobless.

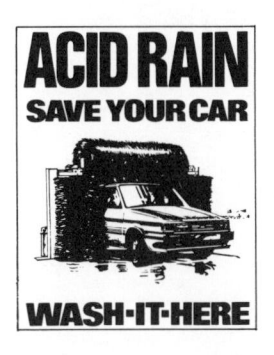

Practically all the work being done on developing a cleaner car is directed at modifying the engine or trapping the gases, instead of stopping the gases forming in the first place. The oil lobby believes the answer to cleaning up air pollution from traffic can be found by staring down exhaust pipes. Many see the advent of the platinum exhaust filter as the final solution. In fact the platinum-based catalytic converter which is now being made compulsory in some countries does reduce hydrocarbon emissions by 87 per cent, carbon monoxide by 85 per cent and nitrogen oxide by two-thirds over the lifetime of a vehicle. But they cannot be the final answer – for one thing, there's not enough platinum to go round. For another, oil is so limited that in 1991 thousands of people were dying in an oil war centred on Iraq.

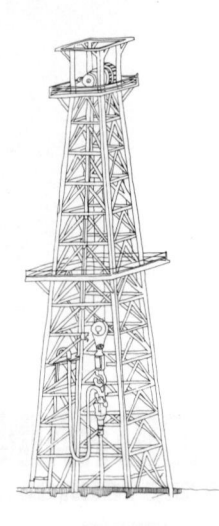

If you own a car here's an inventory of the gases your personal mobile chemical plant releases:

Carbon monoxide – Every year your car – if it is a normal family car and you use it daily for work and, occasionally, for holidays – releases about half-a-ton of carbon monoxide (CO). This odourless gas interferes with one's reflexes and perceptions when it reaches about 50 parts per million – the maximum allowed in working areas in factories. It induces headache and cramp at 200 ppm – a reading one frequently gets in mid-town Johannesburg. Oxford Street in London registered 350 ppm before the present traffic restrictions and New York's busier avenues have surpassed even that – which could explain the crustiness of its cab drivers. At 700 ppm CO kills. CO is suspected of damaging babies in the womb – mentally and physically.

Lead – Over a year your car releases about a kilogram of organic acids and metal oxides such as lead. Lead is added to petrol to boost the octane level which in turn makes the engine run more smoothly and efficiently. Removing lead is no real problem except engines would need modification and fuel costs would rise 5c and 10c a litre, according to John Marriott of Sasol who was quoted in *Business Day* in September 1990. What the motoring community saves on sticking to leaded petrol, other sections of the community may have to pay in terms of their health. Lead, released via the exhaust pipe, is ingested by humans mainly via the alimentary tract and not the lungs. It attacks the central nervous system and kidneys as well as the respiratory system and is known to lower the learning ability in children exposed to traffic fumes. Tests in South Africa have shown city children can ingest so much that it affects their behaviour. Professor Ian Webster, speaking at the second International Conference on Air Pollution (1979) said: "The hyperactive child who can't hold his attention is not an uncommon entity on the Witwatersrand." He pointed out, as did subsequent speakers, that the situation regarding traffic-generated lead in South Africa was far from satisfactory. Blood lead tests on children in Johannesburg's Children's Hospital revealed an average of 16 to 17 micrograms per millilitre – "not far below that of 25 micrograms to the millilitre , the level at which J S Lin Fu (*New England Journal of Medicine*, 1973) suggests that the possibility of a lead problem should be investigated." P S I Barry, chief medical officer of a London metallurgical firm, speaking directly after Webster, said 90 per cent of lead in the environment was from city traffic.

Even so it was 10 years before the Government of South Africa halved the amount of lead in petrol – from a maximum allowable level of 0,836 grams to the litre to 0,4 grams. This brought it in line with European standards. It did so only after Dr Yasmin von Schirnding at the University of Cape Town, demonstrated behavioural disorders in Cape Town children who had ingested lead in areas of heavy traffic congestion. Her research followed research in Britain which revealed that many children in homes for difficult children improved after being treated for lead poisoning. School results also improved in a school near Birmingham's infamous "Spaghetti Junction" after children received similar treatment. The South African Government does not intend phasing out lead as is the intention in Europe. One argument is that engines will then have to consume more petrol.

South Africa's lead standard is the same as Britain, yet in July 1990 Dr Neil Ward of Surrey University, sampling hair and saliva from 31 primary school children in the non-industrial county of Berkshire, found "about half the group had a high level of lead and low reading ability. The children with the highest levels of lead had the lowest reading ability." The children had one thing in common: they all lived next to a heavy traffic stream.

Ironically, although South Africa, with Russia, has the

City air has become a witches' brew of airborne lead, ozone and nitrogen oxides – all from motor cars

monopoly of the world's platinum its motorists cannot use platinum exhaust filters because of the lead in its petrol. In Britain, as in America, unleaded fuel is available to those who want it.

Nitrogen oxides (nox) – the family car dumps 14 kilograms of oxides of nitrogen into the atmosphere each year. These are highly reactive in sunlight and have been recently linked to a range of health problems including cancer and asthma, bronchitis and pneumonia. They also add to the acid rain problem. Nox gases, by combining with hydrocarbons (in unburned fuel coming from exhaust pipes), forms low level ozone. Ozone in the high atmosphere shields the Earth from excessive ultraviolet rays, in the lower atmosphere it damages lung tissue and both the American Lung Association and the British Lung Foundation believe it is more hazardous to health than sulphur dioxide. In the United States and West Germany nox have been shown to damage crops and reduce yields.

Ozone – at ground level, ozone, which is produced from car exhaust fumes by photochemical reaction, is an eye-smarting pollutant. Apart from irritating the mucous membranes and causing coughing and irritation in the lungs, it reduces the body's resistance to colds and influenza and it aggravates heart conditions, asthma and chronic lung complaints.

Other emissions – such as benzines, are known to be carcinogenic and are suspected of causing foetal damage.

The global lack of progress in finding an environmentally acceptable car has a lot to do with the fact that of the top 25 richest companies in the world, 12 are oil companies. Oil companies, so generous in backing environmental causes, perceive, probably correctly, that they have little stake in a world whose hundreds of millions of cars do not use petrol. Another factor is that motor car companies are, understandably, not very eager to retool in order to make a radically different car.

The wild card in all this is Japan, a highly innovative nation with no overpowering reasons to stay with petrol.

Perhaps a breakthrough is possible in liquid fuel. It may, for instance, be possible to develop a membrane to stop nitrogen from the atmosphere being drawn into the engine and thus being converted to nitrogen oxides. This would also give the fuel more kick. Methanol, made from coal, is also a way to cut emissions, and California is trying this direction as a temporary measure. Among the emissions methanol almost eradicates is CO_2 – on the other hand carbon emission from the manufacturing plant itself would probably cancel that advantage.

Professor Wyn Roberts of Cardiff University was reported in August 1990 to be onto a new type of catalytic converter which converts gases in car exhausts into fuels such as methanol and solid carbon. Existing catalysts based on platinum deal mainly with two gases: it converts oxides of nitrogen into harmless nitrogen and carbon monoxide into carbon dioxide (a greenhouse gas). Roberts believes an exhaust filter which converts CO_2 back into carbon and water is "on the cards". The most likely trend will be for governments to set emission standards for cars and for municipal areas to announce tougher and tougher air pollution limits within municipal boundaries. This would have the effect of encouraging "clean cars". On

Experimental solar-powered car

health grounds there is a solid argument for bringing pressure to bear on car manufacturers.

A World Health Organisation/United Nations Environmental Project study in 1989 revealed that 15 to 20 per cent of urban dwellers in the USA and Europe are regularly exposed to "unacceptable" levels of nitrogen oxides, mainly from cars; half the urban population inhale dangerous quantities of carbon monoxide and a third are ingesting unhealthy quantities of lead. In Mexico City, perhaps the most polluted city on Earth, three-quarters of babies have dangerous amounts of lead in their bodies. There are no comparative data for South Africa but it is doubtful the situation has reached such a stage here. For a start we have only about 3,5 million cars with an average 200 000 new ones a year. On the other hand half of these are concentrated in the Pretoria/Witwatersrand region, whose stagnant winter air and strong temperature inversions produce a dangerously enclosed environment.

Governments are not keen to upset the oil and motor car lobby for reasons that may have something to do with party funds, but how long can society tolerate a situation which, according to the United States Lung Association, is responsible for a significant part of the total air pollution problem which costs America $40 billion a year in health care and lost production?

7 Who cares for the public?

The public be damned!
                    William Henry Vanderbilt

AT an Association of Scientific and Technical Societies' debate in Kelvin House, Johannesburg some years ago the managing director of a chemical company assured me that industry puts nothing into the air that nature does not. He said: "You go on about the amount of sulphur dioxide industry puts into the air but have you ever considered how much a volcano contributes?" In other words, "If you think we are polluters, how about God?" The argument is nonsense, but as so many industrialists really seem to believe it, one might as well settle this piece of misinformation right here. Man and the Earth's living systems have evolved to their current state with a certain amount of naturally occurring atmospheric sulphur dioxide, carbon dioxide, methane, radioactivity and so on. Human beings, animals, trees... the entire living world around us, have all learned, not just to live, but also to thrive on certain proportions of gases and other substances. All of them are harmless, providing they are in their natural proportions. Once they exist in excess of those proportions they can be, and usually are, dangerous.

Industrialists might as well argue that because gamma rays and beta rays occur in nature why get fussy when they leak from nuclear power plants? There can be no doubt that industry - albeit with our connivance and due to a common ignorance to which all of us were a party - has radically altered the human environment and we cannot go on in this way. We have altered the nature of the atmosphere without having any idea of what we are letting ourselves in for.

Yet it seems many industrialists, engineers, economists and politicians, especially those over middle-age, would rather carry on the way we are - even if it does mean jeopardising the future of man - if the alternative involves even moderate material sacrifices. There is a cynical, but all too human, saying: "Why should I worry about posterity when posterity has never done anything for me?"

The Transvaal Chamber of Industries, in a bulletin dated 3 October 1986, launched a blistering attack on environmentally aware people, accusing them of hysteria and "trial by rhetoric". It warned that "hysterical outbursts from nature lovers" were causing suffering in the aerosol industry "despite the fact that the whole campaign against the industry is based on a theory which remains unproven to this day." It attacked "a small pressure group possessed of a loud voice and with ready access to the media." Regarding public (and scientific) suspicion about aerosols, Du Pont in the United States in 1974, pledged it would take action, *if* CFCs were proved to be destroying the ozone layer. Its pledge was preposterous. The EPA was so sure CFCs were doing just that that in 1978 it put a ban on the sale of CFC propellants in aerosols in the United States. But industry went on selling such aerosols to countries such as South Africa where the authorities were not so fussy.

New Scientist reported on 17 July 1986 that the Central Electricity Generating Board of Britain insisted that sulphur fall-out was good for agriculture as an antifungicide. "The CEGB says its studies provide more ammunition for its case that expensive technologies to clean up pollution should not be adopted before it is 'scientifically clear' what the effects would be." Here we go again – industry assuming it has some God-given right to introduce into the environment anything it likes and that it is up to the public to find out if it is harmful and to foot the research bill and, meanwhile, suffer whatever the consequences may be.

Many South African industrialists hold the view that pollution is a public relations issue and not a technological challenge. John Egenes, Eskom's former environmental officer, said at a Megawatt Park seminar just before he retired, that some farmers were upset when Eskom cleaned up its fly ash "because it robbed them of a free fertilizer". He said the sulphur fall-out was also good for farmers because "they need to spend less on ammonium sulphate". I was left wondering how Eskom decided which crops needed sulphates and which needed lime and which of these compounds was best for human lungs.

A common ploy of industry is to argue that to clean up will cost the public more than it can afford. Eskom has said that to remove sulphur dioxide from its gases would mean a 30 per cent increase in the price of electricity. I doubt that figure and, whatever the cost, it certainly needs testing against the benefits. Acccording to a report in *Time* (16 February 1987) legislation to reduce sulphur dioxide in the United States could produce 195 000 jobs and $13 billion in sales by clean air equipment firms. In other words it would produce a shift in industrial fortunes and it is that, and that alone, which frightens the polluters.

Iscor, when in 1972 *The Star*'s environmental campaign, CARE, was beginning to put pressure on dirty industries, warned the public that if it had to clean up it would double or treble the price of steel and that the public would have to pay. In fact much of Iscor's waste was simply inefficiency and, therefore, a waste of money anyway. In the event the price of steel climbed but pollution control remained poor.

When Sasol was finally fingered by *The Star* as the culprit behind a sporadic "rotten egg" smell – hydrogen sulphide (H_2S) – which frequently nauseated the Witwatersrand in the mid 1980s (and still does on the odd occasion) a spokesman warned the public of the high cost of cleaning up such gases. *The Star* countered this argument suggesting that Sasol might even get back its money by selling the sulphur "waste". And that is what happened. It seemed to suggest that Sasol had actually given very little thought to economics of installing deodorising equipment otherwise it would have realised it would eventually amortise its costs. If it had given little thought then one must assume it had considered itself to be under no pressure.

I first came across this attitude in Birmingham in the early 1950s when, as industrial reporter on the *Evening Dispatch*, I heard a speech by the head of Imperial Chemical Industries (ICI) in which he announced the company was spending £11 million cleaning up some of its quite appalling pollution. He said: "ICI's decision means that 11 million pounds will virtually be thrown away as far as shareholders are concerned." Patently ICI shareholders lived upwind of the plant's stacks. Another giant, British Steel, was more sensitive. Its spokesman said, on the occasion of announcing huge clean-up plans, "We accept the corporation will be involved in very considerable expense, but we accept this must be part of our social obligations."

Expenditure on cleaning up air pollution is far from unproductive spending. For example, most of the amount spent by ICI on air pollution control equipment was a once off payment and it coincidentally equalled the *annual* amount air pollution was costing Birmingham Corporation in terms of damage to public health and structures.

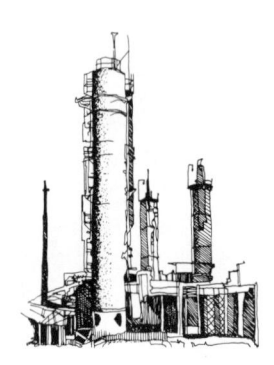

A popular myth among industrialists is that if your factory is far from where people live then pollution does not really matter. A Government environmental official, some years ago, said to me: "Surely a factory in the Karoo does not have to be as strictly controlled as a factory near a town?" I honestly believe he thought there were separate skies for towns and countryside. As the saying goes – "What about the workers?" In September 1990, Eugene van As, managing director of South Africa's paper giant, Sappi, told the President's Council's investigation into a national environmental management system that less stringent pollution measures should be applied for plants which were in "outlying areas where the impact would be relatively low". Impact on what? This may explain what is happening at Sappi's Ngodwana paper mill near Waterval Boven on the main road to Kruger National Park. The mill, site of a huge effluent spillage in 1989 which killed fish for scores of kilometres along the Elands River, is notorious for the way it stinks out a magnificent valley, spoiling the quality of life for thousands of people. I have smelt Sappi's sickly smell from 100 kilometres away. Sometimes it penetrates Kruger Park. Rand Carbide at Witbank, which once had the distinction of being the dirtiest landmark in South Africa because its high stack would daily dump 40 tons of solid material on the surrounding "outlying area", epitomised this myth. One immediately assumes that workers do not count as people, that it does not matter if, daily, they act as human bag filters. Over the years Rand Carbide found itself no longer in an outlying area. When I talked to its management about the way local lawns were blackened by its soot and women were having to do their washing two and even three times a day because it became dirty on the washing line, I was told: "But why have they built there? It was *their* choice to build right up against our fence." I argued that industry had no right to make unliveable land it did not own. What Rand Carbide was doing to its neighbours was tantamount to another industry deciding to use Rand Carbide's premises as a free waste disposal site.

Another example serves to show not only how industry will sometimes be quite shameless in avoiding spending money on cleaning up, but also how the public is not entirely helpless. In the 1960s Union Carbide in Maine in the United States was a notorious polluter. The local mayor received about 80 protesting letters a day. He was told by Union Carbide that for it to clean up would mean dismissing hundreds of workers – and, as the plant employed

Rand Carbide

mostly people from the mayor's town, he decided not to push it. People then complained to the state government. But the state government was also mindful of what Union Carbide meant to state income, party funds and, no doubt, votes. So the state also refrained from pushing the company. Then the Federal Government stepped in: it gave the plant three years to quit polluting. Union Carbide said it would have to sack hundreds of workers. The Government said "Clean up or close down".

Union Carbide's next move was to announce it was having to put off 500 workers. That's when a trade union called in its own pollution expert who found the plant could clean up its emissions without sacking anybody and for a lot less effort than it had been making out. The only person to lose his job was the chairman.

The reluctance on the part of the South African Government to clean up in South Africa is marked and this goes for inside factories as well as outside. Douglas Giles, chairman of Air Pollution Technical Services, in the late 1980s described a really Dickensian scene which he had seen in a Witwatersrand plant where women worked with lead. "When the lunchtime hooter went a number of operators remained seated at their work places, took out food packets and ate the contents without first having washed their hands and without bothering to even wipe off the bench tops". Lead pots, he said, continued to simmer and there was no canteen. Nor did the women have masks or gloves. He suggested the Government set up a ministry of environmental health.

Why is there this reluctance on the part of Government to deal with environmental health hazards? Dr M H Veldman, deputy Minister of National Health, gave a clue in a speech in May 1988 when he inaugurated (or blessed) some clean air equipment at Samancor in the Vaal Triangle, one of the Transvaal's dirtiest plants. "I believe it is very important to realise that South Africa is still a developing country and we can therefore not apply First World standards directly to our situation, nor can we compete with developing countries. In this particular case, Samancor has spent R25 million on air cleaning equipment on which there will be no return on investment." Neither environmental care nor public health appear to figure as worthy of investment in official assessments of environmental spending.

The secret pollutants
When it comes to air pollution control South Africa follows a similar policy to Britain. It relies on co-operation rather than coercion. Sometimes it works, but most times it doesn't. The Atmospheric Pollution Prevention Act of 1965 nowhere obliges industry to be answerable to the public. The Act represents more of a contract between industry and Government than a piece of legislation designed to protect the public. All the major polluters fall under the convenient title of "scheduled industries" which means that because their operations are deemed to be "strategic" only the Government's chief air pollution control officer (Capco) can tell them what to do. They are not obliged to divulge to the public what is coming out of their stacks. The British too have this iniquitous form of industrial protection. The reasoning behind it is that details about stack emissions might provide information to competitors. In some cases the governments concerned do not want other countries to know what is coming out of the stacks of certain industries involved in making defence material. Sometimes, I am sure, it is simply because there would be a public uproar if it became known what the public is inhaling. The most dramatic consequence of South Africa's 25-year old clean air legislation is that it has encouraged "white" suburbs to become smokeless and has led to many gardeners being spot fined for burning garden refuse – even gardeners living downwind from plants which daily emit thousands of tons of smoke annually.

Part of the problem is that the Government's Capco has to police – I use the word lightly – many hundreds of industrial plants scattered throughout the length and breadth of South Africa, plants which carry out about 1 600 "scheduled processes" listed in the Act. To do this he rarely has more than seven or eight inspectors – not enough to look after even an industrial town, let alone a country. When it comes to these scheduled industries, neither local nor regional authorities have any say whatsoever and only the Capco can threaten a plant with closure. In other words, one grossly over-extended official is responsible for the quality of South Africa's air. Mercifully for him, he is not obliged to present an annual progress report to Parliament. The Capco does at least arrange for local health officials to stand in when it comes to inspecting some big industries but this can only be where adequate health departments exist. Witbank, "capital" of the notoriously polluted eastern Transvaal Highveld, has no medical officer of health.

The Department of National Health, under which industrial hygiene falls, spends much of its time defending the state of South Africa's air and assuring people it is not as unhealthy as it looks. For instance it disputes the sulphur dioxide levels given for the eastern Transvaal Highveld in the Foundation for Research Development's report of January 1989 but offers no hard and fast figures of its own. It merely begs the public to believe that the sulphur levels are well within "acceptable" levels and that they are doing no harm. In 1990 it underscored its boundless faith in the situation by withdrawing funds from the FRD for air pollution monitoring. This leaves only Eskom doing monitoring, more or less as a public gesture, for Eskom too is inclined to be dismissive about pollution volumes.

Playing for time

South Africa's clean air legislation, like the British model upon which it is based, calls for factory owners to use the "best practicable means" in abating pollution. A plant owner could claim he cannot afford to clean up and that, normally, would be that. The Capco is the sole arbiter of whether a factory is taking the best practicable means. Worse, it has to be a rule-of-thumb decision for there are no standards laid down in the Act.

Andre Rabie, professor of law at Stellenbosch, once said that a big drawback with air pollution legislation is that a criminal act has to be committed before a plant can be closed. The Water Act, which used to be similar, has been so amended that now a plant can be stopped from operating if the authorities believe it might pollute water. Rabie suggests that fines should be more severe and that each day's offence should be considered a separate offence.

Naturally industrialists tend to take advantage of the present permissive attitude of the Department of Health. When, under pressure to clean up, they call in consultants (who take months); they then go for the cheapest possible equipment (which takes months to arrive and usually many more months to install); they wait for the inevitable breakdown and for the call from the Capco's office, which may well be on first name terms with them. At this stage they again call in the consultants . . .

Some plants illegally close off their filters at night and allow their waste to go straight into the air. This saves some plant managers thousands of rands a month because it avoids having to clean out the filters so often - and it saves on the energy bill. One plant, in the eastern Transvaal, which had a chronic problem with one of its sections which emitted volcanic quantities of dust, used to close the section off at 3 pm every Friday because that was about the time Parliamentarians drove past on their way to their game farms.

The Government allows no tax incentives for industries to clean up but then neither has it ever fined an industry for polluting the air. As a result, one of the most depressed sectors of industry is the very sector which makes anti pollution equipment.

South Africa needs standards. It needs a limit set on just how much of any pollutant is acceptable. As things stand, who knows at what stage the Department of National Health will consider the air to be overburdened? And when it does decide, what then?

The solution probably lies in South Africa having an Environmental Protection Agency (EPA) similar to that of the United States. The American EPA was given Cabinet status in 1990 and a similar agency in South Africa would not only be able to end the all too cordial relationship between the pollution controllers and the polluters (the EPA would monitor the Capco's progress without becoming involved with the polluters themselves) but it could sort out priorities across the whole environmental spectrum.

It also seems reasonable that, with or without an EPA, the chief air pollution control officer should be obliged to table an annual report before Parliament.

Local and regional authorities are allowed to control vehicle emissions and domestic emissions but here again there are no practical emission standards laid down. Smoke density meters can be used only when the sun is shining. Take the case of diesel fumes, a widespread and conspicuous problem on the Rand because of the altitude and its effect on combustion. If a vehicle is found to be smoking excessively it is deemed "unroadworthy" and obliged to be properly tuned and to then apply for a roadworthy certificate at a testing yard.

An international law?

It seems inevitable that air pollution laws will be tightened by countries across the world and that an international treaty will come about. Wild climatic shifts, increasing national disasters and famines will make people more and more fearful of the future. The fear of a greenhouse world will be every bit as worrying to the educated person as the threat of a nuclear war. Christopher Flavin of the Worldwatch Institute, in his October 1989 report on "Slowing global warming" asked:

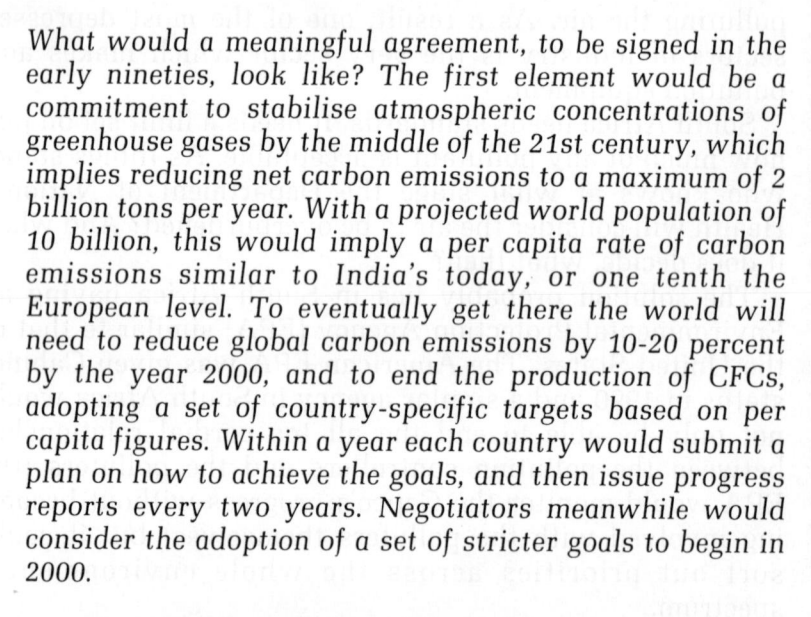

> What would a meaningful agreement, to be signed in the early nineties, look like? The first element would be a commitment to stabilise atmospheric concentrations of greenhouse gases by the middle of the 21st century, which implies reducing net carbon emissions to a maximum of 2 billion tons per year. With a projected world population of 10 billion, this would imply a per capita rate of carbon emissions similar to India's today, or one tenth the European level. To eventually get there the world will need to reduce global carbon emissions by 10-20 percent by the year 2000, and to end the production of CFCs, adopting a set of country-specific targets based on per capita figures. Within a year each country would submit a plan on how to achieve the goals, and then issue progress reports every two years. Negotiators meanwhile would consider the adoption of a set of stricter goals to begin in 2000.

Toronto, the city which hosted the world's first really meaningful conference on the state of the atmosphere and on the possibility of climatic change, has shown the way. Its municipality has adopted the recommendations made at the conference. It has committed itself to reducing its contribution to carbon dioxide by a fifth by 2005, without sacrificing growth. It has inaugurated a red pine tree-planting programme over 20 000 hectares of Ontario. Toronto hopes to mop up 500 000 tons of CO_2. The process will cost $80 million and will be started from the city's Atmospheric Fund financed from city-owned land sales and supported, hopefully, from donations from industry. It says the trees will not only absorb CO_2 but will make the city cooler and, therefore, cut down on air conditioning in summer. Less electricity will mean less CO_2 from power stations.

Co-incidentally, it was Canada which hosted the international Habitat congress in the 1970s which gave rise to the most useful slogan in all 20 years of environmental debate: "Think globally, act locally." This is precisely what Toronto is doing.

8 Fickle rivers

> *All the rivers run into the sea, yet the sea is not full; unto the place from which the rivers come, there they return again.*
>
> Ecclesiastes

WATER, when you come to look at it, is a wonderful substance: it occurs naturally in solid, liquid and gaseous form; it dissolves practically everything – even gold is found suspended in sea water. It is essential in making soil, in releasing new minerals by breaking up rocks and, in the world's oceans, for regulating the Earth's temperature. The human body is mostly comprised of water, so are the various foods we eat. Yet water is made up of two gases, hydrogen and oxygen.

Most of the planet is encapsulated in water and it is in water that life began, protected from an air that was lethal to inhale. There is so much water about that if some explorer from beyond our solar system were to chance upon planet Earth, he, or she (or, I suppose, it) would surely name it the Blue Planet or, maybe, Oceania. Never Earth. The explorer would also assume that the one thing the Blue Planet's inhabitants would never run short of was water. After all, 71 per cent of the planet's surface is covered in the stuff. There is so much water that all the land masses could be dumped well below sea level. But, of the Blue Planet's water, 98 per cent is undrinkable sea water. Another 1,2 per cent, although it is fresh water, is locked in the polar caps and in glaciers. That leaves only 0,8 per cent to drink and with which to irrigate our crops, manufacture our steel, cool our power stations, brew our beer, bath in, carry away our sewage and wash our millions of cars.

Ironically, water is the one thing man *is* running short of.

Saudi Arabia actually imports water for irrigation from the Philippines. It arrives as ballast in its returning oil tankers. About a third of the world's population has no access to piped water and half of mankind would go hungry if irrigation schemes ceased. Part of man's dilemma is that irrigation farmers, who take up three-quarters of the world's available fresh water, actually *consume* water. The little that seeps back into the rivers is usually highly contaminated. By contrast, industrialists and householders merely *use* water before returning it for re-use by others.

The decade of the 1980s focused a great deal of world attention on water. Some countries, including South Africa, suffered the worst droughts in their histories. Not everybody is short of fresh water: the people of Kauai, Hawaii have had an annual rainfall average of 11 400 millimetres this century – more than 30 millimetres a day. Then there's

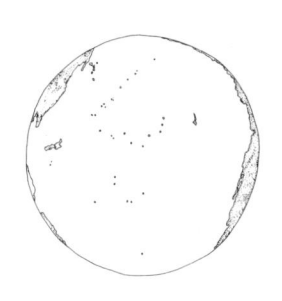

Cilaos on Reunion, an emerald island in the Indian Ocean, which holds the record for the wettest day – 1 869,9 millimetres in 24 hours. While the average rainfall over the entire Earth's surface is about 850 millimetres a year, distribution is very uneven: Kauai has 335 rainy days a year while South Africa's interior, where most of its crops have to be grown, receives not much more than 100.

South Africa's annual rainfall, slightly less than 500 millimetres, puts the country into the category of "semi-arid". One-third of the country – mainly the eastern Cape, Natal and the Transvaal Escarpment – is frequently swept by moisture-laden air from the Indian Ocean and receives from 600 millimetres to well over 1 000 millimetres. In South Africa's two wettest places – in the pine plantations of Jonkershoek, north of the Hottentots Holland mountains, and the Woodbush Forest above Tzaneen – the annual rainfall is around 3 500 millimetres. By contrast, a whole two-thirds of South Africa receives less than 500 millimetres which makes it unsuitable for dry land farming. The region lying along the Atlantic Ocean receives its moisture in the form of night fogs billowing in from the cold Benguela Current, and is the country's most arid region. It is to be expected that the drier a region the more resourceful, in terms of water usage, its people. Bushmen have learned to live without surface water. Some Namibian farmers erect huge kite-like frames on poles and stretch wire gauze across to catch the night fogs. The mist condenses on the wire and drips into a channel along the base of the frame and trickles into a trough for cattle the next day. That's how nature does it – the acacia trees have a screen of feathery leaves and the saplings are festooned with tens of thousands of thorns against which moisture-laden night air condenses to fall into the tree's drip area.

South Africa has no summer snow melt and no large lakes. It has to live off its miserly runoff from rain. As Professor Desmond Midgley, the former Witwatersrand University hydrologist, put it: "Our rivers are wild and fickle." How fickle? Well, South Africa's biggest river, the 2 250 kilometre Orange River, has run dry on occasions. In 1933 it dried up – and in that same year it came down in a flood which swept away farms and livestock. A river cannot get more fickle than that. The Orange has actually recorded a greater flow, on one occasion, than the Zambezi, southern Africa's greatest river. The 1 355 kilometre Vaal, whose water somehow has to supply a fifth of South Africa's population, has also dried up and flooded within the same year.

Climatologist Professor Peter Tyson demonstrated how, in South Africa's summer rainfall region, there appears to be a fairly reliable pattern of wet and dry periods - nine years of poor rains followed by nine years of good rains. Within the dry period there can be a very wet year, and within the wet period there may be a year or two of below average rain, but generally the pattern holds true and it can be traced back well beyond this century. Studies of tree rings - widely spaced tree rings indicate wet years and thinly spaced are a sign of drought years - support the theory.

Professors Richard Fuggle and Andre Rabie in their *Environmental Concerns in South Africa* (1983) said:

> The significance of this elegant and careful analysis should not be ignored ... to do so would be serious in the extreme. We must agree with Tyson that the implications of such changes (from dry years to wet), should they continue to occur as they have in the past, may be profound, particularly for food production in arid and semi-arid areas. Present disregard of these interpretations of pattern in South African climate is disturbing.

Professor Tyson's "elegant analysis" of South Africa's wet and dry cycles

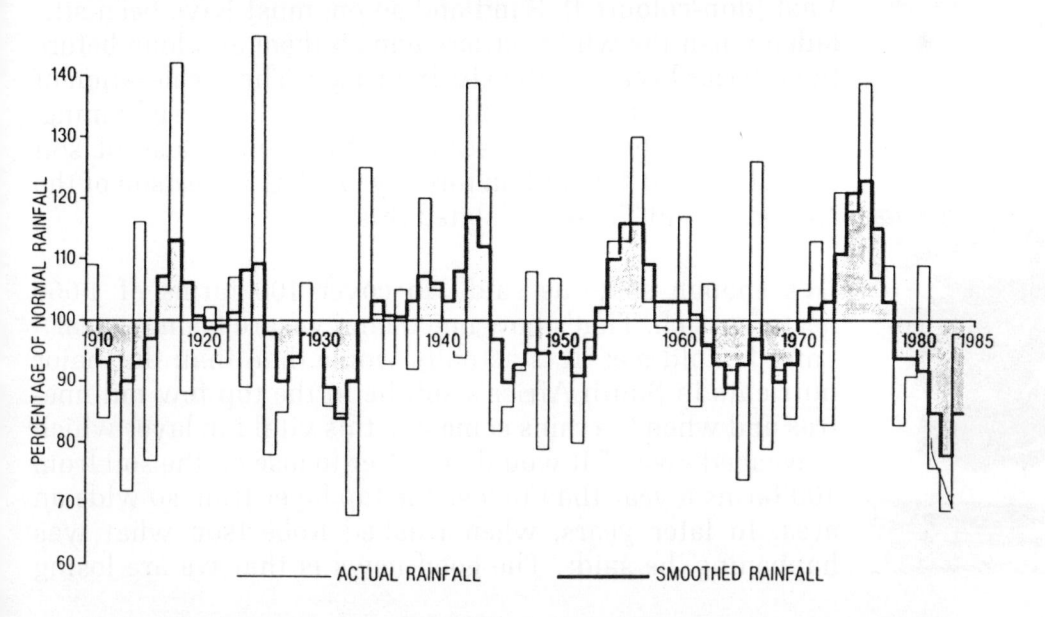

South Africa, in cross section, is, as Midgley has pointed out, like an upturned saucer, the raised rim in the centre being the Drakensberg mountains. This great watershed, centred mostly on Lesotho, gives birth to the three most important rivers in South Africa – the Orange, Vaal and Tugela. From this central rim the land slopes steeply. Thus our rivers are generally fast and scouring and their silt loads become a major factor in that they settle out in dams reducing their storage capacity. The problem of erosion is made worse by the fact that on the inland plateau the winters are practically rainless and, when the rains eventually come in something akin to monsoonal downpours, the dry soil dissolves and is carried away in sickening quantities. The most injudicious thing a farmer can do is to leave his soil naked in spring, unprotected by vegetation. Yet thousands do. Very often it is because the previous season's crop failed in a summer drought and after that nothing could be planted. The land then lies exposed to the winter sun and in August and September the pre-rain winds skin it.

When the rains come the rivers run red with topsoil. The coastal waters, wherever a river empties into the sea, are stained red as if with the lifeblood of the country. The silt can be seen extending 4 kilometres out to sea. Erosion and river silt are, to a degree, natural occurrences and South Africa's rivers, judging by their names – Modder (mud), Vaal (dun-coloured), Sand and so on, must have been silt-laden when the white settlers named them and long before the interior became extensively farmed. The acceleration of erosion since the turn of the century has been frightening. Midgley, in the 1960s, estimated the annual loss of soil could be about 400 million tons a year. T C Robertson of the National Veld Trust translated this:

"It's enough soil," he said, "to cover 100 farms of 1 000 hectares each. That's how much land we are losing a year." Later he told me: "It is actually worse than that: the major nutrients in South Africa's soil lie in the top few millimetres and when the rains come it is this vital top layer which is washed away." It would be better to lose all the soil from 100 farms a year than to lose the top layer from so wide an area. In later years, when I asked Robertson what was happening, he said: "The good news is that we are losing

Natal – a frequent victim of disastrous floods

less soil to the sea these days. The bad news is that this is because there is less soil to lose."

In December 1971 Robertson, speaking at a National Veldtrust conference on natural resources, said that silt studies by the Department of Agricultural Technical Services revealed there were 400 million tons of topsoil going into the Hendrik Verwoerd Dam alone. When the Government announced it was building this dam on the Orange River, farmers, realising much of the land the Government was expropriating would be inundated, began to overgraze it to the point where it was stripped. By the time they handed these exhausted farms over to the nation they had made a small fortune - at the nation's expense - because attempts to repair the damage before the naked soil could be swept into the dam, reducing its capacity, cost the taxpayer R55 million. Even so the capacity loss to the dam was enormous. It was said that the dam's water became too thick to drink but too thin to plough. In 1974 the then Secretary for Water Affairs, Jacques Kriel, denied the Orange was as silted as Robertson had claimed. Kriel, a much respected civil servant, put the figure at 90 million tons. Either way the amount represents an appalling loss of soil and, in a country whose dams are characteristically shallow this silt load, by settling out in dams and reducing their capacity, represents a double blow.

A more recent cause of silting in the upper Orange is

alluvial diamond mining near the top of the watershed in Lesotho where huge earth graders are being used to gouge out stream courses right down to bed rock. The diamonds are said to be the world's finest gemstones but they are costing Lesotho (which gets a tiny percentage royalty from the Far Eastern firm which owns the diamond concession) more than it can afford. The silt is "like melted chocolate" according to somebody who regularly goes up there and it poses a threat to the R5 000 million Highlands Project which entails building a series of storage and hydroelectric dams in the Lesotho Highlands.

Brian Huntley (*et al*) in *South African Environments into the 21st Century* (1990), underscores the silt problem:

> Soil erosion and sedimentation ... cause the loss of 130 million cubic metres of water storage capacity a year, nearly equal to one medium-sized dam such as Midmar or Hartbeespoort. The cost of constructing new dams to replace storage capacity lost to siltation is estimated at between R100 million and R200 million per annum.

One cannot actually lose water as one can lose soil. The Earth will always have the same amount of rain. But one can waste water, render it unusable, and one can reduce a country's capacity to store water. It can be also be wasted by accelerating the already high evaporation process. The shallower a dam becomes (because of being silted up) the more prone it will be to evaporation. Vaal Dam is, on average, about 3,5 metres deep, and it evaporates at the rate of 1,7 metres a year. Dams on the Orange evaporate at the rate of almost 3 metres a year.

A number of techniques have been used in attempts to reduce evaporation including spreading oil on the surface. But the wind breaks the skin. Evaporation is as much a curse as low rainfall in South Africa. One often sees in summer over the Highveld, rain falling high above the ground in strong dark streaks, and then evaporating before it can reach the ground. Good ground cover would reduce the rising heat and allow the rain to reach the ground. Over most of the country the evaporation rate actually exceeds the rainfall, including in the valley where South Africa has its most intensively farmed area, the Vaalhartz Irrigation Scheme in the northern Cape. The valley receives an annual rainfall of about 150 millimetres while its evaporation rate is 3 000 millimetres. The 52 000 hectares scheme consumes as much water as the entire industrialised Witwatersrand.

Because only seven drops of rain out of every 100 find their way into rivers and only four can be stored, South Africa is in no position to waste water. In fact the total runoff from every river in South Africa (53 000 million cubic metres) would fill Kariba Dam only one-third full.

South Africa will, at best, be able to store only 33 000 million cubic metres of water, and it is practically there already. Its largest dam, the Hendrik Verwoerd in the Orange River Project, can store 6 000 million cubic metres, of which at least 2 000 million cubic metres are lost in evaporation.

9 The big drinkers

*We never know the worth of water
until the well is dry.*

Thomas Fuller

ALTHOUGH irrigation uses up most of the planet's stored water supply, without this ancient but still rather crude technology, there would be worldwide famines. More than 50 million Egyptians depend entirely on food from land irrigated by the Nile and aquifers. The grain belts of China, north-western India and the Great Plains of the United States are sustained by supplemental water and their yields would drop between a third and a half without it.

Sandra Postel, a researcher with the Worldwatch Institute, wrote in the institute's *State of the World 1990*:

> *As world population grew from 1,6 billion to more than 5 billion over the last 90 years, irrigation became a cornerstone of global food security. The higher yields farmers could get with a controllable water supply proved vital to feeding the millions added to our numbers annually, especially as opportunities to cultivate new land dwindled.*

Postel believes that the growth of irrigation will decrease this decade as rising costs for new projects increase, as the environmental impacts of dams are questioned and as the global warming phenomenon threatens to reduce supplies of available water. Many irrigation schemes are beginning to founder because rising salt levels are sterilising the soils and because of more demand for water by industry.

South Africa's Vaalhartz Irrigation Scheme in the arid Hartz River valley was started in the 1930s Depression. Vaal Dam was built mainly for that scheme which is 560 river kilometres west of it. The water takes 10 days to get from Vaal Dam to the Hartz Valley and the daily evaporation rate along the Vaal accounts for hundreds of millions of litres. The economic wisdom of supplying 1 100 farmers on the Vaalhartz scheme with as much Vaal water as the entire Witwatersrand uses has often been questioned. The Vaalhartz farmers' contribution towards the nation's income is a tiny fraction compared with the Witwatersrand whose industries produce half the country's income. The comparison is perhaps unfair and I mention it only because one wonders if irrigation schemes, when judged against the real cost of water (for which farmers pay almost nothing) should be required to grow only essential food and not just that which gives the best financial return for the farmer.

Their water, after all, is provided at great public cost.

Nowadays, one of the Vaal's newest dams, built in 1970 at Bloemhof downriver from Vaal Dam, stores water for the Vaalhartz irrigation farmers. It is a shallow dam in a relatively low-rainfall catchment but, with donations from Vaal Dam, it is normally sufficient.

Now that South Africa seems to be able to predict wet and dry decades, Desmond Midgley suggests it should consider encouraging Vaalhartz farmers to expand the amount of land under irrigation in wet years and decrease them in dry years. Farmers could then put income away to tide them over during droughts instead of appealing for State subsidies. Midgley made the suggestion during the Great Drought of the 1980s – just after Peter Tyson had published research results showing that South Africa experiences quite a reliable pattern of wet and dry cycles, each complete cycle spanning 18 years. Just as Tyson's paper had intimated, the drought ended after nine years. I commented in a leading article that the drought had ended in the traditional South African manner – "with farmers sitting on their flooded farmhouse roofs clutching their drought relief papers". For some reason this incensed the Minister of Agriculture who castigated *The Star* in Parliament.

But nothing was done to expand the irrigation areas as Midgley had suggested.

South African irrigation farmers, according to the Department of Water Affairs, have drastically reduced their usage of the nation's stored water in recent years to a point where now they use just over half (50,9 per cent) of the available water. The 1950s were a typical overkill situation with farmers using almost 80 per cent of the country's stored water. It was practically free, after all. Industry and mining and electricity generation use almost a quarter (22,6 per cent) and domestic and municipalities use about an eighth (12 per cent). The forestry industry's pine and eucalyptus plantations take up 7,9 per cent of South Africa's runoff, while estuaries, lakes and nature conservation areas such as Kruger Park get 14,5 per cent.

Conflicts of interests are inevitably arising and they can only increase as the demand grows and the supply remains pegged. Look how afforestation in the eastern Transvaal Highveld and new dams along the Highveld's east-flowing rivers are robbing Kruger National Park of its water. Afforestation of the high savannah above the Transvaal Escarpment (which drains into Kruger Park) has reduced runoff by more than two-thirds. The 20 000 square kilometre National Park, the linchpin of the tourist industry, is the end user of seven rivers before they enter Mozambique and, until the mid 1960s, none had been known to run dry. In recent years most of them have run dry during winter. Worse, the restricted flow during the dry months limits the dilution of effluent from industry and mining which annually grows worse. To date, the Lower Sabie River, biotically the richest river in South Africa, has never stopped flowing, but with two more dams planned for that river and more afforestation, it may be just a matter of time before that tragedy occurs and the river's ecology is shattered.

Dr Henry Olivier, a South African hydrologist who, when he was with the World Bank, was behind the building of such dams as the Mekong River Dam, Owen Falls Dam and the Orange River Project suggested that South Africa should not have placed its irrigation areas and dams in the high evaporation zones on the plateau. He estimated South Africa loses a quarter of its stored water to evaporation and commented that although South Africa, when compared with other countries, is not too bad in this regard, it just cannot afford this loss. He suggested South Africa should concentrate on building smaller, and therefore cheaper dams in the deeper valleys of Natal and in the eastern Cape where not only is evaporation low, but the depth of dams in relation to their narrow surface areas would reduce evaporation to a minimum. He said that Natal, given a mere 250 millimetres extra water a year, would be able to produce optimum yields. Incredibly the Tugela, which contains more water than the Vaal, and which flows through South Africa's most populous area - Zululand - has no major dams in its middle and lower reaches. This has led to a lack of control as far as river flow is concerned and in the floods of the 1980s, not only did the Tugela sweep hundreds of people to their deaths, but it resulted in a huge loss of land through washaways and massive damage to bridges. Annually the Tugela discharges millions of cubic metres of water to the sea and, as we discussed earlier, this river has a latent hydropower equivalent to three Koeberg nuclear power plants. It is a grossly under-used river.

The Great Drought

The Great Drought which did so much damage in the mid 1980s at least focused public and political attention on South Africa's challenging water problems. A month or two before the drought ended civil engineers, under the direction of the Department of Water Affairs, reversed the flow of the Vaal River from Vaal Dam up to the Grootdraai Dam near Standerton which supplies coolant water to some of the Highveld's giant power stations. The R33 million scheme, comprising huge pumps and hastily erected weirs, was in use for only a week or so before the floods came and swept the temporary weirs away, but there had been a very real chance of power stations having to close. Had the Government heeded the advice of experts over the 20 preceding years the emergency could have been avoided.

In 1964 *The Star* assigned me to interview the country's top hydrologists, geologists and historians and prepare a series of articles on the Vaal Valley from its geological beginnings to its cultural history, its economic importance and to look at scenarios for its future. The investigation revealed that the Vaal's assured water supply was, even then, overstretched. Its users had been allocated quotas which there was little hope of fulfilling in a worst case

The Great Drought of the eighties ended in devastating floods

drought. From the advice of the many experts to whom I spoke, it seemed clear the Vaal would "run out of water" by 1984. *The Star* said as much in 1964. It was one year out. But when the Vaal ran dry the Orange River dams were two thirds full. What was needed, said *The Star*, was a national water grid. It took the Great Drought of the 1970s and 80s to underscore the need.

An interesting controversy erupted in the drought-stricken cities of the Highveld in the 1980s. Municipalities stopped people watering their gardens and imposed draconian penalties for overusing water. A burst pipe could cost a householder tens of thousands of rands. The newspaper vigorously protested against such punitive measures and argued, successfully, against a total ban on watering gardens. It argued that the authorities had a social contract to fulfil as far as suburban households were concerned. Gardening is a major pastime in Highveld towns and, on average, a Johannesburg household uses 55 per cent of its water on the garden. This has never been discouraged by the water authorities. A total ban would have wrecked the substantial nursery industry which employed thousands of people. It seemed equally unfair that suburban people were expected to write off their gardens in which they had collectively invested hundreds of millions of rands. The people of the Witwatersrand, singularly lacking recreational facilities because of the absence of mountains, forests, beaches and rivers, tend to "live in their gardens". Indeed, a withered garden, in the case of a house being offered for sale, would reduce its value by thousands of rands.

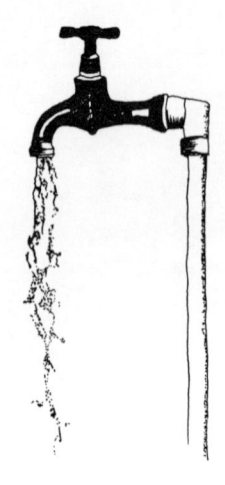

What the drought really revealed was how underpriced water was. It was discovered that Johannesburg municipality had not been reading some householders' water meters for years. It had actually been guessing consumption figures. The state of affairs was exposed when people, having been warned they would pay big penalties for exceeding their water quota, naturally went in search of their municipal water meters to start measuring their own consumption for the first time in their lives. Many found only rusted lumps of metal with antique and often fingerless dials calibrated in "imperial gallons". Some people then found they had been grossly overcharged for water – yet nobody had complained before simply because water had not been viewed as a serious household expense. Johannesburg municipality discovered that much of its reticulation system was rotten (corroded by impurities in the water supply) and that there were massive underground leaks. In Soweto the pumps were pounding in the small hours when few taps would have been on – a sign of massive underground pipe fractures. This all tended to make a mockery of the campaign to heavily penalise people who had the misfortune to suffer a burst pipe especially as the water quality was often to blame for corroding household pipes. But more than anything it revealed the general attitude – that water had, until then, been taken for granted. The Great Drought put an abrupt end to complacency.

As the drought became more threatening, industry found it could save enormous amounts of water. AECI, which appointed its top boffin, Dick Lever, as water conservation chief, managed to cut water consumption by 80 per cent in

In Johannesburg half of household water is used on gardens

some of its factories mainly by switching to boreholes and using less consumptive techniques. Natal firms cut consumption by 70 per cent without cutting production. Power stations fine-tuned their cooling methods and nowadays lead the world in "dry cooling". On the domestic front householders learned all about mulch and how to bath in half the usual amount of water and then how to use bathwater for flushing toilets and for watering the garden. Municipalities began sinking boreholes and Johannesburg hit some big underground supplies.

The Department of Water Affairs began developing vast underground supplies in the extensive dolomitic areas which lie in an arc north of the Pretoria-Witwatersrand-Vaal complex. Here were billions of litres of water which, if conservatively tapped, would not cause sinkholes (a hazard in the Transvaal dolomite regions if too much water is pumped out). Underground reserves of water in the PWV are estimated at 10 000 million cubic metres (the country's biggest dam is 6 000 million cubic metres), but as the annual average recharge from rain is only 270 million cubic metres that's about how much underground water it would be sensible to use. Even so this is a third of the PWV's consumption. It has been suggested that big surface dams could be used to artificially replenish aquifers during flood times. The great advantage of underground water reserves is that they are evaporation free.

The Department also began to look more urgently at developing a national water grid. The upper Orange River in Lesotho, for instance, will in the middle 1990s be linked to the middle Vaal. During the Highveld's Great Drought the Hendrik Verwoerd Dam on the Orange, well to the south of the stricken area, had plenty of water but played no useful role. Certain sections of a future national water grid are today in place. Just as the drought began, a link between the Tugela and the Vaal had been completed – a link which proved vital to the Transvaal's industries. The link is an interesting one: water from the Tugela in Natal, not far from Mont-aux-Sources, is pumped up a mountain into a dam in the Orange Free State where some is allowed to fall back down the mountain at peak hours to provide hydro electric power for the national grid. The rest flows into the Sterkfontein Dam near Harrismith. From there it flows down the Wilge into the Transvaal. Under normal circumstances the Wilge River supplies two-thirds of Vaal Dam's water.

The people of Natal objected strongly to the Transvaal "taking Natal's water to save the Transvaal's industries". The reaction reflected a South African weakness: the lack of an holistic perception and an almost fatal yearning to live in a compartmentalised society. The Transvaalers countered by pointing out how the Transvaal's coal provides nearly all the country's electricity. A ridiculous dispute, but airing it helped underscore that regional *inter*dependence is as important as regional *in*dependence. A national water grid is as necessary as a national electricity grid.

Among other existing "national grid" links is one between the Usutu and the upper Vaal and the Orange and the Sunday's River.

The Vaal Dam has become more of a reservoir than a dam. Although it receives only 8 per cent of South Africa's total runoff it somehow has to provide water to the entire PWV, which in turn provides more than 50 per cent of the nation's income and accommodates 42 per cent of its population.

The Great Drought caused the Government to give more urgency to plans to enter into a contract with Lesotho regarding the R5 000 million Lesotho Highlands Scheme which aims to build a series of storage dams in the well-watered Lesotho highlands. These deep, low-evaporation dams will not only be able to supplement the Transvaal's water supply, but they will provide Lesotho with hydro-electric power for its own use and for sale. The water will not represent "new" water for South Africa as it will merely divert water from the upper Orange to the Vaal, via the Liebensbergvlei River – but at least it will be a welcome infusion of high quality water with which to dilute the increasingly mineralised Vaal.

10 Squeezing the sponge

He seeks water in the sea.
John Ray. English Proverbs

SOUTH Africa has enough water to see it through for, probably, the next 30 years. And after that? After that we run the risk of rationing for periods of three or four years every other decade unless we find new sources – or the population falls.

There are certain remedial measures that can be taken. For a start the Government could address the problem of the drying up of the wetlands – the great sponge areas, for instance, which store rainfall and leak it slowly into the rivers. Half the Tugela River's wetlands have been destroyed. The control over South Africa's vital wetlands has been appalling. Even wetlands right on the coast, such as St Lucia's enormous estuary which feeds directly into the sea, are vital because of their richness of species because of their importance as nurseries for commercial fish species, and because of their great beauty. South Africa, one of the 62 signatories to the Ramsar wetlands conservation agreement (formulated in Ramsar, Iran), had St Lucia listed as a world heritage wetland. But in 1989 the Minister of Environment Affairs was quick to forget St

St Lucia, an internationally protected wetland, is now threatened

Lucia's international status when Richards Bay Minerals asked permission to mine titanium in the coastal dunes above the lake. Water from this sponge had been the only fresh water entering the lake during the Great Drought. It saved St Lucia becoming a salt-thickened Dead Sea. The mineral company was in a hurry to mine and the Minister seemed on the point of giving the go-ahead when the public leapt to its feet. There was a massive national petition and it shook the Minister and the mining company. The battle remains undecided and the Government's attitude to wetlands remains enigmatic.

Meanwhile there is some talk about desalinating sea water to provide towns with fresh water. But while desalination plants might help at small coastal places, they will almost certainly prove too costly if they are used to supply big inland users. A major problem is what to do with the accumulated salt at the desalination plants. To supply desalinated sea water to the Witwatersrand alone would leave a residue of a few hundred tons of salt a day and it cannot simply be dumped back in the sea at the coast. One would have to ship it away from the coast and distribute it as widely as possible out to sea. But as water becomes scarce, and as users are forced to pay the true market value of water, the economics of the situation may change in favour of desalination. My guess is that before this point is reached the population will have ceased to grow.

For South Africa a more likely option is to import water by pipeline from some of Southern Africa's major rivers – the Okavango, the Zambezi, the Chobe or even the Zaire. The 16 000 square kilometre Okavango Delta is nearest but one would hope it would never be used. This inland delta was formed by quite recent earth movements (say within the last few centuries or millennia) which thrust up a natural dam wall blocking the flow of the Okavango, Southern Africa's second largest river after the Zambezi. The Okavango used to flow straight through Botswana into the Limpopo, but now less than 3 per cent gets through the natural dam known as the Second Fault Line. The rest of the Okavango's water spreads out into a huge inland delta transforming the Kalahari desert into a multi-fingered swamp whose crystal-clear water attracts one of the greatest concentrations of wildlife in Africa. This shallow delta is one of Africa's great natural wonders and, if it were drained of even 10 millimetres of its depth, its shoreline would be greatly reduced with negative ecological consequences.

Piping water from the Zambezi or Chobe is feasible but expensive. The Zambezi seems to be the more logical choice. A southbound canal could benefit Botswana along the way. One scenario is that it would be piped into Hartbeespoort Dam and reticulated from there.

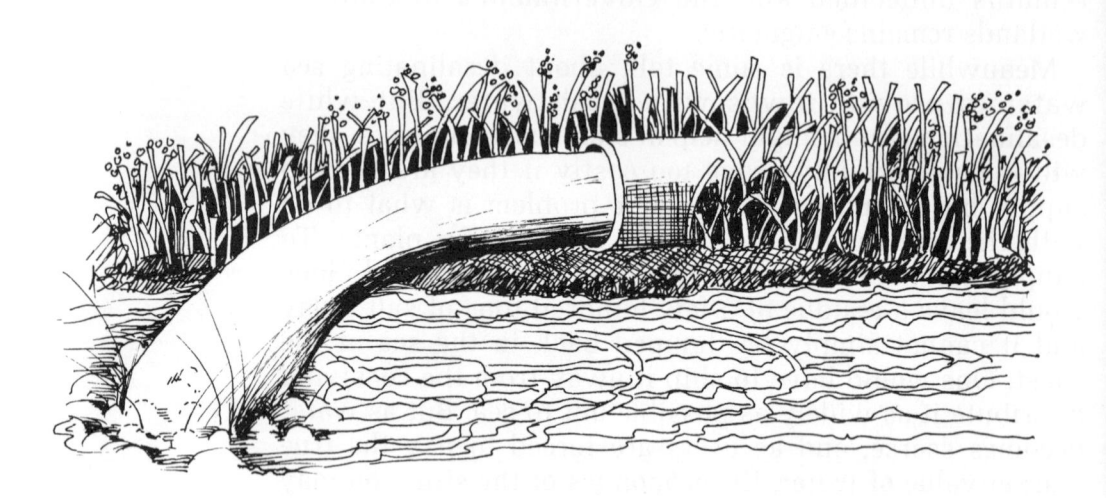

A logical medium-term option is to conserve what we have – to learn to use water more wisely. Farmers can probably cut consumption the most. Certainly many farmers, including big agribiz concerns, have a lot to learn regarding farming in a semi-arid region and some who resort to irrigation could obtain higher yields without that extra water by switching to different crops. John Earle and others, in *New Window on the World* – a marvellously imaginative geography text book for high schools – quotes a story told him by Richard Fuggle, professor of environmental studies at the University of Cape Town:

> *I think I can best illustrate the South African approach to water by recounting a conversation which I had with a school friend who is now a successful farmer. "How are you enjoying farming?" I asked. "Well," he said. "it's much easier now than when I first started. At first I used to rely on rain and I found it hard going as we had droughts four*

years out of five. I then decided not to rely on rain and to farm as if I lived in a desert. Since then things have been easier. Our problem now is the flooding which occurs one year out of five."

Domestic users can also get more from less. For example, it makes no sense at all to use fresh water to flush toilets. The Americans use 19 litres each flush, the Germans nine and most South Africans use six. The EPA has recommended the American standard cystern should be reduced to 5,7 litres. It still makes no sense. We spend millions purifying river water only to use it, well, one does not have to labour the point. It seems likely that a new method of dealing with human waste will one day be developed – possibly using part of the technology developed for space craft. We may, in future, bath less and shower more – using hi-tech showers which use only three litres of water: one litre to soak the body via high pressure mist sprays, one to soap it and the last for rinsing down.

Any further improvements in water conservation would have to be preceded by a rise in the price of water so that water is seen for what it is, a valuable mineral. I am not suggesting that we must make unnecessary sacrifices: when water is plentiful we must enjoy it with a clear conscience. It would be pointless not indulging ourselves because what we save will evaporate anyway. The secret is to be prepared for drought.

There is the question of how much more land can we afford to inundate (through building more dams) in order to irrigate? Resistance against dam building is growing across the world. Too many people are displaced and lose their traditional lands, usually for the benefit of too few. South Africa's huge P K le Roux Dam benefits a dozen farmers.

The Aswan High Dam, built with Russian expertise for the benefit of the Egyptians, has robbed the lower Nile of its periodic natural floods which used to bring suspended nutrients down from tropical Africa, and it has also altered the ecology and productivity of the Nile Delta. It is usually said of dams – particularly hydro-electric dams – that their environmental impact is negligible. But this is nowadays being questioned. Dams cause water to back up for sometimes hundreds of kilometres and this has a profound effect on plant and animal life. Creatures that live in narrow streams sometimes cannot survive in sluggish backwaters. An interesting side effect of Hendrik Verwoerd Dam on the Orange River is that it may eventually bring bilharzia to that river and, possibly, to the Fish River to which the dam is linked by tunnel. Bilharzia has never been found in the Orange because its water temperature is too cold in winter and too hot in summer for the vector snail. But the water below the wall is nowadays drawn from below the surface of the dam where it is insulated against the extremes in summer and winter. One day some water bird will come flying in with an infected snail attached by mud to its leg... Bilharzia is not a fatal disease but it is very debilitating and greatly reduces the quality of life as well as lowers productivity.

South Africa's choice of dam sites has been political rather than intelligent. The Jozini Dam on the Pongola River, built to please sugar farmers, ended up inundating more useful land than it opened up for irrigation. The major irrigation area was to have been the Makatini Flats, which was afterwards found to be unsuitable. The Department of Water Affairs, in the 1960s, had omitted to call in the Department of Agricultural Services to do a soil survey in the Jozini area before commissioning the dam, and the sugar industry, for whose sake the dam was built, suddenly no longer needed the water because the world price had dropped, never to recover. Apart from all that, ecologically the dam was destructive. P B N Jackson, a senior research fellow at Rhodes University and formerly of the Food and Agricultural Organisation, noted that the word "fish" was not mentioned once in the justification for this dam although its impact on one of the most important estuarine fishing areas in South Africa - where the baTonga have fished for centuries - was critical. Likewise, the justification for the Orange River Dam was done almost entirely by engineers and politicians, without liaison with conservation bodies.

Small-scale irrigation schemes, which use reservoirs rather than dams, are becoming more popular as far as international funding agencies are concerned. They do not require expensive pumps or great technological expertise and, like all small-scale farming, they tend to produce far more per hectare - usually twice as much - than large scale schemes because those who run them have a more intimate knowledge of the land under their control.

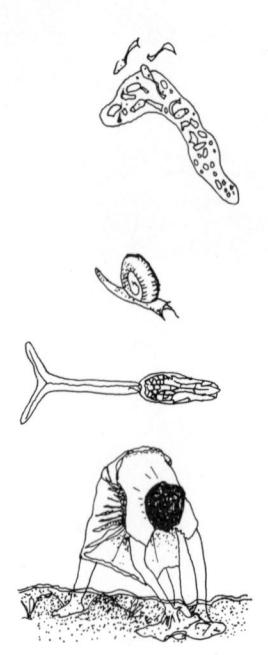

Snail vector, fluke and victim of bilharzia

Squeezing the sponge

The Israelis have developed many methods of making agricultural water go a long way. Drip irrigation is achieving what, in the past, only flood irrigation could achieve. One of Britain's big chain stores daily offers fresh vegetables flown in from South Africa – vegetables grown under drip irrigation by Israeli-trained farmers whose East Rand production line continued, uninterrupted, throughout the Great Drought.

Recycling is a very obvious way of spinning out water resources. Because of it the Rhine in Germany is able to supply several times more water than it actually contains. It is said that by the time the Dutch get their water from the Rhine it has flowed through 50 million German bladders and 30 000 factory plants and that is why the Dutch prefer drinking beer. Recycling is becoming important in South Africa. A third of the tap water on the Rand has been used before.

A rather "way-out" method of augmenting South Africa's water supplies would be to tow an iceberg, several kilometres long, from the Antarctic to the Western Cape

South Africa has two tugs capable of towing icebergs to the Western Cape

and anchor it 20 kilometres offshore. This has been seriously suggested by engineers within the Department of Water Affairs. The iceberg could not be brought closer inshore than 20 kilometres because the bottom of the iceberg, 200 metres down, would snag the continental shelf. The 'berg would have to be anchored to the shelf after being towed at an average speed of one knot (South Africa has two tugs capable of doing this) from the Antarctic. It would then have plastic skirts draped around it and would be "quarried". The chunks of ice blasted away, as well as the melted ice, would fall into the sea and, as freshwater has a lower density than sea water it would float and could be pumped ashore straight into the chronically water-short dams in the Western Cape. According to those who have thought it through the landed cost per litre would compare favourably with conventional supplies.

The towing of icebergs is not a new idea. Rodney Jones, while studying chemical engineering at the University of the Witwatersrand, did a comprehensive study (1981) of "harvesting" icebergs for fresh water and found that between 1890 and 1900 small icebergs were towed from Leguna, Chile to Valparaiso and even to Callao, Peru, a distance of 3 900 kilometres. He believed South Africa would be harvesting icebergs around the turn of the century.

Second hand water

The supply of water has two aspects: the manipulation of the basic supply, and the control of waste. The latter is a major problem and in South Africa, where the "tragedy of the commons" approach is very obvious when it comes to water use, the quality of water is deteriorating in several areas. Mineralised water from mine runoff and from other industries and agriculture is mainly to blame for the pollution crisis which is building up on the Witwatersrand.

Sandra Postel of the Worldwatch Institute says:

> Even the best water supplies typically have salt concentrations of 200 to 500 parts per million (ppm). (For comparison, ocean water has a salinity of about 35 000 ppm; water with less than 1000 ppm is considered fresh; and the recommended limit for drinking water in the United States is 500 ppm). Applying 10 000 cubic metres

of water to a hectare per year, a fairly typical irrigation rate, thus adds between 2 and 5 tons of salt to the soil annually. If it is not flushed out, this can build up to enormous quantities in a couple of decades, greatly damaging the land. Aerial views of abandoned irrigation areas in the world's dry regions reveal vast expanses of glistening white salt, land so destroyed it is essentially useless.

The tds (total dissolved solids) in the Vaal Barrage from where the PWV receives its water is typically about 800 ppm and rises often to 1 000 and, as in America, the salts are more of a threat to soil fertility than they are to human health. Most of us could drink water with 1 500 ppm without stress. But such a concentration could, over a period, kill soil fertility. A farmer in the Standerton district of the eastern Transvaal – whose local stream is polluted by a gold mine – found that by irrigating his farm from the stream he was adding a minimum of five tons of salt a hectare. His crops died. The local mine management was so ignorant of how contaminated its own mine water was that it irrigated some newly installed lawns with it, and when the grass died it complained to the suppliers of the turf who pinpointed the problem. The mine paid the farmer compensation and he went on holiday with the money leaving his land fallow. It is a state of affairs which says little of the morality or the environmental understanding of the mining industry.

In the Far East, Russia and Central Asia, millions of hectares of irrigation land have been abandoned and, according to Worldwatch, a quarter of irrigation lands across the world are experiencing reduced yields because of salination. Irrigation also tends to wash certain natural chemicals out of the soil and pass them into drainage lines and thus, in dangerous concentrations, they enter public water and into the human food chain.

Almost every country in the world has its horror stories about the abuse of water resources. The London *Sunday Times* Insight Team, in 1989, exposed the appalling state of Britain's rivers. One in five sewerage works illegally discharges human waste into public streams. Three thousand kilometres of sewers leak. America's Great Lakes in the 1970s were being contaminated by human waste and industrial effluent to such an extent it was dangerous even to paddle in them. A river in Ohio was so polluted with oil and other residues it caught fire. The latest horror stories are emerging from Russia where the world's largest inland sea, the Caspian, which is about the size of the Transvaal and Orange Free State combined, is rapidly being sterilised. Commercially important fish have been reduced by four-fifths as the sea becomes more and more salty. The salt is building up because, annually, 40 cubic kilometres of fresh water are being denied the Caspian – the water which used to flow in from the Terek and Kura rivers having been diverted for irrigation and industrial purposes. Harmful metals and oil products in the sea's water are, on average, 30 times the permitted maximum. Too late, the courts are turning on the polluters. A steel plant in Cherepovets was, in 1990, fined 20 million roubles (say R100 million) for polluting but, as it was state-owned, the punishment was farcical. Perhaps the worst case of water pollution and abuse in recent years concerns Russia's Aral Sea – the world's fourth largest inland lake being about three times larger than Kruger National Park. Or at least, it was. Now it has shrunk to half its size as its feeder rivers are diverted to irrigation schemes. Two of its major ports, Aralsk and Muynak, are now 32 kilometres and 22 kilometres distant from the shoreline respectively. Agricultural nutrients are washing into the sea causing algae blooms which absorb oxygen and therefore suffocate fish. Annually the winds lift 48 million tons of salt from the dried up bed and deposit them upon the farmland. Thus the sea is exacting bitter revenge on the land.

South Africa has its own problems: in one year as much as 600 000 tons of salts enter the Vaal Barrage from where a fifth of South Africa gets its drinking water. The Barrage area has become the Witwatersrand's sink and into it pours the effluent from the mines – gold mines which mill 88 million tons of acidic rock a year, and coal mines which produce 150 million tons of coal a year. The Department of Water Affairs is not against them using water courses for dumping effluent providing there is enough flow to carry the stuff to the sea and enough alkalinity. The principle of using surface water to dissolve pollutants is much the same as using the air. The department feels if water has the capacity to dissolve pollutants then it would be pointless not to use it. Some may feel that this policy encourages industry to take the easy way out.

Acid can be neutralised, even once it has got into public water. Germiston Lake was for years totally sterilised by mine acids leached from surrounding mine dumps. Then one day the local council was faced with a problem of finding somewhere to dump a load of caustic soda and an official had the bright idea of gradually releasing the alkaline substance into the acid-bound lake. They invited a local high school to monitor the project as an exercise and children watched in fascination as introduced fish thrived, reed beds grew and new species of birds arrived. Today anglers use the dam.

A third of the total dissolved solids (tds) which enter the Vaal Barrage comes from the mines and almost half comes from undefined sources.

In 1960 the Vaal Barrage's tds was 180 ppm. And, as mentioned earlier, by 1985 it had reached 800. Since then the flow of the Vaal, because of good rains, has increased and the flushing effect has relieved the situation for the time being. But at 1 000 ppm, a level it reaches and even surpasses from time to time, the Vaal's water is often below internationally acceptable standards for drinking water. It is generally too polluted for Iscor, the iron and steel plant, to use without diluting it with cleaner water straight from Vaal Dam. But at least the Barrage's water can be flushed out in wet years by opening the Barrage's gates and pouring in fresh water from the Vaal Dam upstream. A happy arrangement, except nowadays even Vaal Dam's water is

Centre-pivot irrigation – is it damaging the land?

becoming increasingly mineralised by runoff from the mine land of the Far East Rand and from farmland.

In the mid 1980s, when the drought was still on and Vaal Dam was not receiving enough water to dilute its mineral load, the problem was particularly severe. As we noted earlier, the gold mines will often allow highly mineralised underground water to go straight into public streams. Massive areas of once reasonable land have been sterilised by the mines which use agricultural land as sites for some of the world's largest mine dumps. It is a cost which, once the gold mines are defunct, the next generation of South Africans will have to deduct from the nation's wealth. Considerable mineral leaching comes from these mine dumps which straddle the southern Transvaal and streams draining the Witwatersrand are lined with mine dump sand, wind-blown as well as alluvial, and acid levels in some streams are on a par with vinegar.

Eddie Koch of the Johannesburg *Daily Mail*, in conjunction with Earthlife Africa - a lively and uncompromising greens group - revealed to what extent some streams are being contaminated. The Klip Spruit, which drains mining land before passing through Soweto and on to the Vaal Barrage, leaches from the mine dumps 8 million micrograms of sulphate per litre (the World Health Organisation recommends a maximum level of 400 for drinking water), 1 900 micrograms of uranium, 520 micrograms of cyanide (five times the recommended maximum); 510 of lead (10 times the recommended maximum) and 60 micrograms of arsenic (slightly above the recommended maximum). Of course, nobody in his right mind would drink from a stream draining an industrial area, but the pollution is such that water purification works are not coping with it. Even Johannesburg's tap water sometimes shows traces of mining effluent: Koch described how subclinical traces of mercury had been found - possibly finding its way in from gold mine dump residues.

Paul Polasek and Claude Mangeot, two water engineers, caused a stir when, in April 1990, *The Star* made public a paper they had delivered some time before in Durban. They revealed that most South Africans were drinking substandard water mainly because the country's "antiquated water works" which, while they are capable of neutralising pathogens, were not doing a very good job on extracting organics from industrial waste. They revealed that South Africa's water quality standards were on a par or lower than some Third World countries; there was bungling by civil engineers who knew too little about the chemistry of waste treatment, there was an "almost total absence of research into water purification technology"; and neither water works nor municipalities carried out daily checks on tap water. *The Star* did a snap check on tap water in the southern Transvaal and found it generally not bad. But it did emerge that daily tests were wanting.

Their accusations were never refuted beyond the water authorities assuring people that the tap water was fine. When Polasek and Mangeot claimed no checks were being made on carcinogenic substances the statement went unchallenged. An interesting indicator of health authorities' attitudes may be found in the case of trihalomethanes (THMs) which are cancer-causing by-products formed when chlorine, which is added to drinking water to disinfect it, reacts with organics in the water. Johannesburgers were assured by the city council in 1990 that on the 127 times tests were made for THMs during 1989 the average level was 50 to 60 micrograms a litre and that the level went over 100 only twice. They were further assured that America allows 300 mg/l. In fact the the US Environmental Protection Agency in the US has, for some time, allowed a ceiling of 100 mg/l but is currently considering lowering it to 25. West Germany and Switzerland are already on 25. In Holland public health researchers are so worried about THMs they allow only 1 mg/l. The European Council may make the Dutch standard binding in Europe.

Polasek insists: "You cannot set standards for these things. Any quantity is harmful." Dr Ronnie van Steenderen of the CSIR discovered that there are places in South Africa (Hammanskraal and Pienaars River are two of them) where the average is well over 200 and many centres are over 100 (Port Elizabeth for instance).

Standards are a vexed subject but in so many categories regarding water quality South Africa emerges as unduly permissive. Take faecal matter: the European Council allows no more than 25 mg/l. The World Health Organisation, mindful of the realities in Third World situations, and not wanting to set impossible targets, says 200 mg/l is safe enough. South Africa allows 600 mg/l.

Algae

Cadmium and mercury, heavy metals which can build up in the body causing anaemia, brittle bones, liver diseases, paralysis and other serious effects, and which enhance the toxic effects of copper and zinc, are very strictly controlled in most countries. The EC limit is 0,005 mg/l for cadmium and 0,001 mg/l for mercury. The South African Bureau of Standards has recommended four times more cadmium and 10 times more mercury.

The Water Act does not set standards for industrial organics at all, except when it comes to phenol compounds which have powerful caustic effects. Here we allow 10 times more than the WHO and 20 times more than the EC.

The Department of Water Affairs, whose officials have a reputation among journalists for being frank and helpful, have an understandable dilemma: whether to spend money on higher standards for the small numbers who demand them, or whether to spend more money on giving more people partly purified water. Polasek's rejoinder when this view was expressed at a conference was: "There is no need to spend more. Just design treatment plants properly." He claimed current treatment was only 30 per cent efficient at removing industrial organics.

A particularly worrying aspect of water pollution in South Africa was exposed by Earthlife Africa and, in fact, brought this anti-pollution group into the public eye. Earthlife, in 1989, found mercury contamination in a stream at Cato Ridge - a crowded black residential area near Durban - and reported it to the authorities in August. Nothing happened, even though the stream fed into Durban's water supply. Earthlife, working with the experienced Greenpeace organisation, found Thor Chemicals of Britain had been given permission by the South African Government to import 35 tons of mercury waste a year from Cyanamid in the USA. Cyanamid obviously found the stuff too environmentally hazardous to destroy in America and so brought it to South Africa. Earthlife, six months after failing to interest the Government, went to the press. Thor's immediate reaction was to downplay the thing as a slight leakage. But within 24 hours the Department of Health ordered the plant closed. The question the public asked itself was why did the health authorities move only after seven months? *The Star* editorialised: "Was it because the public found out?"

South Africa's topography has a useful built-in advantage: its rivers run fast and are thus quite well oxygenated. Because of this they have good self-cleansing properties as far as organic pollution is concerned. But dissolved solids cannot be reduced in this way. Many urban streams are now becoming overwhelmed by industrial contamination, which generally comes down in slugs of pollutants and often causes extensive fish kills. As with air pollution the authorities tend to feel more sympathy for the polluter and although the occasional offender is fined the penalties are very light. In 1990 the beautiful Elands River in the eastern Transvaal suffered a particularly severe fish kill for scores of kilometres downstream of Sappi's notoriously odiferous Ngodwana paper mill, whose settling dam (where pollutants are supposed to settle out) overflowed. The accident destroyed 100 tons of fish and revealed a certain carelessness which is fairly common in South Africa. Industry takes advantage of the rather permissive Water Act just as it does of the weakly-applied Atmospheric Pollution Prevention Act. The mill was fined R6 000, which underscores the point.

The Water Act of 1965 starts off by laying down standards for trout streams. It's a nice little idiosyncrasy. Imagine if the Soil Conservation Act started off by laying down the law about replacing divots on golf courses. But the trout stream clause was prophetic because, shortly after, there suddenly appeared a distinct threat to South Africa's trout streams: cold water soap powder. Up until these detergents became popular, 20 years ago, villagers in the mountains did their washing by bashing their clothes on smooth rocks in the stream. The new wonder detergents have transformed washing day as well as the water quality in some areas.

Trout

Worldwide, water management seems to be moving in a clear direction – PPP, or the polluter pays principle. In the long run of course PPP stands for the "public pays principle" because fines will be added on to production costs. The Germans have a scheme in the Ruhr Valley where all industries pay into a single river system authority which carries out anti-pollution works. It constantly monitors the water and can "sniff" a slug of pollutant back to the offending pipe. Factories are taxed according to how much oxygen demand their effluent places on the river and the money pays for treatment plants as well as for devices such as storage tanks for fresh water which can be released when the river is low, thus increasing the dilution of waste material. The tax for such schemes has to be high, high enough to exert pressure on industrial economists to urge factory owners to stop the pollutants entering the river in the first place. One of the first results of the Ruhr tax was that the canning industry began to recover and re-use the vinegar it used to dump in the river. It also resulted in paper plants recycling 90 per cent of their wastes which are particularly high in oxygen demand.

The South African Department of Water Affairs stated in its comprehensive book *Management of the Water Resources of the Republic of South Africa* (1986) that in keeping with international practice, the Department of Water Affairs had adopted the principle that the polluter pays for the abatement of his own pollution. One cannot help thinking that if ever this was applied to the mining industry it would do awful things to its profits. Nevertheless the Department has given notice of possible new measures requiring industry to implement new water efficiency technologies "within a reasonable period of time".

As in air pollution, where sulphur emissions and smoke often represent recoverable and even profitable resources, so it is in water pollution. In 1970, in the state of Washington, an engineer fond of fishing downstream from a paper mill, which was slowly polluting the river, decided not to complain but to strike a deal instead. He built a plant next door, filtered out the mill's effluent and sold it back to them for re-use at a profit of $1 million a year.

A less constructive approach, but quite effective, was when an Ohio angler walked into the plush downtown foyer of a large paper company carrying a bucket containing filthy water and dead fish. He then startled the mid-morning crowd by swishing the contents across the marble floor. He walked up to the receptionist and handed her a note telling the company that this was what they had done to a perfectly good river and that there was plenty more where that came from.

Dying lakes

South Africa, being at the tip of a relatively undeveloped

continent and surrounded by huge expanses of ocean with turbulent winds, is fortunate in having to deal only with its own acid fall out – this contrasts with the land-packed northern hemisphere, where most nations are heavily industrialised and sulphur pollution is freely exchanged. Canada and Scandinavia now report many tens of thousands of lakes which have become too acidic to support life, and both regions blame their neighbours to the south for the problem. The phenomenon of dying lakes is widespread and is part of the reason for the current debate on how much and how fast the industrialised countries should clean up acid-creating sulphur air pollution. In 1986, after almost 20 years of procrastinating, Britain's Central Electricity Generating Board accepted it was partly to blame for Scandinavia's huge fish loss. Lord Marshall, chairman of the CEGB, flew over hundreds of dead and dying lakes in Norway before announcing the CEGB would spent £600 million curbing sulphur emissions from its coal-fired power stations. CEGB scientists discovered why acid rain affects some areas more than others: it appears that aluminum leached from soils by acid waters is the real toxin which is killing fish. It was also discovered that conifers, by capturing on their needles both dry acid fallout as well as acid raindrops, make the soil more acid and add to acidic runoff.

Apart from Lake Sibaya in Zululand, South Africa has no large natural lakes but it does have several dams and many of these, especially in the eastern Transvaal, are showing signs of acidity. Judging by the amount of acid fallout – either via rain or in dry form – it is only a matter of time before the dams of the eastern Transvaal begin to show signs of biological deterioration. We have already discussed how increased mineralisation, especially severe in the areas which receive runoff from mine properties, is becoming a problem. Perhaps only when acidification begins to attack the popular trout waters in the Transvaal Escarpment, thus affecting the recreation of the Rand's mining and industrial executives, will anybody get worried enough to do something.

Another problem is eutrophication, a process triggered by too many nutrients entering a body of water. Nutrients from sewerage works, industrial effluent and fertiliser-impregnated runoff from farmland cause "blooms" in dams

Water hyacinth on Hartbeespoort Dam

– blooms being sudden flushes of algae growth. Thus, from time to time, Hartbeespoort Dam turns pea green as gelatinous volumes of algae build up. Cattle have died drinking from the dam – poisoned by blue green algae. The more life in a dam, the more death, and as the dead algae and water weeds sink to the bottom so they begin to decay; in decaying they take up oxygen and this eventually suffocates the fish. The end result of eutrophication is for the lake to die and become a stinking swamp giving off methane gas.

The problem is not easy to address, especially when it comes to phosphates and nitrates from sewerage works – both potent fertilisers. The idea of treating sewage is to turn harmful organic waste into "harmless" inorganic waste. The process is very expensive. But what happens then is that the inorganic by-products, phosphates and nitrates, boost plant life and end up in some downstream dam as organic waste after all.

The 1989 annual report of the Water Research Commission stated that "in the long term the deteriorating water quality and the resulting decline in its usefulness can become a bigger problem than the availability of water" in South Africa. It saw "salinisation and eutrophication" as the worst problems and pointed out that South Africa's dams are increasingly subjected to enrichment with plant nutrients such as nitrogen-containing compounds and phosphate. The resultant algae blooms cause problems. But here the WRC saw an opportunity: algae is rich in protein and can be used as a cattle food additive. It can be more productive from a water input and space consuming point of view than growing fodder under irrigation. Indeed, in the 1970s AECI, a big contributor to the algae blooms which discolour Hartbeespoort Dam, began a big and bold experiment to use its waste nitrogen (its biggest waste problem) to grow algae in the grounds of the company's huge dynamite and chemical plant at Modderfontein. The experiment was stopped during the drought and, sadly, never reinstated.

Hartbeespoort Dam

The bigger problem in causing algae blooms is phosphate and standards differ for phosphate pollution depending where one is in South Africa. We are likely to see tougher restrictions being introduced regarding phosphate pollution, half of which comes from industry. Certainly South Africa has made some considerable strides in developing a technology to remove phosphate at sewerage plants.

Another problem associated with sewage disposal is the question of what to do with the sludge left over after sewerage works have removed the pathogens. This is yet another example of where an environmental problem can prove to be an environmental opportunity. Throughout the world sludge is either incinerated (in the USA a third is incinerated) but this creates air pollution; or it can be used as landfill (Japan does this with half its sludge while Russia dumps as much as three quarters) or it can be dumped in the sea. The United Kingdom dumps a third of its sludge in the North Sea. Taiwan, with only one sewerage works, dumps nearly all of its raw sewage in coastal water to boost fish production. Or sludge can be used as a soil conditioner and fertiliser.

In the 1960s Chicago was paying $60 a ton to bury its sludge. In the early 1970s it was *receiving* $12 a ton from California's citrus growers who dig it into the soil. Seattle in the State of Washington – a city about the same size as Johannesburg – uses all its annual 100 000 tons of sludge on a 2 000 hectare piece of city-owned land on which it grows trees. Municipal horticulturalists say trees, fertilised by sludge, grow twice as fast and, through the eventual timber sales, Seattle should make a profit. Calcutta runs the biggest aquacultural scheme in the world by dumping its sludge in special ponds and growing 40 tons of fish a day for the local market. China produces 3 million tons of fish a year using mainly untreated human waste. The Taiwanese have found that after washing and gutting sewage-fed fish, in just the same way they wash other fish, the fish show no more pathogenic contamination than those from the open sea.

According to Marcia D Lowe, a researcher with the Worldwatch Institute, test plots of wheat, rice and cotton show that urban wastewater irrigation boosts yields 25 to 50 per cent above those achieved using ground water and commercial fertiliser.

Planting rice

Paying through the hose
What of the future? Obviously water will move up in price, probably very steeply, until it reaches its true market value, and then it will be so pricey that water conservation will become fashionable.

A future supply of water – underground water – is, in several places in the world, being sadly depleted and contaminated by toxins leaking from waste dumps in many parts of the world. In some parts of China water tables are dropping 1 to 4 metres a year. In the southern Indian state of Tamil Nadu, heavy pumping for irrigation has caused the water table to drop 20 to 30 metres in a decade. South Africa, lacking widespread development, has so far avoided disastrous dewatering. In the Karoo, where borehole water can be thousands of years old (fossil water it is called), and where replenishment of aquifers is extremely slow, 100 towns which are entirely dependent on borehole water are careful not to extract more than is wise. Indeed, humans and livestock depend on borehole water in over two-thirds of South Africa.

We have already mentioned how, in the southern half of the Transvaal, massive subterranean caves in the dolomitic rock – some with a capacity greater than Vaal Dam – are filled with water which could be exploited. The gold mining industry, to stop water flooding into its mine workings, has dewatered several dolomitic areas of the Transvaal causing sinkholes as the now empty underground cavities collapse. The small western Transvaal town of Bank was abandoned in the 1960s because of the threat of sinkholes. A nearby gold reduction plant, with 38 workers, was swallowed up by a sinkhole. In the mining town of Blyvooruitsig a house, with its occupants – father, mother, three children and a maid – disappeared one night into the earth. So did a tennis court, one Sunday afternoon in mid game, swallowing a player. Once the gold mines are exhausted of their metal these natural dolomitic reservoirs could be refilled and tapped.

There is also the opportunity to use more groundwater from the fissures of the granite dome which occupies the space between the Witwatersrand ridge and Pretoria. Some of these are huge and they rapidly fill after a few storms. Many gardeners use boreholes (some have struck 100 000 litres an hour at less than 10 metres depth) and, in time, there's no reason why municipalities should not sink neighbourhood boreholes and recoup the cost by selling the water for gardening purposes and for topping up the region's many swimming pools.

South African water engineers have warned from time to time that South Africa's assured maximum supply (that which its dams can guarantee to provide even in a worst case drought) is enough for only 40 million people – a population level we have almost reached. T C Robertson of the National Veld Trust said in 1971:

> *Planners must liberate their ideas from the present bondage (and) from the safety device of arithmetic average. Only then can they harvest and use the wasted abundance of the flood years. While cities and industries are chained to an assured supply of water, the thirsty earth can adapt its work to the unpredictable cycle of drought and flood. Planning is already advancing towards a concept of irrigation water use that will accept the penalty of drought and eagerly exploit the gift of the floods. This is South Africa's ultimate water dilemma, the challenge that must be faced as the nation turns from dam building and the re-use of water to the last resort, of de-salting the sea.*

Liberated ideas? How about rain-making? Dr Jacques Kriel, when chairman of the Water Research Commission, believed cloud seeding (dropping dry-ice on clouds) had potential, but only in years to come. More research was needed. In the early days of cloud seeding – around the late 1940s – cloud seeders made more money than they made rain. In the US the general opinion seems to be that cloud seeding does not work. But the Israelis claimed a 15 per cent increase in rainfall and actually built small dams to trap the extra water. South Africa, after 43 years, has made little convincing progress and may be doing as Professor Lourens Heimstra of Stellenbosch suggested that if you precipitate the clouds before they hit a range of mountains, which is their natural trigger, you just move the rainfall backwards and don't achieve much. You simply make rain fall somewhere else.

Desalination? Perhaps, as water is recognised for the important mineral that it is, we will find a way of economically de-salting the sea. But the more likely course is first to increase recycling and for industry and agriculture to upgrade even further their attempts to produce more goods from less water and then to bring in the Highlands Project. This should take us through to 2030. After that the Zambezi. After that? Desalination. But, by then, one would hope, South Africa will be an industrialised First World country and will have reached zero population growth.

Who should control water?

Originally water control measures came about because of public health issues – the avoidance of cholera and typhoid which, right into the early years of this century, were still common diseases in Europe and America. Now the scene has changed. It is taken for granted that advanced countries will maintain water supplies that are free of the old diseases and now the question is how to ensure water gets to all those who need it, including industry and farming and to ensure it is free of toxins. For that one needs standards and standards need constant reviewing.

Professors Fuggle and Rabie feel that with regard to pollution control "it seems desirable to abandon the idea of country-wide standards and, with it, the role of the South African Bureau of Standards." They believe that regional controls are better and that standards should be set regionally. Indeed this is now Government thinking too. While less central Government is always desirable it is impossible in some categories – air pollution control must, for instance, have national standards and, ideally, international standards. Water is not that much different. Hydrologically there must be central control otherwise who is to stop one region robbing the people downstream? The eastern Transvaal Highveld region may decide to double its forest plantations and thus jeopardise the country's biggest tourist attraction, the Kruger Park, by taking up its water supply. Likewise it might be tardy in monitoring certain pollutants and thus pass even more problems downstream.

Regional control would work only if there was a strong environmental protection body with cabinet status, or, even better, "super ministry" status. Its job would be to look after broad national interests; to be responsible for health research and the constant review of standards regarding dangerous substances, and to act as arbiter.

11 The last resource

Roll on, thou deep dark-blue Ocean, roll!
Ten thousand fleets sweep over thee in vain;
Man marks the earth with ruin, his control
Stops with the shore; upon the water plain
The wrecks are all thy deed, nor doth remain
A shadow of man's ravage.

                                    Lord Byron

HOW wrong Byron was. And how unmistakably the fate of the seas bears out Hardin's theory of the tragedy of the commons.

To some the sea is their life, and the fish in it their livelihood. To others the sea is a medium - a testing and sometimes dangerous one - on which they travel in ships. To others it is leaping marlin, a summer holiday, a yacht race. To the geographer it is 70,8 per cent of the Earth's surface, and deeper than Everest is high. To the botanist this is where life began when the air was too poisonous to inhale. To the demographer this is from where 2 000 million humans get 40 per cent of their protein.

The North Atlantic alone has enough fish to equal the world's grain harvest 20 000 times. In the soup-like seas of the Antarctic the Russian trawler SS *Knipovic* landed six tons of live krill in 30 minutes. Off Peru, in 1971, the anchovette shoals of the biggest fishery known to man yielded 12 million tons. The following year, nothing.

Byron obviously never believed man could "mark the sea with ruin". The ruin really became obvious only when Thor Heyerdahl crossed the Atlantic in the raft *Ra* in 1969 and found a 2 250 kilometre long belt of unbroken pollution. There were times when the crew had difficulty plucking up the courage to dip their toothbrushes in the water. Further south a flotilla of destroyers seeking a missing submarine found the Atlantic so coated in oil that it was pointless trying to find the submarine by looking for any oil slick it might have left. And in the Puerto Rican trench, 9 kilometres deep, scientists recovered the deepest vertebrate ever found - a 12 centimetre long fish - and brought to the surface with it old paint cans, batteries and other goodies. Nearer home, Alan Heydorn watched turtles in Zululand hatching and making their way to the sea. Not one of the hatchlings survived because many became stuck in gobs of oil on the beach and fell prey to ghost crabs.

As for the fishlife, for decades we have been intensively exploiting sealife with insufficient knowledge and enormous greed which sometimes bordered on frenzy. It has been like farming livestock from above an inpenetrable layer of thick cloud, using fleets of helicopter gunships and bombs. Look how mercilessly we hunted the whales until a last minute international agreement stopped all whaling. Even then the Japanese continued killing hundreds "for

Whaling off the South African coast in the 1950s. Source The Argus

scientific research". Scientific? They were all killed by the same old commercial whaling firms who processed their meat into pet food and for the delicacy market. Honour has never been a strong point in the industry.

Not only have we plundered the seas, but we are in danger of radically altering its character. Over the next 40 years, because of the mistake of using ozone-destroying chlorofluorocarbons (CFCs) for aerosols, refrigerants and solvents, we can expect up to a 20 per cent increase in ultraviolet radiation which will slow down photosynthesis and growth in phytoplankton. In 1988 the air above the Antarctic suffered a 15 per cent drop in its ozone level. Ozone shields the Earth's surface from excessive ultraviolet light. The thinning corresponded with a 15 to 20 per cent drop in surface phytoplankton, according to the Worldwatch Institute journal (July 1989). Phytoplankton is the sea's version of grass meadows, but the minute organisms float freely and drift with the currents. Like land plants, phytoplankton takes in carbon dioxide, releases the oxygen and retains the carbon which eventually sinks when an organism dies, thus usefully removing carbon from the industrially overloaded air. Reduce phytoplankton and one reduces the planet's ability to remove excessive carbon dioxide and thus the greenhouse effect is increased. Reduce phytoplankton and one reduces the primary food source of the oceans which directly, or indirectly, affects every living thing in the sea.

The coral reefs, which are also being destroyed, can be equated with the rain forests of the land. They are rich in species – at least a million species including more than 2 000 types of fish found nowhere but in coral reefs. Reefs are being dynamited for various reasons. In Mauritius fishermen used to toss sticks of dynamite into coral reefs simply to flush out one fish. Around the world many reefs have been suffocated by silt which fans out from river mouths. The Japanese and Taiwanese smash reefs with weights (bobbins) attached to their nets to stop the nets snagging. These bobbins are used, legally, in South African waters.

From South Africa's point of view, the most shameful chapter of all was the 1960s and 1970s when enormous damage was done to its uniquely large sardine (pilchard) stocks. In 1968 Professor Jan Lochner of the University of Port Elizabeth, a systems dynamics expert, speaking at an Oceanographic Research Institute conference on coastal ecology, warned that although the sardine shoals off Namibia could, if properly managed, annually yield 2,5 million tons, they were in imminent danger of collapsing. He said the catches would become increasingly erratic and then suddenly crash. The only politician who understood what he was saying was John Wiley, National Party MP for Simonstown, who was openly scathing of the Department of Economic Affairs which was in charge of setting sardine quotas for Namibia. In 1968 Namibia landed its biggest catch in history – 1,4 million tons.

In 1969 the Government, despite Lochner's warnings, increased the quota to 1,75 million tons. But only 1,2 million

Pilchard

tons were caught, a drop of 280 000 tons from the season before. Unnerved by its miscalculation the Government reduced the 1970 quota to 810 000 tons. Again the catch fell short of quota. Lochner pleaded for more drastic cuts, so drastic that they would have temporarily brought the fishing industry to its knees. But Thornton Booth, director of the world's biggest fish cannery at Walvis Bay, said: "We are expanding our plant. We would not do this if we had doubts about the industry."

In 1971 the sardine (pilchard) catch dropped to 646 000 tons, the lowest in years. Omaruru MP, Boet Botma, said: "It is obvious to anybody that all is well." He said the drop was the result of skilful management.

In 1972 the quota was raised to just under 1 million tons. John Wiley rounded on his own party saying they must know there had been falsified figures "with the intention of making it appear that Dr Lochner's forecast for the year were incorrect. He was within one per cent of accuracy." Wiley, a man of considerable courage and who later made an intelligent and committed Minister of Environment (he died in office) pleaded for the quota to be slashed. The quota of almost 1 million remained but the catch dropped to half of that. In 1973 the catch rose to almost 706 000 tons but Lochner had forecast this final upward surge. He said that under pressure nature tended to compensate by rapid breeding. What had also happened was that less nutritious anchovies now made up a great deal of the catch. The Government expanded Walvis Bay harbour and, in 1977, upped the quota to nearly a million again. That year the catch reached only 400 000 tons. Two fish factories closed. In 1978 the season was stopped halfway through. Eastern Transvaal tomato farmers had to retrench workers because 80 per cent of their crop was for canned sardines. In 1978 414 000 tons of sardines and anchovies were hauled in and the following year the sardine quota was lowered to 337 500. Willem Barends, a big fishing concern, asked for a higher quota because profits were disastrously low. By 1980 only two fish factories remained open. The quota was down 99,2 per cent on 10 years before – a mere 12 500 tons. Even so the trawlers came back with less than half of that. Even the anchovy were in steep decline. In 1981 the last factory closed. Eight thousand men had lost their jobs. The trawlers were sold to Chile and South Africa was now importing canned sardines. A lot of men behind the scenes made good money from the rape of Namibia's coast.

South Africa's own sardine shoals, between the Orange River and Cape Agulhas, were also reduced by more than 95 per cent and they too never recovered. South Africa was not alone – West and East Germany, Russia, Britain, Norway, Belgium ... they all helped plunder Southern Africa's waters. As recently as 1989 South Africa's sardine catch comprised 81 per cent juveniles. The anchovy catch too was three quarter juvenile fish.

There was, even in 1990, still little understanding of what had happened. The then Minister of Environment, Gert Kotze, in opening a marine exhibition in October said:

Tuna

> ... after the Second World War, off both the Republic [South Africa] and Namibia, the catch from the south east Atlantic rocketed to over 3 million tons. Since those halcyon days of the late 1960s, the catch has dropped, not due to overexploitation but by means of rigorous control and careful scientific study. I believe that we have achieved as healthy a state of fishery as can be found anywhere else in the world.

There are a number of problem areas in South Africa and a number of opportunities too, waiting for the right sort of leadership. False Bay, for instance, is becoming badly polluted and its fish stocks are threatened by a lack of adequate control. The Western Cape Marine Conservation Society says there has been a large drop in the number of yellowtail, a big and popular angling fish. Vic Kabalin, founder and president of the society says one reason is that trek (seine) netting has swept up whole shoals of these fish. "This wipes out whole communities of fish and so makes the job of regeneration extremely difficult," says Kabalin. "The situation is aggravated by the fact that the height of the trek netting season coincides with the yellowtail spawning season." He sees inshore trek netting as a particularly crude method pointing out how non-target fish are pulled in, how the sea bottom is denuded and how the "nursery fish" in the surf zone are destroyed. Kabalin, a Fish Hoek councillor, would like to see False Bay become a national park. The 40 kilometre wide, mountain-ringed bay is important to the ecology of the entire south-west corner of Africa. It is a nursery to many species and is a good place to see huge southern right whales which come close in shore, dolphins, seals, jackass penguins – even flying fish. Apart from overfishing the bay is assaulted by serious sewage pollution in parts.

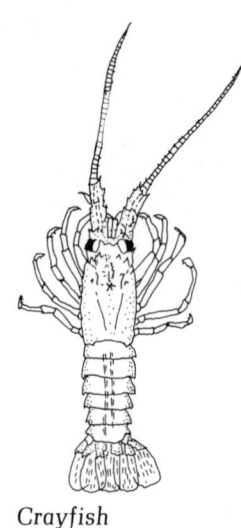

Round the corner in Walker Bay, former Minister John Wiley, aware of the damage seine netting was doing, banned it. Minister Kotze, claiming there was no scientific evidence to justify banning it, reinstated netting. Today, says Kabalin, 11 species of fishes have almost disappeared, the great white shark has become rare and this has led to an upsurge in seal numbers. In other words, bottom-dragging nets have created ecological chaos.

Although the annual fish catch off South Africa, in terms of tonnage, is fairly constant nowadays the fluctuations and downright population crashes in some species is worrying. Hake used to yield 1 million tons a year but now yields 87 per cent less. Tuna, a line fish which must not be caught with nets, are down 60 per cent, almost certainly because of foreign trawlers using illegal nets. Tuna fishing employs 5 000 South Africans. Crayfish have entirely disappeared from some parts and the ones South Africa catches now are tiny compared with 25 years ago. International poachers, mostly Taiwanese, have an easy time simply because there is no coastguard and penalties are tantamount to a slap on the wrist. Minister Kotze instituted R1 million fines for poaching in 1990. "This is proof of the Government's zeal," he said. No, its zealousness will be demonstrated only when the first heavy fine is imposed and the offender's trawler is confiscated.

The fish crash along the south-west coast in the 1970s was not unique. Much the same happened off Peru where the anchovette fishing grounds in the late 1960s were yielding 10 million tons a year. A US scientific commission warned that the catch rate was unsustainable. But the fishing frenzy continued and the following year the catch climbed to 12 million. Then it crashed to nil. The industry claimed that the failure was due to a natural fluctuation in the strength of the Humboldt Current which normally caused huge upwellings of nutritious material to rise from the depths. The anchovettes fed in these upwellings. Yet even when the upwellings returned to normal the fish did not return.

Crayfish

Anchovy

The worldwide commercial catch reached a record level of 84,5 million tons in 1988 according to the Worldwatch Institute – up from 21 million tons in 1950. But the picture is not rosy. The probable sustainable catch is 100 million tons. But when one considers subsistence fishermen also pulled in 24 million tons, plus the fact that many fleet owners still falsify their figures, we are probably witnessing global overfishing. The Worldwatch Institute says:

> The recent upswing in catches is attributable to the use of more efficient fishing techniques and the increased exploitation of less desirable species in the herring and sardine family. Also, the world's fishing fleets have intensified their exploitation of remote regions in the Southern Pacific Ocean. As fisheries decline, family income and even food intake, will head downward for more than a million people who depend on the oceans for their livelihood.

The Law of the Sea, signed by practically every country in the world (159 signed) has still not been ratified. The stumbling block arises from international jealousies and suspicions regarding the mineral riches which lie on the ocean bed beyond the continental shelves, in the deep sea. Eight years after the Law of the Sea was framed only 40 of the 60 countries needed to ratify it have done so. But at least the nations agreed on the "200 mile EEZ" – the exclusive economic zone which extends offshore for 200 miles (360 kilometres) and over which each nation has total jurisdiction regarding offshore living and non-living resources. This takes in 90 per cent of the world's fisheries.

There are also regional agreements to control certain activities such as dumping sewage in the sea and to reduce agricultural runoff which carries fertiliser which overstimulates sealife causing eutrophication and red tides. Red tides are becoming more and more common. Sewage and fertilisers cause massive population explosions among dinoflagalettes (of the phylum Protozoa) which may give off a toxin which discolours the sea. The poison wipes out fishlife and even sea birds (as happened in Britain in 1968) and shellfish accumulate it and become lethal to man if eaten. South Africa has experienced several minor red tides but may start getting more now that towns are being allowed to discharge sewage into coastal waters. More and more South African factories are being allowed to discharge waste into the sea. Eighty per cent of the world's commercial fish are caught in the shallower waters off coastlines – the waters most affected by pollution.

It is this sort of permissiveness which has led to the recent disasters in the sea around industrialised countries in the northern hemisphere. The Adriatic, perhaps the most beautiful sea on Earth, in 1989 became in parts a foul and stinking mess because of eutrophication (massive algae blooms which then die off and putrefy). Nearly half the Baltic's bottom waters are now biologically dead. More than 17 000 seals died around northern Europe in 1988 and three-quarters of the female seals in the Baltic are believed to have been sterilised by polychlorinated biphenyls (PCBs). More than 3 000 dolphins were washed up along the United States' eastern seaboard and were found to have high concentrations of PCBs and pesticides and, as in the case of the seal epidemic, it was concluded that the animals had been killed by a measles-like virus which was able to attack the pollution-damaged immune systems of the sea mammals. Whale populations, hugely reduced by the twentieth century overkill, are now dying in some areas from mysterious diseases, especially off North America where one finds contamination by mercury, cadmium and various chemicals as well as biocides which either get washed into the sea or are deliberately dumped.

Southern right whale

Some industries do not just have a low level of social conscience, they have none at all. The sea is to them the final sink for all wastes. The most horrifying story remains that of Minamata, the coastal town in Japan where Chiso, a big chemical company, had knowingly been dumping mercury in the bay from which the populace collected shellfish which were a daily part of their diet. From 1953 to

1968 many hundreds of residents died of "Minamata disease" and hundreds were born deformed or became partly and permanently paralysed. It mystified medical science but Chiso's directors knew what it was all about. The company's medical chief had demonstrated to the board of directors the precise cause: in front of them he fed milk, laced with Chiso effluent, to the office cat. The cat went into convulsions and died. The firm transferred the doctor, moved the effluent pipe to an adjacent bay and got lawyers to go into town and get relatives to sign indemnities agreeing not to sue the industry. To this day thousands have received not a penny in compensation.

The Wafra *sinks off Cape Agulhas.*
Source The Argus

The most dramatic pollution incidents usually involve giant oil tankers breaking up and smothering coastlines. It was the sinking of the *Wafra* in 1971 which made *The Star* decide to advance the launch of its environmental campaign, CARE. The sinking of the *Wafra* was a particularly messy job. South Africa sent in strike aircraft to sink it and, hopefully, burn up as much oil as possible. Even so the oil slick did terrible damage to the Agulhas coastline. In 1989 came the incident of the *Exxon Valdez* in Prince William Sound, a rich Alaskan fishing and wildlife area.

The oil, in places a metre deep, smothered almost 1 000 kilometres of shoreline. The oil company, which had been warned about the possibility of such a disaster by environmentally concerned people, had dismissed such a possibility and was consequently totally unprepared for it. Exxon executive Don Cornett said it was "just another cost of doing business". In March 1991 Exxon was fined $1 billion and it paid out $3 billion to clear up.

All the same, such disasters are probably less serious, worldwide, than the daily runoff into the sea of oil washed off streets and from industrial factory premises, and the daily flushing of ship's tanks at sea. A US National Research Council survey estimated in 1985 that the equivalent of 21 million barrels of oil annually enter the sea. By comparison, an average 600 000 barrels are accidentally spilled annually by wrecks and burst pipelines. The Council warned that oil concentrations as low as one part in 10 million parts of seawater can affect fish reproduction and plankton growth.

There is also the question of plastic. The South African coast is badly polluted by floating plastics and daily sea creatures and birds are washed up entangled in plastic or are killed swallowing it. Some predators mistake floating plastic bags for jelly fish. Each year, in the northern hemisphere, 30 000 fur seals are strangled by plastic. The Worldwatch Institute in Washington estimates that about 500 000 plastic containers are daily thrown overboard from merchant ships.

In 1990 Peter Ryan of the Percy Fitzpatrick Institute for African Ornithology at the University of Cape Town, found 3 500 floating plastic objects to the square kilometre in the sea off the Cape. More than half were tiny match-head-sized pellets made by the primary producers and which are transported to 2 000 secondary manufacturers around the coast in inadequately stitched sacks. Ryan estimated 45 000 pellets to the metre on the West Coast's beaches. The yokes of beer "six-packs" will continue ensnaring animals for 20 years and more.

An enormous problem is the thousands of kilometres of indestructible nylon drift nets which the Taiwanese and Japanese annually cut adrift when they become damaged or entangled after a storm. They may chop loose many kilometres at a time. These nets are banned in their own national waters yet their trawlers carry up to 100 kilometre-long lengths for fishing elsewhere – including in South African waters. The mesh, because it is small but elastic, can ensnare small and large animals including small whales, dolphins, seals, turtles and birds. Floating lengths of these 12 metres deep "walls of death" will float for years until the weight of the corpses pulls it down. In 1989 it was thought there were 20 000 kilometres floating unattended in the Pacific alone. They are banned in South African waters but South Africa, like every other coastal nation in Africa, is totally unable to patrol its EEZ which covers well over 750 000 square kilometres. And, as I have indicated, even when foreign trawlers are caught red-handed (such as a Taiwanese skipper who dumped his drift nets over the side and ran for it and was fined R1 000) they are fined tiny amounts – just as international smugglers are when they are caught with illegal rhino horn and elephant ivory.

Although the picture as far as the sea is concerned is cause for concern, there are signs of a turn around in international thinking. Even the fatalistic Japanese have cancelled the building of an international airport on top of the world's finest example of blue coral reef. There are several regional agreements between different nations to curb dumping plastic from ships and to curb sewage and industrial wastes. The worldwide ban on dumping radioactive wastes has been in force for years. But it is surely significant that governments have to restrain industry. There is little doubt that without legal restraints industry would sacrifice the sea, and indeed the long-term survival of man, for the sake of making maximum profits in the medium term.

There is the question of farming the sea, as opposed to hunting it as we do at present. Once we learn to treat coastal waters in the same way we try to treat the land – in other words not using it for dumping sewage and industrial waste – we can begin to farm the sea. Results to date have been surprisingly poor when compared with the potential. For instance, where one hectare of inland pasture might produce 250 kilograms of beef, an oyster bed of similar size should yield more than 40 000 kilograms of oyster flesh or 200 000 kilograms of mussels.

Freshwater fish

In passing it is worth noting that, inland, fish farming or aquaculture is capable of producing 250 kilograms of freshwater fish per hectare of dam water in the Highveld region and double that in frost-free areas. This is in waist high water. Currently, 100 000 Transvaal fishing license holders catch an annual average of 500 tons – mainly from dams. A large proportion of this is trout meat, trout having been introduced to South Africa almost a century ago. Carp were also imported and introduced but they did not prove popular and have now become a nuisance in inland waters where they grow to world record sizes. They could, with processing and good marketing, become a useful food – especially as they eat algae which is a problem in itself in our overstimulated dams.

The FAO says there are 40 million hectares of high potential fish farming dams in the Indo Pacific area alone. China already obtains half its fish from inland sources and Malacca's Tropical Fish Culture Research Centre has obtained yields of 1 500 kilograms a hectare – 68 times the natural yield.

Coastal development

Seeing that most of the sea's living resources are in the shallower water around the coastlines it is imperative that we watch what we dump in the sea and that we analyse the probable impacts of coastal development plans before we go ahead with them. There is also the consideration of tourism. South Africa's coastline with its dune forests and, in the Cape, its soft hills blanketed in fynbos, is one of the most attractive in the world. As the world's more popular coastal areas become overcrowded or badly polluted – the French, Italian and Yugoslav coastlines are fearfully contaminated with all sorts of gubbins – so the jet-setting tourists are likely to come here. At a world conference on sandy beaches held at the University of Port Elizabeth in 1979 a Californian delegate described the eastern Cape beaches as "probably the finest examples of sandy beaches on Earth." Yet only Durban, East London, Port Elizabeth, Mossel Bay and Cape Town employ professional planners. One of the worst planned seaside resorts, Amanzimtoti, just south of Durban, relied on its town clerk to make planning decisions. Several years ago I interviewed him

Seine net fishermen

and he said he really could not see there was a need for a professional town planner along the South Coast. His own town had allowed towering and unsightly skyscrapers to block the sun from the beach from around mid afternoon each day. Many people who built their homes in the hills just back from the beach have lost their sea view and, instead, stare straight into the drainpipes of the buildings along the front. All the way down that once beautiful coast, as far as Ramsgate, development has been tawdry. Developers have stripped many dunes of their forests to make way for holiday flats which, in some cases, are seriously at risk as the now destabilised dune sand shifts beneath them. Pathways down to the sea have also been poorly planned and have caused slumping on a huge scale.

In recent years there have been some quite fierce and emotional battles between coastal developers and the public. The fiercest was that which raged throughout 1990 when a mining company attempted to develop an opencast titanium mine in the wetland dunes next to St Lucia Estuary. The mining company, half-owned by Rio Tinto Zinc (RTZ) of Great Britain, was anxious to go ahead before proper environmental impact studies were carried out. When the public discovered what was going on the company, Richards Bay Minerals, refused to discuss its plans. It was its policy not to speak to the public I was told. Only when RTZ discovered that the London *Sunday Telegraph* was about to splash the story did the British directors order Richards Bay Minerals to fly an executive up to Johannesburg to speak to Fred Bridgeland, the newspaper's Southern African bureau man. Richards Bay Minerals continued to ignore South Africans until, eventually, the public's anger boiled over. Pressure groups raised well over 300 000 signatures protesting the mine plan. The mining company then spent R5 million on a public relations drive to persuade the public that an opencast mine could be an asset. It doled out large sums to wildlife conservation including quite frivolous grants such as R10 000 to count rhino in the tiny Zululand game reserve of Ndumu. The company has now been forced to produce a genuine environmental impact analysis before the Cabinet decides the issue.

The public is also engaged in a battle to save Chapman's Peak Drive in the Cape Peninsula – certainly South Africa's most scenic marine drive – from having an opencast kaolin mine. Battles royal were fought to successfully save Robberg Peninsula nature reserve from a marina; St Francis Bay from a marina and fishing harbour; a plan to fire experimental "live" missiles into the sea off Betty's Bay, and so on. Many conservationists feel that the analysis is irrelevant because St Lucia should be considered sacrosanct.

Former environmental Minister, John Wiley, using the old Environment Conservation Act of 1982, declared a limited development zone along the entire South African coastline. He declared nobody could develop anything inside a belt extending 1 kilometre inland from the high tide mark without Ministerial approval. The dictum seems to have been invalid and was probably pure bluff. But it acted as a shot across the bows for coastal development. The rewritten Environment Conservation Act of 1989 went a step further and empowered the Minister (by now it was Gert Kotze) to determine policy in respect of the "protection of ecological processes, natural systems, and natural beauty." It also empowered the Minister to declare "limited development areas". Jan Glazewsky of the University of Cape Town's law faculty commented that in view of the confusion caused by John Wiley's attempt to impose coastal zone regulations now was the chance for the new Minister to declare the entire coast a limited development area.

Glazewski, a young and committed environmental lawyer, welcomed the new Act's Board of Investigation idea which would be chaired by a judge, magistrate, advocate or attorney, as a "valuable technique for accommodating differing public interest groups." Alas, Minister Kotze never got around to implementing this section of the Act and lost his portfolio at the end of 1990.

In February that year Roelf Botha - South Africa's first professor of landscape architecture at Pretoria - as chairman of the Council for the Environment, produced a document titled *A Policy for Coastal Zone Management - Part One*. The council is still to come up with the vital Part Two which will provide guidelines for land use in the coastal zone as well as focus on the utilisation and conservation of components of the coast such as estuaries, dunes, beaches, rocky shores, the intertidal zones, islands and so on. Meanwhile the Department of Environmental Affairs has set up a Coastal Management Advisory Programme based on part one of the policy document. It offers lectures, publications and, soon, it will come out with a manual for coastal zone development giving "easy to understand" advice on how developers can avoid causing damage when, for example, building on a dune or cutting paths through coastal forest.

The real problem along the coastline is greed and overkill. There is an aggressive commercialism which, too often, sees the public as overemotional and obstructive. Therefore, until the Environment Conservation Act is properly armed (Glazewski describes the Act as a gun which the Minister now has to load with bullets - the bullets being regulations) all these great intentions will have a limited effect on curbing the continuing damage along South Africa's 3 000 kilometres of coastline.

12 The red blood of the earth

> The great red hills stand desolate, and the earth has torn away like flesh, the lightning flashes over them, the clouds pour down upon them, the dead streams come to life, full of the red blood of the earth. Down in the valleys women scratch the soil that is left, and the maize hardly reaches the height of a man. They are valleys of old men and old women, of mothers and children. The men are away, the young men and the girls are away. The soil cannot keep them anymore.
>
> Alan Paton (Cry the Beloved Country)

The red blood of the earth

THE greenest land I have ever seen is New Zealand where I lived for a year or so in a clapboard house tucked in a deep forest in the rounded hills above Wellington. Here is a gentle land where 16 sheep can graze on a hectare of shining grass. By contrast, over most parts of South Africa's sheep country, that many sheep would need anything up to 160 hectares. At first glance New Zealand, somewhat underpopulated as countries go, appears to be, if there is such a word, "unerodable" – an unerodable paradise of year-round soft rains and warm sunshine, snowy peaks, emerald valleys and fat, ever-busy rivers.

Yet, ecologically, New Zealand is a disaster. The Maoris who arrived 1 100 years ago made short work of the flightless moa – the world's biggest bird. It was a typical case of overkill. They hunted down every last one of these almost giraffe-sized birds which had no defence. The person who did the most damage to New Zealand was probably Captain James Cook, the English explorer and pioneer dietitian, even though he never stayed there. New Zealand, like most of the Pacific islands, had no mammals, except a couple of species of bats, and so Cook put ashore some pigs and goats in the hope they would increase and thus provide decent meat for passing ships. The pig and goat populations did not increase. They exploded.

Then came the rats and mice, and the opossum, introduced by the colonists who arrived from 1822 and who also brought in the wapiti, red deer, fallow deer, chamoix and thar – even moose. These creatures invaded many eco-niches previously occupied only by birds, and they began to make deep inroads into the islands' beautiful primeval forests. The pigs rooted on the forest floor, the goats and deer ate the saplings and the opossums ate the tree tops. Without tree cover the hillsides began to collapse and in many areas the soil came away "like flesh", as Alan Paton would have said. Today one receives a bounty for whatever one shoots in New Zealand in the way of wild mammals.

New Zealand's experience provides a useful lesson. If such a fertile, well-watered, thinly populated land is so vulnerable to careless land use, what of South Africa's highly erodable plateau, baked by the sun all winter and lashed by the storms of summer?

On the other hand, when one compares South Africa with Israel and contemplates the agricultural miracles performed there – rich orchards, planted woodlands, grain fields, all growing from former deserts and using a minimum of irrigation – one has a glimpse of the potential of the South African veld.

Cities buried by sand

Globally, and certainly locally, soil loss is man's most serious environmental problem, yet it is the one which receives the least political attention. The shock statistics which are occasionally trundled out have little impact on the public mind and almost none at all on the minds of politicians.

Sadly, in an urbanised world, man has become divorced from nature. Most people no longer realise how totally dependent they are on what goes on beyond the city's edge. It is tempting to say that it was different in ancient times when even the world's biggest cities were but a few hectares in size. They would have been acutely aware of agriculture; they would have known from where their milk came, unlike today when urban people are fundamentally ignorant of agriculture and children grow up not knowing that milk comes from cows. A former colleague, novelist Mike Nicol, proved it once by randomly asking children in Hillbrow, Johannesburg, from where they thought milk came. "Many thought it was a silly question," he said. "They said it came from the corner cafe and was made in a factory." As a result of this Nicol and I then arranged with Benoni dairy farmers Ron and Alan Diesel to set up a farmyard in a Hillbrow park for a weekend. Twenty thousand people turned up to see cows being milked. It became an annual event.

The irony remains that the people of biblical times, even though they were closer to nature, were just as agriculturally short-sighted as we are. They allowed their lands to be overgrazed and overcropped until finally they wrecked their own civilisations and created deserts. The highlands of central Mexico, according to an archaeological study by Alayne and Alan Street Perrot of Oxford University (*American Antiquity* 1990) were first devastated by maize farming 3 500 years ago. Then, 1 000 years ago, there was again a period of gross erosion. Some of the land devastated 3 500 years ago is still useless.

Across vast stretches of the once green and productive Middle East, soil erosion has done its worst. In Syria 400 000 hectares of man-made desert have buried many ancient settlements. Archaeologists are digging through deep sand to unearth the secrets of at least 100 towns and settlements which were once on waterways. Where the Babylonians grew two wheat crops a year there is now desert and the tall Mediterranean forests, whose timber played such a vital role in building the great naval fleets which forged the successive Mediterranean-based empires, are no more. In their place are bleached boulder strewn hillsides whose remaining natural vegetation is of interest only to goats. Well to the south, the Sahara advances down Africa at 2 kilometres a year along a 3 000 kilometre front. The United States Agency for International Development says more than 650 000 square kilometres of land along the southern fringe of the Sahara – known as the Sahel – which was once suitable for agriculture, is now a desert. It has happened over the last 50 years.

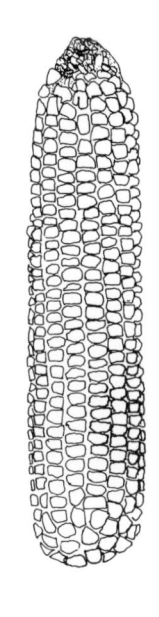

Soil erosion near Senekal, Orange Free State. Source *The Star*

According to Kai Curry-Lindahl, Unesco's outspoken Swedish biologist and conservation philosopher, during the last 100 years water and wind erosion have destroyed an estimated 20 million square kilometres world wide – it is equivalent to 16 South Africas and amounts to a quarter of the Earth's farmland. Since he made that assessment in his book *Conservation for Survival* (1972) nothing has changed. Because of overgrazing and overcropping – a result of both the overkill compulsion and the Tragedy of the Commons – almost every country today has suffered extensive damage. The United States had, by 1940, destroyed 40 million hectares of former farming land which is one-sixth of its total available farmland. Practically all of the damage took place this century.

Perhaps not all of the world's desiccated former farmlands are lost for ever. After the Israeli Six Day War, when the Arabs evacuated a part of the Gaza Strip and took their goats with them, plants began appearing and today some of those areas are, once again, covered in vegetation. Vegetation cover tends to greatly reduce the volume of hot air rising from the land and thus allows more rain to reach the ground. And the moisture does not evaporate so rapidly, but has time to soak down into the shaded earth to feed the plant roots and increase the ground cover. In today's parlance – a positive feedback system. But where man has allowed soil to be eroded right down to the lithosphere, as is happening in Africa, it takes nature 6 000 years to build up another ploughable layer.

About 20 years ago the scanning cameras aboard the first Earth Resources Technology Satellite, ERTS-1, revealed some peculiar white geometrical patterns, many kilometres across, in what was then Rhodesia. When a land area shows up white on these images, it usually denotes bare rock. Pink reveals grasslands and deep red reveals dense vegetation such as rain forests, riverine growth and irrigation schemes. The puzzling, unnatural white shapes turned out to be tribal trust lands. Overgrazing had exposed the soil – the sun, wind and rain had done the rest. Around the squares one could see the healthy pink of better managed land. More recent satellite images have revealed similar destruction in South Africa's homeland areas. Lebowa's geographical shape is the most pronounced and is etched out in a ghostly white on the surface of South Africa.

If soil is left bare, such as after a crop failure due to drought, the sun dries it, the wind picks at it and the rain carries it away. Curry-Lindahl said that data from Zimbabwe in the 1960s showed that where bare soil was exposed to the rains the annual soil loss rate was between 10 and almost 100 tons a hectare on land that was even only slightly sloping (slopes of between 3 and 6,5 per cent). By comparison, loss of soil from healthy grassland slopes is about 250 kilograms per hectare. One has to appreciate the power of rain: a quite normal South African thunderstorm, which yields 10 millimetres, will dump, on one hectare, 100 tons of water at 50 kilometres per hectare. Rich, deep and vegetated soil can absorb such an impact, and retain a useful percentage of the moisture, but thin powdery shallow soils are swept away.

Professor Micheil Laker, soil scientist at Pretoria University, says: "Deep soils act as reservoirs. They hold water for long periods. Our soils are becoming thinner with erosion and thus dry out more rapidly."

Africa was a paradise when the colonialists arrived. As Victor Supeng, Minister of Agriculture for Bophuthatswana pointed out, there had been no man induced extinctions until then. The great forests were intact. True, the land was underpopulated but even where populations were concentrated there was a reverence for nature.

It seems there came a point when the "culture" went out of agriculture among black and white farmers alike. That "mood of indifference" with which people exploited nature

Grainlands in the western Cape. Source The Argus

(to which Lyn White Jnr alluded), became manifest. Indeed, with the notable exception of the south-west Cape, and those farms in Zimbabwe which are still managed by well-educated farmers, there has been widespread severe damage and desertification throughout sub-Saharan Africa.

For aeons the indigenous people of Africa practised a system of shifting agriculture and nomadic cattle herding. It made sense. Land would be tilled for three, four or five years until its nutrients ran low. Then the village would move its fields. It would be decades before that land would be farmed again, by which time it had recovered. But the imposition of political boundaries and the massive increase in population have now made shifting agriculture and nomadic herding largely impracticable.

Africa is a severe test of a farmer. Even nature sometimes seems to struggle! Look how, in the more benevolent temperate regions of Europe, the United States and Asia, the large quadrupeds are able to move down into the valleys in winter and then back on to the hillsides in summer. There's always food and water. To survive in Africa, quadrupeds such as wildebeest and zebra have sometimes to migrate hundreds of kilometres in search of seasonal grazing.

13 The death of the forests

Momento fit cinis; diu sylva. (In a moment the ashes are made, but a forest is a long time growing).

Seneca, Naturales Quoestiones

IT is interesting to conjecture what sort of vegetation the now bare South African Highveld had a few centuries ago. In Sandton, north of Johannesburg, archaeologists from the University of the Witwatersrand discovered at Lone Hill the biggest Iron Age factory so far unearthed in Africa. It must have operated for three or more centuries according to Professor Revil Mason. Mainly it made hoes and spear blades from the ferricrete nodules which still crunch like gravel underfoot. Mason says that to smelt and forge each spear blade would have needed charcoal from two mature trees. From where did these trees come over all those centuries? It seems the Highveld used to be open forest.

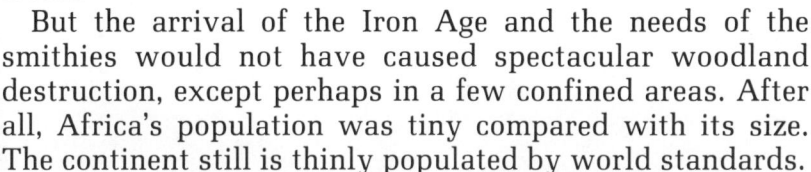

Iron Age hoe

But the arrival of the Iron Age and the needs of the smithies would not have caused spectacular woodland destruction, except perhaps in a few confined areas. After all, Africa's population was tiny compared with its size. The continent still is thinly populated by world standards.

Fire - extensive veld fires - would have been a natural part of the veld's ecology long before man, or even ape man, emerged. The Highveld, in particular, would have been prone to burning because of many factors, including the very high incidence of lightning storms and the presence of flint-like quartz rocks which are frequently rattled loose from hillsides by earth tremors which send them bouncing down the slope firing off sparks. (The Witwatersrand System is shaken by 10 earth tremors a day, although most of them are undetectable except by instruments.) The Tulbagh earthquake in 1969 sparked off 45 veld fires caused by rolling stones. Baboons also deliberately dislodge stones in the mountains as they seek the scorpions which live beneath them. And then man himself has been around for 2 million years and has probably used fire for most of that time. The earliest use of fire, according to Glenn C Conroy of Washington University, St Louis, Missouri (*Primate Evolution* 1990) has been found in fossil material at Swartkrans near Sterkfontein in the Central Transvaal and dates back beyond 1 million years to possibly 1,8 million. Runaway fires, started by hunters who, for millennia, utilised fire to trap animals, or to bring on early grazing to attract antelope, would have greatly influenced woodland distribution. In fact the early Portuguese navigators knew South Africa as "the land of smoke".

There is a great deal of controversy about the necessity or otherwise of using fire as a veld management technique. In many lightly grazed areas where, for years, fire has been kept out, the grassveld has become choked by bush encroachment. A former warden of Kruger Park, Colonel J A B Sandenbergh, who took over the National Park from 1946 to 1953, banned veld burning and although he was in charge for only seven years the effects of his policy remain evident today in areas severely degraded by bush encroachment.

Fire has an ecological role. Source The Argus

But, of course, fires, especially when aggravated by man-induced factors, do indeed do damage and South Africa's worst ecological disaster was caused by such a fire late last century. It destroyed our last great forest. But let's look first at the character of the original South African canvas.

Jan van Riebeeck, in his journal of September 1652, wrote of the forests he found during his explorations around Table Bay and Hout Bay: "They are the finest forests in the world and contained as long and thick spars as one could wish to have. It is surprising to see the fine forests which are scattered all about the mountainsides."

Sir John Barrow, in the eighteenth century, wrote about "an extensive forest" at Algoa Bay which he said came close to the shore. He described yellowwoods so tall that there were no branches for the first 12 metres and which had trunks 3 metres across. The entire coast was, according to early records, thickly forested. The presence of isolated, centuries-old specimens of trees found in the coastal pocket forests (such as in the Umtamvuna Gorge near Port Edward) - trees which are uncommon here but common in the Central African rain forest - reveal how the South African forests were probably connected to the Zaire Forest by a contiguous strip centuries ago.

In the Transvaal interior, the Victorian hunter-explorer, Cornwallis Harris, wrote of the "stupendous forests" he saw in 1835 in what is now the Pretoria district.

That prolific botanical writer, Eve Palmer, in her *Trees of South Africa* (with Nora Pitman in 1961), points out that "fine strong timber was the foundation of the country". She describes how early Cape Town swallowed up the great cedars of the Cedarberg and, of course, all the forests of the peninsula. The great fleets of Voortrekker ox wagons which sailed north across the Karoo to settle the interior were made from the giant yellowwoods, stinkwoods and assegai trees of the southern and eastern Cape. The diamond diggings around Kimberley spelt the end of the camelthorn trees - some of which were centuries old - that were a feature of those dark plains. The small town of Vryburg, alone, burned up 10 000 tons of camelthorn wood according to T R Sim's *Native Timbers of South Africa* (1907). The gold mines of the Rand led to the destruction of thousands of trees for buildings and railway sleepers, although most of the pit props were from plantation timber.

Apart from "overkill", carelessness played a tragic role in reducing South Africa's native forest to what it is today – a mere 0,25 per cent of the land surface. In the Cape drought between 1865 and 1869, a series of devastating fires swept the southern Cape rainforest from end to end. In those times the forest extended from the Hottentots Holland mountains to Transkei. Stacks of fuelwood had been carelessly stockpiled along the forest edges and these began several conflagrations. The 1869 fire was the worst. The only extensive patch of forest to survive the fires was around the Knysna/Tsitsikamma area. Eve Palmer describes it as "one of the greatest calamities of South African history" and quotes a contemporary report:

> From Swellendam in the south, up through Riversdale, Mossel Bay, George, Knysna, Humansdorp and Uitenhage, red hell flared, and tales of death and desolation mounted as the days passed. Human lives and much property were lost. Hundreds of people who were in more or less comfortable circumstances were reduced to the verge of starvation: homes were left as rubble. Mile after mile of country presented a melancholy and desolate appearance.

Another contemporary report quoted by Eve Palmer said:

> This was a clean sweep of everything. Houses, trees, gardens, orchards, forests, all gone. Nature never can, nor will, restore the grand old trees, not a few of them 30 feet in circumference.

One beehive hut takes 400 staves

It would be wrong to assume that forest destruction was solely the fault of white settlers. In Zululand great tracts of forest were wiped out by the Zulu who, to build a single beehive hut, needed 400 staves. These were, according to Sim, mainly saplings. He said that around 1890 there were more than 91 000 of these huts – so that's around 3 million young trees destroyed. The huts would probably have needed replacing at least every 30 years. Zulu cattle kraals used stouter timber and for these, hardwoods must have been felled by the tens of thousands. Today, in parts of Zululand, women have to walk 40 kilometres to fetch and carry fuel wood. Many resort to burning tufts of grass or dried cattle dung to heat baby food.

The twentieth century sugar farmers irrevocably changed the Natal and Zululand coastal landscape by clearing its forests to grow cane – even to the extent of razing many of the tiny riverine pocket forests that were left. While many of the big planters are now aware of environmental considerations there are some who even today are quite mindless in their approach.

Keith Cooper, director of conservation for the Wildlife Society told me of how he had gone to a farmer in the Mkuzi Valley in 1985 after hearing that he intended felling all the indigenous sycamore fig trees along a river bank in order to grow bananas. Cooper warned him that the act would be illegal and the Wildlife Society would lay a charge. Apart from it being illegal it would also cause the destruction of the bank in the next flood and so damage the river permanently. Despite this the farmer felled the fig forest. He was fined R5 000. The following year, when the bank was washed away, the farmer claimed, and received, R70 000 compensation from the government for the loss of the land. It revealed a deplorable gap in environmental control laws, which exists to this day, and a terrible cynicism among some farmers.

Massive forest destruction has been a feature of the twentieth century throughout Africa and the world. At the 1990 International Tropical Timber Organisation's conference in Bali, delegates from 45 nations were told that at current rates of extraction the forests of Southeast Asia, West Africa and Latin America could reach a point of no return by the year 2000. The FAO in Rome believes that for

Erosion in the Karoo

every hectare of forest presently being planted, 10 are being deforested. In Africa the FAO puts the ratio at 1:29. Zaire, in the first 10 years of independence, destroyed 25 000 square kilometres of its rain forests to bring into agricultural production what turned out to be very shallow soils. Within a few years the land was abandoned, useless for crops and useless for trees. Since then tens of thousands more hectares have been destroyed. The trouble with the usually very shallow soils in which rain forests are rooted is that they singularly lack nutrients. The sustenance for the giant trees lies in their own detritus, the natural litter of the forest floor. Yet rain forests are the most stable, and complex, of ecosystems. Their secret lies in "species diversity" which is the most fundamental need of any healthy ecosystem. The areas with the least species diversity are, of course, deserts. Those with the most diversity are the tropical forests. While a desert produces almost nothing the Amazon jungle can produce something like 1 100 tons of growth in the space of a hectare every year according to Dr Mike Meadows of Rhodes University. Meadows, in his 1985 book, *Biogeography and Ecosystems of South Africa* quotes a British botanical geographer, P A Stott, who estimates that the trees produce 11 tons of litter a hectare.

Variety is not just the spice of life, it is its very essence. Every living thing – and recent estimates are that the Amazon might have as many as 20 million species of living things (mostly invertebrates) – plays its part in the survival of the forest. When death overtakes the smallest insect, the noblest jaguar or the greatest tree, it dutifully returns its nitrogen to the common pool.

Take a farmer into a rain forest and most of the insects and birds he will recognise will be the ones he considers to be "pests". Yet in the forest each creature has a positive role. Remove that forest, and plant grain, and suddenly the only creatures left will be those that eat grain. And when you have sprayed poison to defend your crop, and it has matured, you then reap it and remove it thus robbing the soil of natural compost and tilth. The soil has to be given an annual fix of fertiliser for as long as the soils hold out, which is not long because, in the absence of compost, the soil's crumb structure breaks down into powder which is easily carried away by wind and dissolved by rain. Desertification follows.

The Amazon Basin has lost 5 per cent of its forest as a result of man's activities. The Amazon forest's total area is larger than the United States and it can easily sustain this 5 per cent loss, but as the threatened large scale deforestation of the Amazon Basin could have a significant effect on the global climate, the destruction must be controlled.

Philip Fearnside of the National Institute for Research in

Brazilian loggers cart away their prize.
Source Panos Publications

the Amazon at Manaus (Brazil) told me of plans along a tributary of the lower Amazon to establish iron smelters using charcoal from tropical hardwoods. The furnaces of this industry, the Grande Carajas Development Programme, would need almost a ton of timber a minute. It will amount to the biggest deforestation process in history. The last I heard, the programme was being re-evaluated.

The Amazon overkill – a large part of which has been the fault of the United States which converted hundreds of thousands of hectares into short-lived pastures for beef for hamburgers – is now declining. According to Fearnside, most of the current slashing and burning being carried out by peasant farmers involves secondary growth, in areas which have been farmed before. The tropical forest around Panama – extensively cleared between 1904 and 1915 when the Panama Canal was built – is now so recovered it is difficult to believe it was cleared so recently. I saw for myself in smoke-filled Brazil how the Atlantic coastal forest, whose great life-filled canopy filled Darwin with "wonder and astonishment", is today 99 per cent gone. And although much of the grazing which replaced it has been abandoned the forest can never come back because the seeds of the ancient forest are just not there any more. In many places only rock is evident. How can one measure such damage? The loss of species, habitats and soil?

Slash and burn techniques which are applied by peasant farmers need not be destructive provided, when the soil is exhausted and the people have moved on, the native tree seeds have remained in the ground or at least can be naturally dispersed over the cleared land from nearby virgin forest. That has happened in the Amazon.

The tropical forests of Brazil, Zaire and Indonesia add up to 43 per cent of the world's canopy forests. The rest are found in Central America (14 per cent), Central and West Africa (19) and Australasia (24). J P Lanly (*Tropical Forest Resources* 1982) estimates there were 16 million square kilometres of tropical forests up until this century. Now, he says, there are 11 million square kilometres. The 11 million is, according to some, a very optimistic assessment.

Judith Gradwohl and Russell Greenberg in *Saving the Tropical Forests* (1988) wrote:

> *What we do know is that deforestation is now proceeding at an annual rate of at least one per cent - up to 2 per cent if one includes areas under selective logging - and that extrapolating from these figures, 20 to 40 hectares are disappearing every minute.*

The rate of destruction in West Africa is, they estimate, 5 to 6 per cent a year. But an undated FAO table used by the authors shows the Zaire jungle is disappearing only at 0,2 per cent, which is half the rate shown for the Amazon.

A great deal of forest destruction is to extract hardwoods bound for Japan which re-exports them. Japan, which for years has been considered an international environmental hooligan, is also now reconsidering its attitude. There is a promising trend towards a more conservative approach to the world's forests. It is not that conservationists want the exploitation of forests to cease. That is not what conservation is about. The rain forest resource needs careful management so that future generations will also be able to enjoy, as we have done, the bounty of the forests as well as their beauty and wonder.

Kokerboom

The protection of the rain forests' species diversity, and the avoidance of wiping out species which we may not even know exist yet, is important. Who knows how many as yet unresearched plants and animals in the rain forests may provide us with drugs and substances which can cure cancer, AIDS, slow the ageing process and so on? Of the 20 million or so organisms believed to be living in forests not even 2 per cent have been properly studied by science.

There is also the aspect of carbon dioxide absorption and oxygen generation which is described elsewhere in this book. But it should be noted that the impact of the Amazon, in particular, on the global oxygen supply has often been exaggerated. I have been guilty of this myself in Our Fragile Land (1974). If the Amazon were to disappear it would certainly deplete the world's oxygen by a few per cent but it would merely mean that people living at sea level would be inhaling about the same quantity of oxygen as the people now living at Pietermaritzburg's altitude are inhaling. The importance of saving what is left of the world's rain forests is because of their huge ecological influence, their diverse species and their sheer wonder.

There needs to be a moratorium on deforestation but it must bear in mind Third World countries whose income depends on selling forest hardwoods to the industrialised nations. The industrialised world must share the blame for much of the destruction so far. Thus a moratorium would have to have an aid package to go with it.

The search for Supertree

Superman may be a figment of the imagination but geneticist Peter Schon of White River, in the eastern Transvaal, is hoping to clone Supertree. Through genetic engineering he is aiming to breed a hardwood tree – a eucalyptus hybrid – which could halve the amount of land needed for hardwood plantations in South Africa. He has produced a row of 10 trees which, although only two years old, appear to be reaching harvestable size in half the time other eucalyptus trees take.

Schon's work is vital, economically and scenically. Commercial timber needs high rainfall areas, and, in South Africa that means scenic, mountainous areas. Already 1,2 million hectares are under plantations. This is actually a mere 1 per cent of the land surface but, nevertheless, it is a conspicuous 1 per cent. The industry, perceiving a future shortage of pulp wood as well as hardwood, has said it must double the amount as soon as possible. The timber industry is a lucrative industry. In 1989 exports of sawn timber and wood products were worth R2 billion. But one must consider the sacrifice South Africans are making in the way of losing characteristic scenery – now smothered by a monotonous black pelage of same-size trees. Until quite recently planting was often injudicious: it dried up vital wetlands for instance, and millions of trees were allowed to stray – to seed themselves in river beds and in native forests. The Government itself actually planted pines in the wetlands in the coastal dunes of Lake St Lucia, thus robbing this huge estuary of much of its freshwater supply.

Unfortunately exotic trees tend to overpower even our stoutest native trees. The biggest tree in South Africa, an 84,2 metres *Eucalyptus grandis* (a blue gum known in its native Australia as the ghost gum), grows inside one of the most important natural forests in South Africa, the Woodbush Reserve near Magoebaskloof in the north-eastern Transvaal. The Woodbush forest, pathetically small though it is, is the largest inland remnant of indigenous forest to survive, but it is infested with pine and gum which have invaded it from the adjacent plantations.

In the nearby Blyde River Canyon, a prime scenic area noted for its beautiful natural forests, stray pines are shouldering aside native trees in the krantzes. The Garden of Eden – part of the Knysna Forest – is, along the N2 roadside, heavily infested by giant pines.

A problem has been that timber plantations are arranged in blocks, each managed by one man who is responsible only for the plantation and not for what his plantation might be doing to the river running past it, or to a neighbouring wetland or scenic area. If trees started seeding themselves in the river, it was not the forester's affair nor was he given a budget to curb trees which strayed. Anyway, who was to say the trees had come from his neck of the woods?

At Woodbush, Government foresters, some years back, deliberately planted long fingers of pine plantations thrusting deep into the native forest. When I asked the Department of Environment for an explanation I was told, officially and in writing (1989) from the director general's office, that the pine forests had been planted on grassveld (which, I gathered, the official considered useless ground) to reduce the risk of the indigenous trees being destroyed by grass fires! The reply revealed a lot about the Department of Environment's public relations but it also revealed an abysmal ignorance. To begin with, the grassveld in this high-lying mist belt, noted for its ground orchids, is one of the rarest biomes in the country. It is significant that of 16 species of birds, about which the CSIR's Red Data Book has expressed concern, 10 are grassland and wetland species indicating serious changes in these ecosystems. As far as grass fires are concerned, the grassveld has been subjected to fires for millennia and the forest edge has coped. But should the pine plantation burn it would destroy much of the Woodbush reserve.

The Department, in 1989, gave the go-ahead for three-quarters of the farmland in Natal's fire climax grassland to be planted out to softwoods. The Department of Agriculture had in fact planned these farms for agricultural purposes in that it had identified the zones on each farm suggesting where prime pastures should be, where arable lands lay and where land should be left alone. This would have cost the taxpayer a fair amount over the years – but it would have been worth it had the farmers stuck to the plan. Indeed they were obliged to by law. But the Department of Environment (under which forestry fell) allowed farmers to plant 75 per cent of their land to trees. This would include *all* grazing and crop land because by the time one excludes river banks and servitudes there is only about 75 per cent left. Obviously the Government does not see food-producing land as important when it can be sold off to industry. Timber-growing being essentially an industry.

In 1990, on paper at least, there appeared to be a change of heart in the forestry industry. A new code of practice was drawn up by the Forestry Council, a council set up by private growers in conjunction with the Government's foresters. It ruled out the practice of growing plantations up against indigenous woodland and called for a mutual effort to root out stray trees. It also encouraged the establishment of nature trails through forestry-owned land. All the large timber companies now employ conservation officers who advise on environmental aspects and who help prepare environmental impact reports before new areas are planted. But unless these EIRs are made public and allow for public comment they are tantamount to self-policing and that almost never works. The industry has banned the use of hormone herbicides (unlike the cane industry) and now assists in establishing village woodlots for fuel and for traditional building material. It has pledged to clear riverine forests as well as wetlands of invading foreign trees, to step up research into hydrology and catchment management and to preserve heritage sites. It has inaugurated many hiking trails and started education programmes.

Missing from its code of ethics is aesthetics. I raised the topic at an informal meeting arranged by HL&H Mining Timber and attended by Sappi and Mondi in White River in July 1990. I pointed out that the industry had, in the recent past, greatly degraded the ambience of the eastern Transvaal. Great chunks of the "Jock of the Bushveld country", as well as vast areas in the green hills of the Natal Midlands, the Amatole Mountains of the eastern Cape and the equally gracious hills of the southern Cape have been transformed into parodies of Canada or, where eucalyptus and wattles have been planted, Australia. In some mountain passes and along tourist routes trees have been planted right down to the roadside thus wiping out the vistas altogether. There was a general agreement among those present that the matter of aesthetics needed to be reviewed.

What is really needed is for timber firms to produce a public environmental impact report on each new plantation. They must demonstrate that what they are doing is in the long term interest. After all the industry is irrevocably re-arranging the character of South Africa's scenery, altering drainage patterns and soils, and destroying the food-growing potential of thousands of hectares. As a great deal of timber products are for sale overseas we are technically exporting the country's fertility.

This is where Peter Schon's work is so important. He works for one of the "big four" timber firms, Hunt Leuchars & Hepburn (HL&H) who specialise in mining timber for which they grow hardwoods (eucalids). Daily 5 000 to 8 000 tons of timber are taken into South Africa's mines. There is also a great need for timber for construction (South Africa has to double its housing stock in the next 10 years). Schon has developed a very promising hybrid which appears to grow twice as fast as the average *Eucalyptus grandis*. It is hybridised from *E. grandis*, a tree noted for its good timber and drought resistance, and *E. nitens*. In two years the hybrid has grown to 13 metres high with a 10,9 centimetre diameter at breast height. In two more years it will be ready for harvesting. Normally it would have taken eight years.

Schon's Supertree usefully sheds its lower branches as it grows and its crown architecture is shaped like an assegai – its volume of leaves just enough to provide optimum photosynthesis with minimum water need. When I saw it at the halfway stage it was growing 18 millimetres a day. The saving in water uptake is important: the plantations which now dominate the eastern Transvaal's hills are partly to blame for the drying up of rivers entering Kruger National Park and Mozambique which could ultimately affect the tourist industry to the tune of millions of rands a year.

14 The tragedy of the Platteland

> The logical outcome of it all is the
> Great South African Desert
> uninhabitable by man.
>
> 1914 Drought Investigation
> Committee report

ARCHAEOLOGISTS excavating sand dunes in the Indus River Valley in 1922 found, to their surprise, a magnificently preserved walled city of exquisite brickwork. It had been abandoned for no immediately apparent reason. The story behind this 5 000-year-old city, Mohenjodaro, in Pakistan's Darkana district of Sind, is a forewarning for modern man. For millennia it lay buried beneath desert sands yet, 5 000 years ago, it was the biggest city in this once thriving and productive valley. There were no signs of it having been sacked by an enemy. It had waterborne sewerage, bathhouses, libraries, multi-storey buildings, a business centre – an incredibly modern city – but why had its people fled? The answer lay in its bricks.

To bake those bricks the people needed fuel and the fuel was wood. And the wood was from the thick forests which coated the hills along the Indus River. The Indus itself would, in those days, have been a strong but gentle river fed by snow melt from the great peaks of the Hindu Kush and with a strong flow the year round. When the storms rolled down the valley the forest sponge would absorb the heavy rains and ensure a steady, controlled runoff. The river would slowly rise and its swollen waters spread over the floodplain and deposit new nutrients. But, as the forests were felled to feed the brickworks so the monsoonal rains would have come off those now stripped hills with a greater velocity. As deforestation spread, so each storm would have triggered a flash flood, faster and higher than the last. Instead of the flood waters fingering out across the croplands they now rolled the croplands back and dumped them in the Arabian Sea. The city's brickwork shows signs of the ever-rising floods – nature's writing on the wall.

Man's history is filled with such stories. The walls of Jericho were not brought down by trumpets and nor where they built solely against a human foe. They were a defence mainly against floods and it was the ever-increasing volume of the floods – man-enhanced floods – that destroyed them.

In January 1981, in the valley of the Buffels, the century-old Karoo town of Laingsburg was hit by an unprecedented – but not unpredicted – flood. Two hundred and fifty million tons of water swept through the town in one slug, carrying more than 100 people to their deaths and clearing away all riverside homes as well as bridges. The survivors

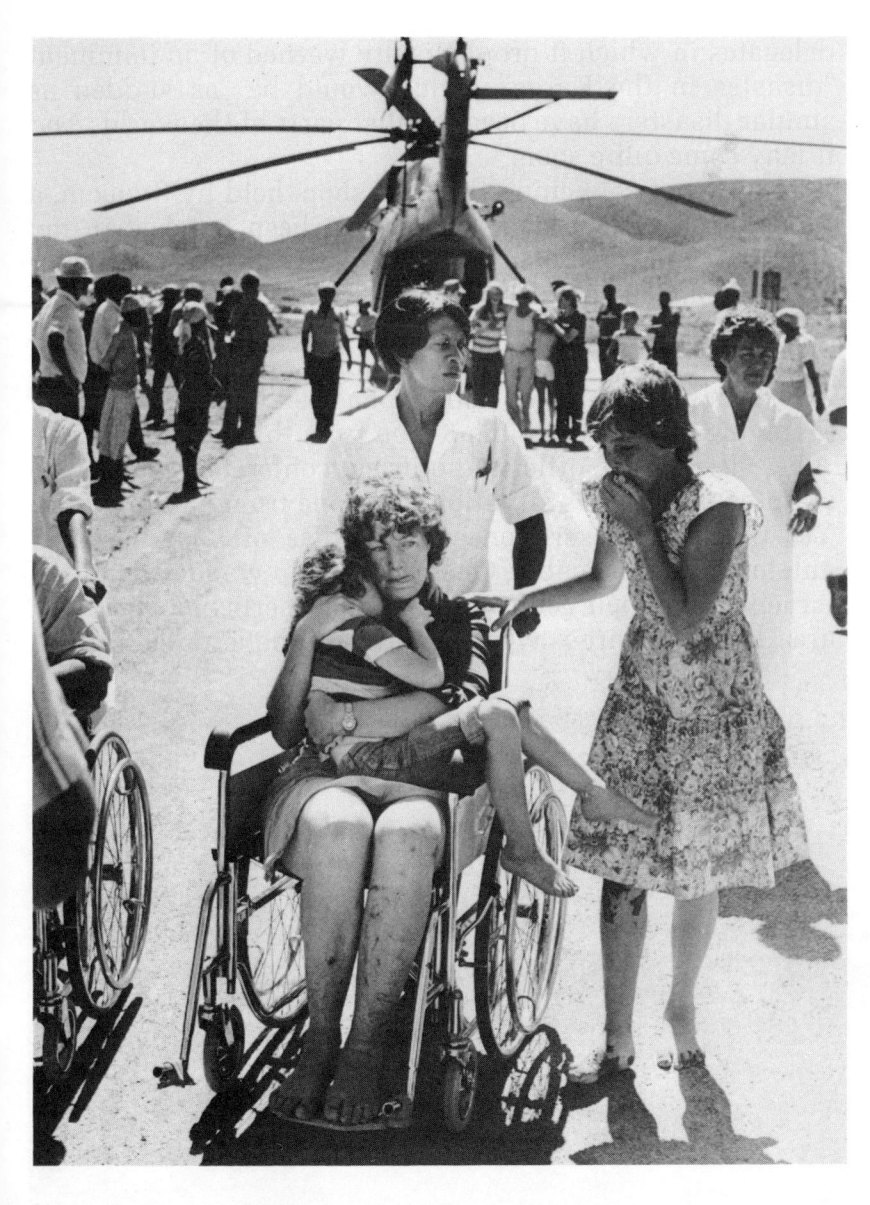

Survivors of the Laingsburg flood are airlifted to safety. Source The Argus

crowded the churches wondering why God had punished them so. The insurance companies also talked of an act of God. But God had been blameless. This was an act of man. Over the years man had destroyed the vegetation which once covered the hills along the Buffels River and he had drained the spongelands. Fourteen months before, on 27 November 1979, at a workshop in Graaff-Reinet to examine the future of the Karoo, a situation report was handed to delegates in which it prophetically warned of an imminent "disaster in the Karoo" which would be "as sudden as similar disasters have been in other parts of the world. And it may come quite soon."

The idea of convening the workshop, held by Syncom, a think tank organisation, had in fact been hatched in my garden in Sandton when I expressed to the founder-director of Syncom, Andre Spier, the need for a future holistic plan for the Karoo which takes up a third of South Africa. Spier, a dynamic Hollander who specialises in economics and futures research, agreed and emphasised the importance of involving the people of the Karoo from the very beginning. After decades of official inquiries, conferences and even statutes the Karoo's situation had gone from bad to worse. Yet this semi-desert, once a paradise of vast herds of antelope, is redeemable. One cannot help wondering, if the Israelis, with their genius for making deserts bloom, had an area like the Karoo, what they would have done with it.

Drought in the Transvaal. Source The Star

Instead the Karoo is spreading northwards and eastwards and the economies of its pretty little towns are, like the landscape, drying up.

The workshop achieved two things: for a flickering moment South Africans became aware of the Karoo; more constructively, it gave birth to the Rural Foundation, which is working on a strategic plan aimed at rural upliftment and which includes working out action plans, with those directly involved, for stressed areas such as the Karoo.

The Karoo presents an intriguing challenge to South African ingenuity. Its problem has so many facets that every man, woman and child could find a role to play. To revive and restore this 400 000 square kilometre region would need the co-operation of as many institutions as possible – universities, government, business sector, agricultural circles, engineers, energy research and development boffins, biologists, the National Parks Board, hydrologists, schools ... By using human-scale technology, as opposed to expensive large scale technology, the Karoo could be made to thrive again. Massive fruit tree-planting projects, along the lines of the projects organised by the Jewish National Fund in Israel, could be organised with volunteer labour during holiday times. Woodlands to break the power of the desiccating westerly winds could be planted. There is donga filling to be done. Such programmes could be organised via schools, nationwide. The villages themselves could offer mentally restful and physically active holidays. Derelict houses and farmsteads could be renovated for people on working holidays. Spier, incidentally, suggested permanent "new" rural societies:

> Being one third of South Africa, the Karoo's greatest asset could be space. With the doubling of the population over the next 25 years, the enormous pressures on the cities and the job market could be relieved by a network of semi-self-sufficient novel communities spread more evenly over our entire available space. Communication technology will overcome distances and isolation and give access to the basic services of health, education and entertainment. Energy-frugal and ecologically sophisticated uses of the natural resources of the arid zone, could form the basis of higher population densities and, therefore, rural stability. The Karoo could house and feed 10 to 20 times its present population of 300 000 bringing wealth and stability

without the glaring disadvantages of high density urban living.

In Britain there is a national register of people who are prepared to give their time free for such working holidays. Most of the volunteers are highly skilled and include scientists and technologists, so that teams of varied expertise can be tailored for all manner of projects. The work camps – the tents or other accommodation are usually organised by the sector which stands most to gain (usually a local council) – are visited by local experts who give lectures, or show slides, or chat about the locality. In America, during the Depression of the early 1930s, the Californian Conservation Corps was established and for $5 a week (of which $4 had to be sent home) workers were fed and housed as they helped establish hiking trails, plant timber and built small dams. Today that timber is maturing and is worth hundreds of millions of dollars. Again the Israelis, faced with squeezing food out of the desert, have evolved a profit-making system called the *moshav* in which people own their own homes and earn money, but share equipment such as tractors and jointly buy fertilisers. As Spier pointed out in his preamble to the Karoo conference, the opportunities are there and the water is available but needs to be drilled for and carefully conserved. There are opportunities for raising livestock by planting *Acacia karoo* at densities of up to 40 a hectare to produce an annual 4 tons of pods, for fodder. On a collective basis springbok could be farmed and then cropped at up to 25 per cent a year.

   T C Robertson did a lot to draw public attention to the way the Karoo was spreading, like an amoeba, across the land. He described in the journal he edited, *The Veldtrust*, how the western Karoo was drying out and, like a furnace, was super-heating the westerly winds which were then sweeping across the eastern Karoo desiccating its plant cover more and more. In the past the Karoo was coated with a fine silvery grass which, when the winds blew in from the dry northern Cape, would flatten itself against the soil thus protecting it from the hot breath of the west and, at the same time, like a space suit, its silvery sheen would reflect the fierce rays of the sun away. The wool price had changed all that. Earlier this century it rocketed and

The tragedy of the Platteland   181

Dust storm in the Transvaal. Source Sarel van den Berg

farmers crammed sheep into the Karoo and, although the sheep grazed the Karoo out of existence (that silvery grass is now extinct), the farmers made a fortune. Many then sold up. Now, when the winds blow, they pluck at the denuded soils and they dry out the Karoo's margins helping it to spread northwards and eastwards. In the 100 years up to 1970 the Karoo invaded 207 000 square kilometres, according to Robertson. John Acocks, author of *Veldtypes of South Africa* (1975), estimated that overgrazing had caused the Karoo to advance 290 kilometres in the first half of the twentieth century. In May 1973 the Earth Resources Technology Satellite (ERTS 1) images confirmed that since 1953 the Karoo had overtaken another 70 kilometres of grassland.

The Karoo is probably still being overgrazed. According to Dr Johan Serfontein of the Department of Agricultural Technical Services, who addressed the Karoo conference in Graaff-Reinet in 1979, the Karoo then had 7,8 million sheep and almost 1 million goats and cattle. Counting the 300 000

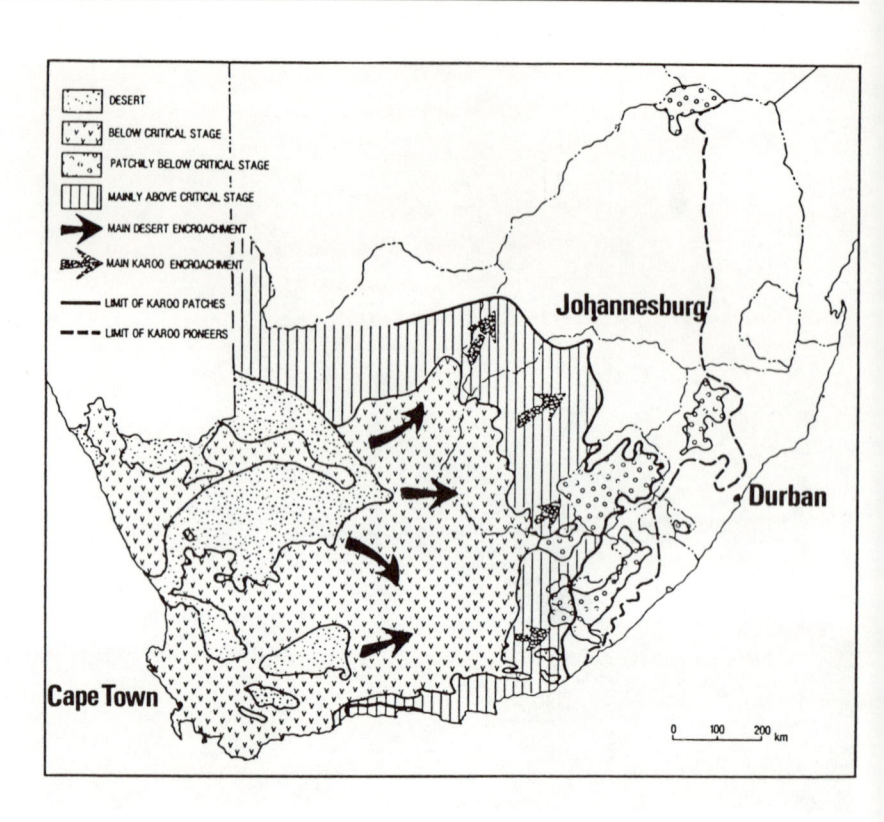

The spread of the Karoo. Source The Star

head of game, there were 10 million large grazers which each had to exist off 2,6 hectares. Serfontein said each animal unit required at least 4 hectares.

Robertson described South Africa's high inland plateau as having "the worst soil in Africa". He said it was mostly wind-deposited sand and lacked, almost entirely, the benefits of flood plains periodically enriched by waterborne nutrients. The average yield per hectare across the whole of South Africa was less than half that of Zimbabwe (then Rhodesia) and only a third of the United States - a combination of poor soil and indifferent farming. In truth the great plateau is more suitable for ranching than ploughing. In fact 85 per cent of South Africa's agricultural land is grazing country which once supported one of the most breathtaking wildlife concentrations in the world. By 1990 three-quarters of the country's grazing had been seriously degraded. Acocks identified 72 "veld types" in South Africa and tried to describe them as they would have been in their climax, before man began to till the earth. Apart from the veld types Acocks described 75 variations.

The point of his exercise was that he believed that it was necessary to know how nature "farmed" each area before we ourselves farmed it. After all, nature had had millions of years to experiment with a balance of plants and animals which were suited to the soil and climate. Alas, very few reliable examples of original veld have survived the twentieth century. Nobody is sure, for example, what "typical Highveld" was like. What we do know is that the once large areas of sweet Highveld grasses have, through injudicious grazing policies, been overtaken by much less nutritious sourveld.

The agriculturally exhausted granite-based plain between Johannesburg and the Magaliesberg, despite having "the poorest soil in Africa" (in this case it is just decomposed granite), used to support a dozen species of antelope, buffalo, zebra, giraffe, elephant, two species of rhino, lion, cheetah ... Today, apart from a few small farms, its soils are exhausted and its landscape an arboretum of foreign trees. Look also at how the Karoo is veined by dried-out stream beds named the Renoster, Buffels, Olifants and even Seekoei (Hippopotamus). Every species had its role in maintaining the interior's ecosystem, even if it was only to donate its droppings and, eventually, its carcass. Today these creatures have been entirely shot out. No longer do elephants push over thorn trees so that their barbed wire canopies protect the last patches of grass against desperate grazers in times of drought. These shaded and protected grass nurseries became a source of seed so that when the winds of spring came, new seed was scattered over the bare soil. No longer do hippo keep the channels clear of reeds. In any event there are no reeds and the rivers are dust.

South Africa must have supported an enormous tonnage of meat on the hoof before organised farming was introduced. It was able to because a wildlife population utilises all the vegetation, trees, grasses and herbs while cattle eat only certain species of grass. Giraffe eat the high tree crowns, kudu eat the middle tree, impala and other buck feed off the lower branches; porcupine eat the bark, all manner of creatures eat the fruit and the tree litter on the ground; buffalo eat the coarse grass and so open up the lower grass storey for zebra who open up the even finer grasses for wildebeest. The lowveld is rich in animal species, one of the richest regions on Earth, but it takes 11 years to "improve" the lowveld for cattle – cattle which, unlike wild bovines, are prone to many diseases. Wildlife is far more productive and far kinder to the veld. Why then is wildlife not farmed more? For two simple reasons: first it is difficult to market because South Africans prefer beef and mutton. (In the late 1980s the hotel trade began buying more. Guinea fowl was common place, kudu was common and crocodile tail – a very bland white meat – appeared on menus). Second, there is still the problem that nobody can own a wild animal – unless it's dead. True, game ranching is slowly catching on and wild animals are fetching high prices at game sales. All the same, if you raise eland (which, incidentally, can grow to a marketable weight in two years in a situation where a cow would starve to death) and they all leap the fence, they will automatically belong to the person next door. What is beginning to happen is that farmers are mixing game with cattle to get better utilisation of plantlife and they are also forming conservancies. Conservancies have become popular in Natal which was the first province to establish them in 1978. By 1990 there were more than 100 covering 850 000 hectares. They mainly comprise blocks of contiguous farms whose owners wish to encourage wildlife. They are advised by provincial nature conservation experts who also train their 350 game guards.

South Africa's wildlife has been largely replaced by cattle. The Department of Agriculture estimates 6 sheep or goats as being the equivalent of one head of cattle and by using "cattle units" estimated South Africa had 13,5 million cattle at the last count in 1984. Twelve million live off the veld, the rest are raised in factory farms. Yet natural grazing in this country can sustain only 8 million.

Just as South Africa has replaced the rich variety of naturally occurring wild animals with cattle, sheep and goats, so it has "simplified" plantlife: it has destroyed the variety and replaced it with a more easily manageable monoculture. In unfarmed areas the plant variety at this southern end of Africa is mind-boggling. It so fascinated the early botanist-explorers that some never went back to Europe. There are 22 300 species of plants in South Africa, which is about the same number as is found in the world's largest country, Russia, and 30 per cent more than in the United States, which is seven times the size of South

Africa. The contrast is explained by the fact that much of the northern hemisphere was smothered by the Ice Age up until about 10 000 years ago. The ice cap would have come close to wiping the botanical slate clean. South Africa has not been smothered by an ice age for 200 million years.

As South Africa's soils deteriorate so more and more species of plants are threatened with extinction. When G V Jacks wrote his report *The Rape of the Earth* (1939), after flying over much of South Africa in a biplane during a world survey of erosion, he noted that nowhere on Earth did he see an area where "national catastrophe, due to soil erosion, was more imminent" than in South Africa. He said that the tragedy of South Africa was the "appalling rapidity with which soil erosion followed inconsiderate farming" and that "soil erosion strikes at the very roots of South Africa's existence and is the most urgent problem confronting the country at the present time." Jan Smuts once said, half seriously, that the soil erosion problem was more important than politics. It remains South Africa's most dangerous environmental problem.

The 1939 Government of South Africa recorded, without any sign of alarm among its many farmer Members, that since the beginning of the century 25 per cent of South Africa's croplands had been wrecked by erosion. Nothing was done about it. In fact the situation had been recognised since 1914 when a select committee was appointed to investigate, among other things, why droughts were becoming so severe. This Drought Investigation Committee and subsequent investigations found nothing to suggest that less rain was falling and blamed poor land management and overgrazing for causing the soil to lose its moisture-retaining abilities. The drought committee had concluded:

> *The simple unadorned truth is sufficiently terrifying without the assistance of rhetoric. The logical outcome of it all is the Great South African Desert uninhabitable by man.*

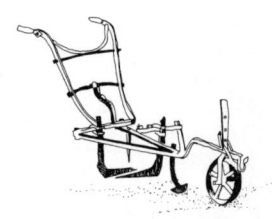

Dr Gerry Garland of the University of Natal's environmental sciences department, in a brilliantly conceived university publication, *The Rotating Cube - Environmental Strategies for 1990*, remarked that it was a pity soil had no market value. The Americans have tried to find some sort of figure by totting up the value of all the nitrogen, phosphorous and potassium in one ton of soil. If one were to buy it in fertiliser bags it would come to the dollar equivalent of R30. On this basis, Garland judged Natal's soil losses to be about R500 million a year. The Australians worked out that for each millimetre of soil lost, wheat yields declined 4 kilograms a hectare. Brian Huntley, the ecologist who is now director of Kirstenbosch Gardens in Cape Town, says that for every ton of grain produced in South Africa, 20 tons of soil are lost. That estimate is the most scary of all. South Africa, except in unusually dry years, can feed itself. It needs 6 million tons of maize (the national staple food) and usually produces a surplus. But many traditional maize-growing areas are deteriorating. Transkei, which should be able to produce 3 million tons of maize under ideal conditions, is producing only 100 000 tons, which is not enough to feed itself. Zululand too, twice ravaged by floods in the 1980s, is also grossly underproducing and what it does grow is often at great cost to the soil. Fortunately its government has established a Bureau of Natural Resources which is enlightened and knowledgeable and it is going to be interesting to see how it goes about stablising this very stressed region.

Land, once it is bare of vegetation, often cannot retain rain water long enough to absorb it, and the faster the runoff the more the scouring effect. Aquifers are no longer replenished. Springs dry up. Riverbeds become silted and the rivers become shallower and more prone to evaporation and flooding. Dams become silted up. The soil which gets washed out to sea tends to smother marine life on the floor of the continental shelf. As Jacks said, there is an "appalling rapidity" in the events which follow careless farming.

The extent of the damage

South Africa has 1,2 million square kilometres of land and of these 120 million hectares, about 15 million are almost useless desert. Of the 103 million hectares available for agriculture only 15 per cent is fit for ploughing – a mere 15 million or so hectares of arable land. Of this 15 million hectares, a quarter had been written off by the time G V Jacks flew over in his Gypsy Moth in 1939. T C Robertson later worked out it would take only 80 years, at the rate erosion was taking place in mid century, to remove all of South Africa's topsoil. As recently as April 1990, in the Minister of Agriculture's annual report, it was stated that the carrying capacity of South Africa's grazing land was still decreasing and that farmers continued to overstock cattle and game.

It was estimated by John Acocks that the stock carrying potential of South Africa had been reduced 75 per cent. Professor Desmond Midgley, the Johannesburg hydrologist, worked out from silt samples that the total soil loss in South Africa was, in the 1960s, almost 400 million tons a year. But at the 1971 Conference on Natural Resources at Jan Smuts House in Johannesburg T C Robertson stated that silt-sampling in the Orange River revealed that 400 million tons a year were going down that river alone. This was denied by Water Affairs, who put the figure at Hendrik Verwoerd Dam at 90 million tons. Robertson, a great one for using statistics as illustrations, said that the 400 million tons was the equivalent of losing 15 centimetres of topsoil from 137 000 hectares of farmland.

In 1947 Dr C E M Tidmarsh of the Department of Agriculture found that a number of Karoo plants wiped out by sheep could no longer be regrown when reintroduced to their former habitat. He feared the rainfall must have deteriorated and suggested this could have been because with less veld cover the Karoo's albedo (its ability to reflect heat) was drying out the air.

This led to the Government appointing yet another official enquiry. In 1948 Dr D F Kokot was appointed secretary to the Desert Encroachment Committee to investigate "the steadily increasing severity of annual droughts." The committee found, just as the 1914 select committee had found, that the rainfall was not diminishing. It concluded that the desiccation of the soil was not due to worsening droughts but to poor farming. The committee comprised seven scientists and their conclusions, published in 1951, reminded the public that South Africa's topography and very seasonal rainfall made the land difficult to farm:

> One third of South Africa receives less than 20 inches [500 mm] of rainfall per annum and only 3 per cent receives more than 40 inches [1 000 mm]. But not only is the rainfall inadequate in quantity, its bad seasonal distribution is such that it is seldom possible to grow crops throughout the year although temperatures will allow this nearly everywhere.
>
> More than two thirds of the country receives 70 per cent or more of its rainfall during six months of the year only.
>
> The unique seasonal distribution of the rainfall, combined with its erratic occurrence from year to year, has provided the stage for some of the most spectacular deterioration which has taken place anywhere in the world in so short a time. A powerful factor aiding the deterioration is the elevated character of the central plateau with its steep river gradients to the sea.

Kokot, in a telephone conversation many years later, told me he felt the Karoo was still "triumphantly on the march". He said farmers on the periphery of the Karoo were inviting it in by practising insensitive farming. His committee had felt the Karoo would reach the Vaal River by the turn of the century and would have surrounded Bloemfontein by then. To an extent this has happened: Karoo vegetation is now found in the northern Transvaal. In the western Transvaal sand dunes have invaded former mealie fields. Karoo precursor plants have appeared in the eastern Transvaal too.

Kokot pointed out in his committee report how "many estuaries where small sea-going vessels could freely enter, are today so blocked with silt that even a small rowing boat runs aground."

The Kokot report had no impact. It failed even to give the country's first Soil Conservation Act of 1946 the urgency it deserved. Even 20 years later the vast majority of farmers had failed to comply with the mandatory section in the Act which required them to have their farms planned with regard to soil erosion and water storage measures. Nobody was ever fined under the Act. T C Robertson was among many who wanted soil erosion, when caused by wilfulness or carelessness, to be considered a serious crime. "Thefts from the storehouse of nature should be regarded as a more serious crime than thefts of private property," he said. The 1969 Soil Conservation Act was stronger in its terms but equally useless except that it did allow for a stock reduction scheme and farmers began getting paid not to farm.

In 1971 Dr S J du Plessis, policy adviser to the Minister of Agriculture, accused bad farmers of "treasonable activity". At about this time, Dr W A Verbeek, Secretary for Agricultural Technical Services, reported to Parliament that in 10 years the decline in average soil cover in the Karoo had been 40 per cent. He said that in the particularly dry and fragile northern Cape area of Vryburg/Mafikeng 82 farmers had overstocked their farms and at Christiana in the western Transvaal, the average farm carried double its stock-carrying capacity.

In 1972 the first two farmers were brought to court and although their fines were a slap on the wrist it at least signalled the beginning of the end of the love affair between the State and the farmers. Yet even to this day no farmer in South Africa has ever been adequately punished for wrecking land. Professor Andre Rabie of Stellenbosch suggested that the State adopt the same attitude towards farmers as it did towards would-be bottle store owners. A prospective bottle store owner had to pass a written test and prove he was a man of means. Prospective farmers had to prove nothing. When a farmer died his farm was often split up among his sons and so on into less and less economic units. In some cases the cleverest sons were sent off to university to become lawyers or doctors while the dumbest stayed home to run the farm. One doubts whether this applies anywhere today: of the 140 000 registered farmers of 1966 only 70 000 have survived.

What could be done? Throw money at the problem? In 1948 the National Veldtrust estimated that R200 million needed to be spent by the State by 1973 if soil erosion was to be checked. Yet even by 1980 only half that had been spent. Education? In 1978 a survey showed that **only** 15 per cent of farmers in the Aliwal North area straddling the Orange River were "actively" interested in conserving soil; 12 per cent were passive; 28 "didn't care"; a third were "antagonistic about their soil" – and 88 per cent of farms in the district were denuded of grass cover. Those statistics refer to white-owned farms whose owners had the advantage of compulsory education. With black farmers the situation is worse: the average black farmer is an overworked woman with a baby on her back.

There is not enough time to save the situation by education alone. In any event, one would have to start by educating the Government. One of the worst things that could happen is for collectivisation to be introduced. Nowhere has this succeeded in feeding the people. The world's big food producers – those who help feed Russia and the helpless countries of Africa – are all free-enterprise countries. But even in the United States, the most agriculturally advanced country of all, soil losses have been appalling and almost wilful. Lester Brown, head of the Worldwatch Institute, warned that while the world could survive a loss of fossil fuel resources it could not survive the loss of its soil. He said in 1984 the world was losing 23 billion tons of topsoil annually. The US was losing 2 billion tons. These tonnages were over and above that which nature was replacing. The reason was that continuous cropping, rather than crop rotation, made soil more vulnerable. The effects of insidious soil loss on crop productivity may remain hidden for a time because fertilisers can be used to artificially squeeze more out of the thinning soil. But sooner or later productivity will collapse.

But before looking at solutions, there is one more fundamental problem with land management in South Africa – that of wetlands. These are the sponges that soak up the rains, store them, filter them and slowly trickle them into river courses the year round. Dr George Begg of Natal University believes all wetlands should be "public resources" including most of those in private hands.

South Africa's attitude towards wetlands is one of almost total disregard, yet they are vital to urban and rural water supplies and to food production. In the United States 150 professional scientists are engaged in mapping and monitoring wetlands and the US Clean Water Act which controls wetland conservation is a very powerful piece of legislation. South Africa has nobody officially monitoring wetlands. Begg, at a Sandton conference on wetlands sponsored by Sappi in 1989, said 90 per cent of "bottom lands" in the northern Transvaal have been planted out with poplars by a match company. Farmers are happy because the trees will dry out the "useless marshland" so that it can be put to the plough. Half of the Tugela Valley's wetlands have gone and Natal's sugar farmers, says Begg, "are absolutely not interested in managing this resource – and blacks have learned from whites." (In fairness to this sector, it was obvious in 1989 and 1990 that the sugar farmers were adopting a more conservative approach.)

According to Begg, some individual wetlands might be split among as many as 50 or 60 farmers, each of whom might have a different policy regarding it.

The Government owns most of the South African sections of the soaring Natal Drakensberg, the nation's most important watershed, and years ago it recognised the need to protect this magnificent area. Yet even here, especially in the foothills, there has been devastation in places. Carl Zunckel who farms near Bergville built a 4 metre high bridge over the upper Umlambonja River in 1980. When I saw it in 1987 it had disappeared. Not washed away but buried beneath 3 metres of silt. I looked up river and between Zunckel's farm and the great wall of the Berg was a strip of land belonging to the Amazizi, a colourful Zulu tribe. It had been converted from a soft, green landscape to a surrealistic sepia moonscape. Sheer overgrazing is wrecking this vital watershed. Reg Pearse, author of *Barrier of Spears* (1973) who took me to Zunckel's farm, in describing how damage was mounting up in all black-owned land along the 180 kilometres of the Berg, described it as having been "goated". A few kilometres down river from Zunckel's buried bridge is Driel Barrage. This is a vital component of the Tuva pumped storage scheme which, in bad droughts, is used to supply the industrial hub of South Africa – the Witwatersrand – with water. The dam, one of South Africa's newest, is now 50 per cent silted.

Near Champagne Castle, one of the Drakensberg's better known hotels, a land owner – a professional man – built a dam high up in the hills. The river dutifully piled up behind the dam wall and then, as soon as the dam filled, the river spilled over the side, instead of over the wall, taking the hillside with it.

The huge Drakensberg massif, all 270 000 square kilometres of it, is half-owned by the Department of Forestry (150 000 square kilometres), with the Natal Parks Board owning 50 000, KwaZulu 50 000 and 20 000 in private hands. Lesotho owns the plateau, the fount of the Vaal, the Tugela and the Orange rivers. While the headwaters in the Berg have their problems, the estuaries at the rivers' ends are also being abused. Natal has 69 dead or dying estuaries, says Ian Garland, sugar farmer and doyen of South Africa's environmental educators. Garland and seven other sugar farmers got together to rehabilitate the estuaries which are choked and even dammed up by silt.

When it comes to saving the country's wetlands Begg offers two suggestions: the Government must either acquire all wetlands, or pay farmers not to use them.

As I commented earlier, if we are to avert the Great South African Desert there is no time to use education. The difficulty with the education approach emerged from a study, discussed by Gerry Garland. Garland pointed out that the International Federation of Institutes of Advanced Study, using Nigeria, the Philippines, Colombia and Peru as its base, discovered:

> [That] in these areas many farmers did not recognise symptoms of erosion like gullies as evidence of agriculturally related erosion. They realised that land fertility was falling along with crop yields from year to year, but few, if any, ascribed this to cumulative soil loss. Such attitudes were unrelated to fundamental educational attributes like literacy, suggesting that the solution does not lie simply in elementary education.

In a letter to *The Star* in 1989, J R Jerman of Pennington on the Natal South Coast described how he was a member of two South Coast Government-appointed soil conservation committees composed almost entirely of sugar farmers. He said they had, over many years, "pleaded and demanded" that action be taken against farmers guilty of soil exhaustive farming. No action was ever taken "because they say the education process must continue. Why? After all, it's been 40 years since the The Conservation of Agricultural Resources Act of 1932."

Robertson, exasperated by the lack of remedial action in KwaZulu, suggested to Chief Mangosuthu Buthelezi, who was then designing the Zulu capital of Ulundi, that he should rather build the Zulu capital between Durban and Madagascar, because that was where his country was going to end up in 50 years' time. Robertson saw a dangerous problem in Zululand where soil erosion was, and still is, appallingly rapid. He foresaw "the seeds of bitter strife" in the situation. He condemned Hendrik Verwoerd's "Grand Apartheid" policy for short-sightedly jeopardising the future viability of South Africa as a food-producing state. Verwoerd, he said, had handed to the homelands – which were virtually Third World states which the Government wanted to establish and then economically cast adrift from "white South Africa" – some of South Africa's most precious but vulnerable agricultural land as well as sensitive catchment areas. Three-quarters of the homelands were in the "over 500 mm" rainfall region and a third were in high potential regions. But the farms produced yields of between one-sixth and one-seventh of white-owned farms in similar areas. Bophuthatswana, the most technologically advanced of the homeland areas, produces less than 10 per cent of its potential. Venda can produce 64 kilograms of grain to a hectare – white-owned farms on the Highveld produce 2 300 kilograms per hectare. The world average is 3 600 kilograms per hectare.

I have already mentioned Transkei's abysmal production, but it would be unfair to leave the matter there. It is not that Transkeians are bad farmers. It is that they cannot begin ploughing until the first good rains make the soil soft enough for their cattle-drawn ploughs. Sometimes the rains don't come until January and then there is barely time to grow a maize crop before winter starts. And even in a year when the rains are early they do not have an adequate number of draught oxen. There are precious few tractors, which might be just as well, because tractors in the wrong hands can devastate land.

Robertson, after his retirement, wrote to me from his home in Scottburgh in 1978 saying how the Government, having itself failed to control disastrous farming techniques on white-owned land, was now handing the task over "to the independent Black states, jealous of their newborn sovereignty". He went on:

> *The Bantu have a cultural background of shifting agriculture. When the land is ruined by herds or by the hoe they simply move on to ruin more land. From this follows the demand for more land instead of a campaign for better agriculture. In white areas, after a 25 year old campaign, we found it impossible to introduce conservation farming by education, propaganda and persuasion. It was only when the power of the platteland stemvee decreased that compulsion was introduced and prosecutions began.*
>
> *Bantu politicians, like Gatsha Buthelezi, firmly in the grip of cattle kraal politics, would risk ruin if they introduced compulsion.*

Robertson's barb concerning shifting agriculture was perhaps unfair. Less than a century before, the British, following the defeat of the Zulu, had compressed the Zulu people into the area north of the Tugela. Their cattle herds grew but there was now nowhere to move them. No people can change their traditional way of farming overnight. To a Zulu cattle represent wealth rather than meat. Huntley, Siegfried and Sunter, in their *South African Environments into the 21st Century* wrote that two out of every three Zulu cattle die of natural causes. In other words they are not slaughtered for protein. The Zulu's love of cattle is often scorned in the same way that people sometimes deride the Hindu who would rather starve than kill their sacred cows. On the other hand those "sacred cows" perform a huge ecological service: they supply fertiliser and fuel (dried dung), they supply milk and they provide draft in a land which not only cannot afford tractors but whose often soft and muddy lands would be wrecked by the weight of tractors.

Oxen play an important ecological role

Nevertheless cattle numbers must be reduced if Zululand and other regions are to survive. Can it be done? The Panos Institute in London reported in *Panoscope* (July 1990) of a case in the Mvumi district of central Tanzania where the government, in a last ditch attempt to save the collapsing veld, ordered the removal of 68 000 cattle from 1 800 square kilometres. The social cost was high. Schools emptied as boys followed their fathers driving the cattle to new pastures. No impact study was done on the areas to which they were sent. Families no longer had milk, meat and manure. Manure was used for fuel, floor construction and fertiliser. The grass recovered and this brought back antelope which began eating crops. After a while people were allowed to bring back only approved cattle for milking purposes. Pastures of better-type grasses were prepared. The results are enigmatic. Panos quoted a local man, David Mzuri, who posed the most important question of all – he said destocking the land helped it to recover "but was the problem merely exported?" The ideal would be to slaughter. What politician would dare suggest that?

Ina Perlman of Operation Hunger in Johannesburg, interviewed in *The Star* in November 1990, said that while independent Zimbabwe had reduced malnutrition to 6 per cent, it remained at 20 per cent in South Africa. She believed part of Zimbabwe's success was because it brought back subsistence farming. Peasant farmers are usually far more productive, hectare for hectare, than large scale farmers. They know every corner of their small holdings and what it will grow best. Perlman pleaded for the early scrapping of South Africa's notorious "Natives' Land Act" of 1913, which had confined black land ownership rights to 13 per cent of the country. She said that would immediately make available almost 6 million hectares of land for subsistence farming – assuming the capital could be found – which could relieve a lot of hardship.

Whatever the final arrangement the problem still remains of how to stop South Africa's scarce croplands and scarcer good pastures from being ruined by poor or greedy farming practices. T C Robertson suggested at the 1971 Natural Resources Symposium at Jan Smuts House in Johannesburg the establishment of a bureau of ecological standards (BEST). He said BEST should employ scientists of such excellence (and of all colours) that their judgement would be respected by all countries south of the Limpopo as an international authority for the protection of the environment and for the increase of agricultural production without doing harm to the renewable resources of water and soil. "It will have to be a unity that has its roots in the ecosystem, not in the statute book." He considered that until such a unifying bureau was established a soil conservation programme in Southern Africa would remain an organisational impossibility.

Robertson's BEST would first establish standards and then send out an inspectorate to ensure they were applied.

> The standards would not be a political policy, subject to deductive logic and all the emotions of Utopianism. Today's scientific method makes it possible to quantify the environment and its welfare – and there can be no argument with exact measurements. That is the main reason why conservation must be kept out of the political arena.

Robertson saw BEST as in no way being connected with the Department of Agriculture but having jurisdiction in matters concerning water, soil and pollution. It would set up model farms. It could also, one supposes, take the burden off the politicians if it became necessary to tell a Zulu farmer to reduce his cattle.

Richard Fuggle and Andre Rabie point out that in 1970 South Africa had only 0,86 hectares of cropland per head of population while the world average was almost double – 1,63. Of the available land we had cultivated three-quarters (0,6 hectares) leaving only a meagre 0,26 hectares compared with 1,29 for the world as a whole. By 1980 the amount, because of population growth, was down to 0,5 per head and by 2020 it will be down to 0,2 hectares. This is why it is so important that the Department of Forestry reconsider its policy to plant prime agricultural land to softwood timber simply because there is a good export market for it.

Industry versus agriculture

The battered Highveld which grows 80 per cent of South Africa's maize, 75 per cent of its sorghum, 65 per cent of its sunflower (oil), 58 per cent of its dried beans, more than half its potatoes, almost half its wheat and a third of its beef, has the bad luck to have some of the world's most extensive near-surface coalfields. Eskom, the nation's generating corporation, has learned to exploit even the meanest of coals which engineers know as "top soil". They are joking of course. But, in a sense, South Africa is sacrificing soil for power.

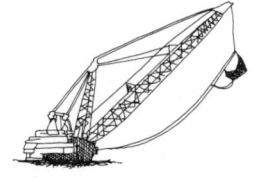

Dragline mining

When one travels across the gently undulating Highveld, especially, but not only, in the eastern Transvaal, one occasionally sees above the profile of the land the enormous crane-like arms of draglines jutting from mobile factories which look like a cross between a battleship and an enormous tank. Each scoop of the dragline's bucket gouges out a piece of land the size of a swimming pool. The topsoil is put aside and the machine gradually eats its way down to the coal seam and the coal is sent on its way by conveyor belt to some giant power station. Open cast mining began in 1970 in the Witbank area and, since then, the Department of Agriculture has demanded more and more safeguards regarding rehabilitation of mined out farmland. Johan Greeff, manager of safety and technical services at the Chamber of Mines says it cost R20 000 to R50 000 to restore a hectare of land after open cast mining, which is far more than the market value of the land. There have been suggestions that it is not worth restoring some land. Rather the mines spend the R20 000 a hectare on improving more promising land elsewhere for agricultural production.

There is also the question of mine dumps – gold mine dumps in particular – which, at present, smother 1 500 square kilometres of former agricultural land and which contaminate farmland with acidic runoff. The Chamber of Mines now insists that mines adopt a policy of integrated environmental management (IEM) which forces mines to establish how they will minimise environmental impacts in the short, medium and long terms and what will happen when the mine is decommissioned. A likely technology is that mine tailings will in future be dumped underground but there has been little pressure on the mines to seek bold answers.

In terms of the Mining Rights Act 1967 the government is powerless to stop mining taking place even if it happens to be prime agricultural land. As long as a person can prove the existence of a mineral, and his ability to extract it, he must be awarded a mining permit according to law. As with the open cast coal mines the Minister can insist on certain conditions being met – such as restoring the land afterwards – but that's as far as he can go. What the Minister could do, but never has, is to bar prospecting in certain categories of agricultural land. The National Parks Act in fact has adopted such a clause for all parks established before 1980. These cannot be prospected and therefore mining rights can never become an issue.

Air pollution　　　　PLATE 1

An Eskom "six pack" power station. Annually, each of these coal-fired plants pumps tens of millions of tons of greenhouse gases into the atmosphere. (Jon Hobbs)

An eastern Transvaal opencast mine feeds a nearby power station with 40 000 tons of coal every day. (David Molesworth)

Koeberg nuclear power plant: no coal, no ash, no smoke and no greenhouse gases. (Eskom)

PLATE 2   *Air pollution*

Highveld Steel, a major polluter in the eastern Transvaal Highveld, has improved since this scene in 1981. But it remains a conspicuously smoky landmark. (The Star)

The notoriously smelly plume from Sappi's Ngodwana paper mill fans out down the Elands River valley towards Nelspruit. (Jon Hobbs)

Air pollution PLATE 3

Morning Glory in a Pretoria garden – blemished by acid rain. (L. Prozesky-Schultz)

A typical Highveld temperature inversion traps Soweto's domestic smoke. (Julie Clarke)

Soweto's main road on a winter's morning. (Herbert Mabuza, The Star)

PLATE 4   *Air pollution*

As the greenhouse effect raises sea levels these dolosse – invented in South Africa and named after African toy cattle made of clay – are being used worldwide to protect shorelines from heavy seas.

Water PLATE 5

A soggy northern Transvaal banner advertises a prayer meeting to end the drought. (Sarel van der Berg, The Star)

Laingsburg in the Karoo photographed 10 years after the 1981 flood disaster which swept away many homes and people. Denuded valleys upstream increased the river's velocity.

PLATE 6   Water

The Umfolozi bridge on the N2 highway gives way under silt-laden waters in the 1987 floods which killed hundreds. (Daily News)

South Africa's largest dam, the Verwoerd Dam on the Orange River, is taking in 90 million tons of topsoil a year.

Water   PLATE 7

TOP Millions of South Africans still have no reliable water on tap. (Urban Foundation)

LEFT Karoo windmill pump: more than 100 towns exist entirely on groundwater. (David Molesworth)

Irrigation uses about two thirds of South Africa's stored water – much of it wastefully. (David Molesworth)

PLATE 8   Water

Looking towards the mouth of the Mkomazi River with Umkomaas visible on the skyline to the right. Note in the top picture, taken in May 1987, how sugar-cane has been illegally planted right down to the river's edge. In the lower picture, taken the following October, the sugar-cane and the soil have been swept away to cause further ecological damage offshore. (Edward Beasley)

Soil PLATE 9

The horrific result of injudicious cultivation and overgrazing on a Natal hillside. (Jon Hobbs)

Looking more like the San Adreas Fault, a deep erosion gulley snakes across a Natal farming area draining the soil of moisture and fertility. (Jon Hobbs)

PLATE 10   Soil

TOP *It is doubtful that open cast mining in agricultural areas – despite these attempts to restore the veld afterwards – is worth the temporary benefit obtained from the coal.* (Jon Hobbs)

ABOVE RIGHT *The Karoo, having conquered this former maize field, advances under a fence near Hertzogville, Orange Free State.* (Jon Hobbs)

Dongas near Itala Game Reserve, northern Natal. (Jon Hobbs)

Soil   PLATE 11

Monocultures, whether pine plantations, canefields or these cattle fattening camps cause irreversible changes to the land and limit the options for future farmers. (Jon Hobbs)

Mining activities have made South Africa relatively wealthy but they have also robbed it of future wealth. Here sinkholes due to mining have wrecked farmland. (Jon Hobbs)

PLATE 12   Soil

When Nasa first saw these unnaturally-shaped white patches on images transmitted from a satellite over central Zimbabwe they were puzzled. It was later discovered the shapes coincided with tribal trust lands. In these artificially-coloured images red denotes vigorous vegetation such as rainforest or irrigation schemes and white denotes bare ground – in this case land which has been overgrazed and exhausted. (Landsat image of July 1985, produced by the Satellite Applications Centre of the CSIR)

Soil   PLATE 13

The ghostly white shape of Lebowa is revealed by this Landsat image transmitted from space to the CSIR's Hartebeeshoek tracking station. The whiteness indicates an almost total lack of ground cover due to soil erosion and overgrazing; the dark shape in the centre is the thickly forested Blouberg range. Pietersburg is the blueish area to the bottom right. (Landsat image produced by the Satellite Applications Centre of the CSIR)

PLATE 14   Forests

A mere 0,25 per cent of South Africa is covered by indigenous forest such as this coastal forest in the Cape. (David Molesworth)

Forests   PLATE 15

Inside Johannesburg's suburban "rainforest" created by gardeners using hosepipes and the plants of four continents. Into this rich new ecosystem have come many new bird species kept in check by domestic "jungle cats".

Afforestation has irreversibly changed parts of South Africa into a foreign landscape reminiscent sometimes of Canada, sometimes of Australia. (David Molesworth)

PLATE 16   Forests

Wood is the main fuel for most South Africans. Some women walk 40 kilometres three times a week to collect it. (David Molesworth)

Sylviculturalist Peter Schon clones trees for fuel wood and especially species for traditional medicines which have become rare. (HL&H Mining Timbers)

Plantlife   PLATE 17

Watsonias at Silvermine, south west Cape.

Leucospermum blooms above Constantia, Cape.

Part of South Africa's heritage is an extraordinary variety of plantlife – a field of flowers near Calvinia, north western Cape.

PLATE 18   Wildlife

South Africa is one of the few countries which has to cull elephants. In the Kruger Park and abutting private reserves such as Sabi Sabi live Africa's biggest tuskers. (Sabi Sabi Game Reserve)

White rhino, once nearly extinct, are off the endangered list after the Natal Parks Board developed a technique for capturing and redistributing them to former strongholds. (David Molesworth)

Coastline PLATE 19

Idle fishing boats at Lambert's Bay. More and more vessels are chasing fewer and fewer fish.

Devastated coastline. Diamonds are found in the rock crevices so diamond miners dig down to bedrock in these high security areas along the west Cape coast. (Jon Hobbs)

Dredging the sea-bottom for diamonds — is the ecological damage worth it? No environmental impact studies have been made public. (John Hobbs)

PLATE 20   *Coastline*

Richards Bay Minerals (RBM) titanium mine. The dunes are entirely removed, sifted and replaced. Here treated sand has been planted to timber. (Jon Hobbs)

Before: the high dunes which once existed at Richards Bay will be rebuilt and replanted.

After: a reconstituted dune 12 years later. RBM now wants to mine at Lake St Lucia and replace existing grassland and pines with indigenous bush. The announcement sparked a huge public protest.

Coastline PLATE 21

Cape seals swarm on the beach at Kleinsee. Among the most prolific mammals on earth the question is whether it is moral to harvest them, like fish. (John Hobbs)

BELOW *Oil slicks from passing tankers threatening the jack-ass penguin. (The Argus)*

LEFT *This woman, whose diet depends on sealife, has witnessed the near sterilisation of Transkei's coast by organised poaching. (David Molesworth)*

PLATE 22   *Coastline*

False Bay from Silvermine. Some would like the 40 kilometre wide bay to become a national park.

Coastline PLATE 23

South Africa's coastline lacks a vernacular style architecture. Fish Hoek shows a typical and bland mixture of styles.

PLATE 24　　　　*High density living*

Squatters who are drawn to the towns are sometimes incredibly resourceful. This tin cathedral graces Crossroads squatter camp outside Cape Town. (Urban Foundation)

CENTRE *High density can be attractive; Observatory in Cape Town has a greater population density than Soweto.*

BOTTOM LEFT *High density living, Lisbon style, has worked for centuries.* (Julie Clarke)

BOTTOM RIGHT *Soweto's "51/6" homes were an apartheid government's answer to housing "temporary" blacks.* (The Star)

High density living   PLATE 25

Granada, Spain – an attractive vernacular style; there is a human scale and privacy despite high density. (Julie Clarke)

Suburban Germiston – designed around engineering requirements; 40 per cent of space is for "traffic sewers". There is no transition between public and private space and no sense of community. (Julie Clarke)

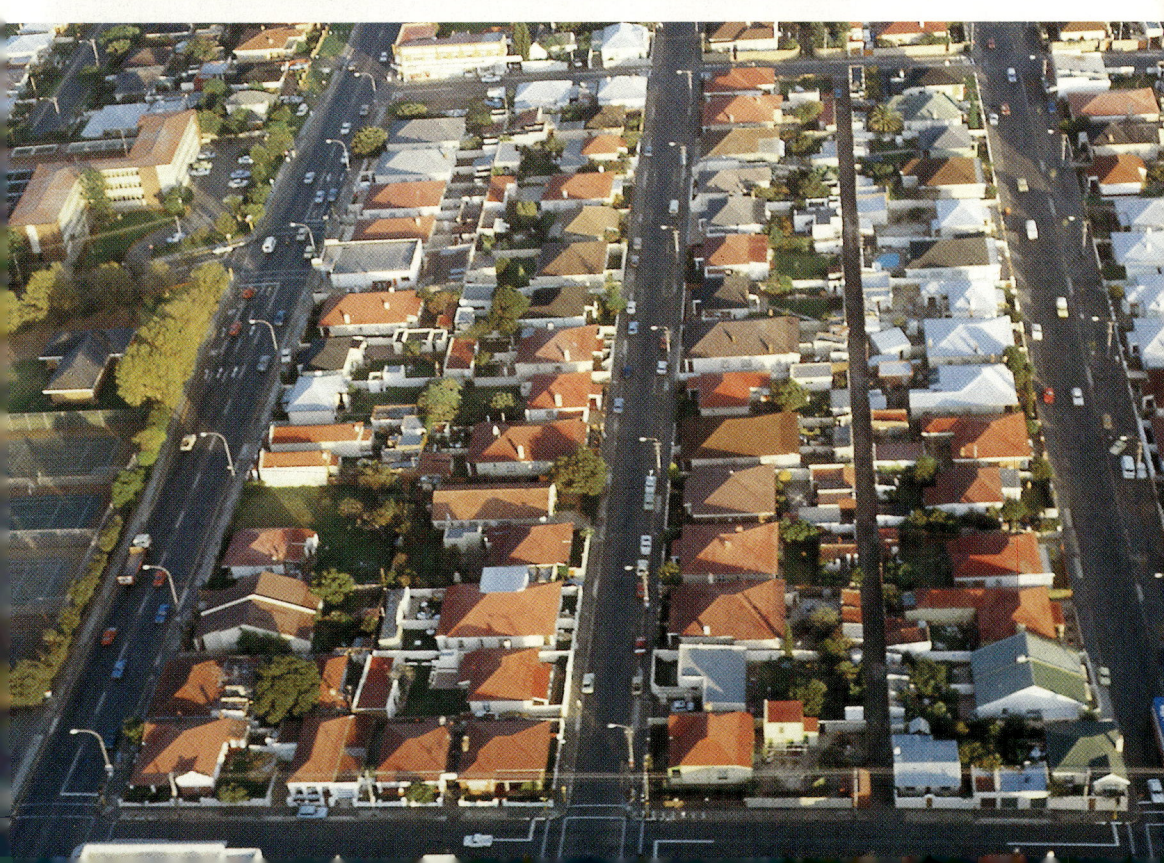

PLATE 26   Cars versus people

Residents demonstrate against new major roads whose sole purpose is to speed up suburban traffic. The opposite is needed: squeeze points and speed bumps.

CENTRE *Abandoned motorways in Cape Town. Traffic has ruined many South African urban areas – without solving the traffic problem.*

BOTTOM LEFT *Lisbon, where people come before traffic. When a car comes along people move their chairs.* (Julie Clarke)

BOTTOM RIGHT *Sandton's "High Street" – designed solely for cars.* (Conrad Berge)

Urban rivers PLATE 27

The Braamfontein Spruit trail through Johannesburg, Randburg and Sandton – people began to create it themselves. The politicians came later.

The growth of paved urbanised areas is increasing the volume of stormwater runoff. Engineers nowadays slow down runoff by allowing it to flood parks and playing fields. (Stephen Davimes, The Star)

PLATE 28   Office environments

Central business districts such as Johannesburg's whose streets give no thought to environmental quality, are slowly losing custom to the suburban business nodes. (Julie Clarke)

ABOVE The developers of Woodmead Park believe people prefer tranquility and "genuine air" at work. (Environmental Design Partnership)

Sick building syndrome can result in hermetically sealed buildings if ventilation is not controlled.

Softening city centres PLATE 29

An early Johannesburg building will be incorporated into the façade of a modern city block. (Etienne Rothbart, The Star)

BOTTOM LEFT *Small Street Mall – a Johannesburg street won back from traffic for pedestrians.* (The Star)

BELOW *Trees help soften the city scene.* (The Star)

PLATE 30   Landscape planning

The main rest camp and conference facility at Itala Game Reserve in northern Natal. Skilled environmental design has neatly recessed it into a wooded hillside. Note how thatched roofs and naturally-occurring rocks harmonise. (Environmental Design Partnership)

Landscape planning   PLATE 31

LEFT Eskom, instead of cutting a service lane through indigenous forests, now strings its pylons over the tree tops using helicopters. Here cables rest on the tree crowns ready for installation. (Jon Hobbs)

ABOVE Eskom used to shoot Cape vultures because their excreta coated pylon insulators causing power failures. Now they install special vulture perches. (Jon Hobbs)

Flamingos clear high tension cable made more visible by using cistern ball valves as markers. (Jon Hobbs)

PLATE 32   Waste

ABOVE *A mounted specimen of a rinkals which was found dying with its head in a can.* (Etienne Rothbart, The Star)

TOP RIGHT *Waste glass: Glass is entirely reusable.*

RIGHT *A Botswana hut insulated with beverage cans prior to being coated with mud.*

BELOW *At the Robinson Deep refuse disposal site gases from decomposing garbage are turned into methane gas for the gold mining industry.* (Stephen Davimes, The Star)

15 Silent spring

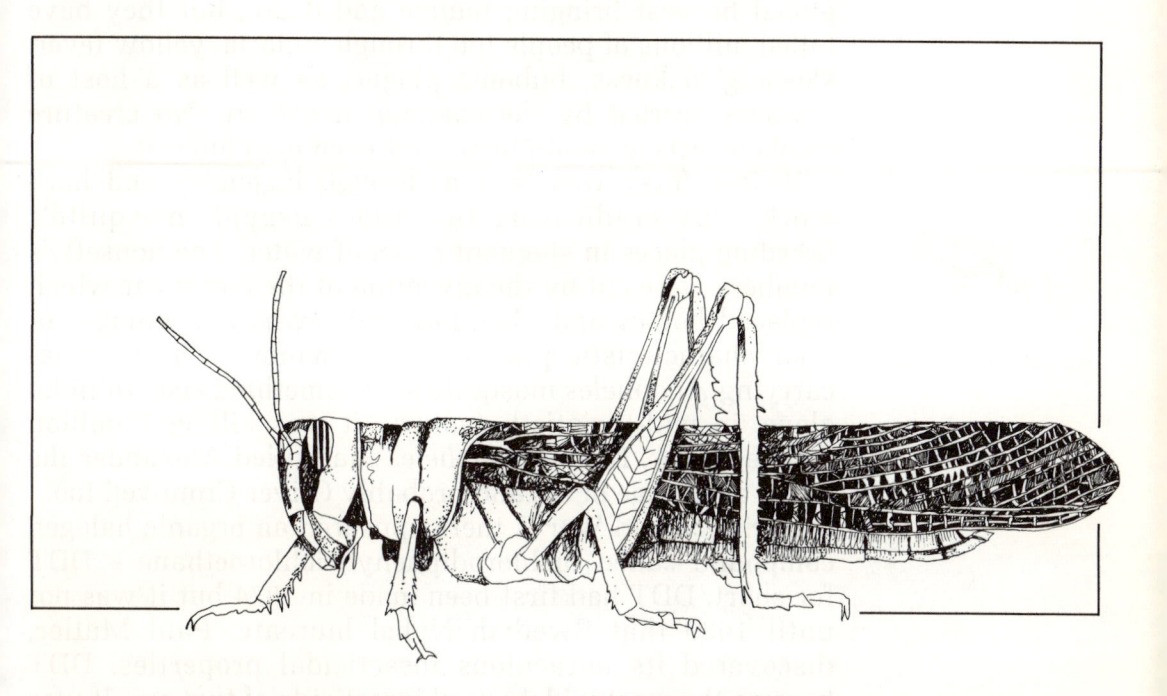

A coward's weapon, poison.
　　　　　　Phineas Fletcher in Sicelides.

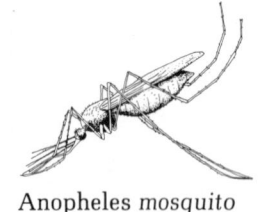

FOR sheer numbers, or even going by weight, this is not the age of man, it is the age of insects. It has never been anything else for 400 million years. Insects, through the ages, have not only eaten a large percentage of man's global harvest bringing famine and death, but they have killed millions of people too through malaria, yellow fever, sleeping sickness, bubonic plague, as well as a host of diseases carried by the common house fly. No creature rivals insects as mankillers – not even man himself.

Yellow fever was beaten through ingenuity and hard work – by eradicating the *Aedes aegypti* mosquito's breeding places in stagnant pools of water. The housefly's numbers were cut by the invention of the motor car which replaced horses and, therefore, rid towns and villages of their characteristic piles of horse manure. The malaria-carrying *Anopheles* mosquito was something else. In India alone, in mid-twentieth century, it was killing 7 million people a year. It was *Anopheles* that killed Alexander the Great at the age of 33, and probably Oliver Cromwell too.

Anopheles *mosquito*

During World War II there appeared an organic halogen compound called dichlorodiphenyltrichloroethane – DDT for short. DDT had first been made in 1874 but it was not until 1939 that Swedish Nobel laureate, Paul Muller, discovered its miraculous insecticidal properties. DDT became the most widely used insecticide of that era. It was incredibly successful against the malarial mosquito and was found to be effective against almost all insects including many that were agricultural pests. It appeared not to be poisonous to man. Throughout the 1940s and 1950s it came to be used extensively and by 1965 traces of it were to be found in almost every living organism from Marilyn Monroe to Japanese oysters. It was found in the fatty tissues of animals in Antarctica, 3 000 kilometres south of the nearest point of application. The fact that it had impregnated the marine environment was ominous: only a few parts per million (ppm) were needed to decrease photosynthesis in marine phytoplankton – the source of 70 per cent of the Earth's oxygen. It was coming down in rain and was borne on the wind.

Rachel Carson, author of *Silent Spring* (1962), a book which helped spark off the new age of environmental awareness, shocked the public and angered chemical companies by pointing out that of the 3 million tons of DDT which had, up to then, been sprayed on insects, at least 2 million tons were still swishing around the rivers and tides of the world killing non-target organisms far from the original target zones.

By 1970 the World Health Organisation found 120 species of insects were resistant to DDT and many of DDT's early and dramatic victories – such as the way it reduced malaria by killing the vector mosquito – had been reversed.

DDT was the hydrogen bomb in man's anti-insect arsenal – effective when on target but its "fallout" was environmentally disastrous. It, at first, produced in the public a faith and great expectancy in chemical controls. "Conquering nature" was still popular stuff in those days. Nature needed taming – just look how the Billy Chipperfields and Moscow State Circuses were able to tame Bengal tigers and get seals to balance balls on the ends of their noses.

Biocides were big business – hence the industry's anger when Rachel Carson rocked the boat by drawing public attention to the fact that DDT, and many other biocides, were not behaving as advertised. The chemical companies set about trying to destroy Carson's reputation but they were up against an astute scientist who used her sense of humour as a weapon against her unamusing detractors. Carson revealed the story of Clear Lake, California which became one of the classic stories of the early "green" movement. Clear Lake was a popular picnic spot but was notorious for its clouds of tiny midges. DDD, a form of DDT, had been used to kill the insects. A test of the lake water confirmed no harm had been done. The insecticide residues were in a safe concentration of 0,05 parts per million (ppm). But then the lake's grebes – an attractive water fowl – were found dead with up to 1 600 ppm DDD in their bodies. It was discovered that plankton in the lake were absorbing the DDD from the water at about 5 ppm (representing a 100 times greater concentration than the water). Plankton-eating fish showed a concentration of between 40 and 300 ppm. Carnivorous fish carried up to 2 500. Within a short time almost no trace of the insecticide could be found in the water. It had, as Carson put it, "passed into the fabric of life which supports the lake". The midges developed resistant strains and came back in force.

Carson was not against the use of agricultural chemicals

– she was against sloppiness in applying them. Her concern about the ill-researched chemicals and the way they were handled was vindicated after her death from cancer. She triggered worldwide concern and in 1964, the year of her death, tests in Johannesburg revealed that every man, woman and child had DDT in their adipose (fatty) tissues. The average level in Johannesburg adult males was 7,16 ppm for whites and 5,94 for blacks. In Israel the count in males was 19,2 ppm – the same as Americans living in Miami. Even Eskimos carried 3 ppm. In California it was found that mothers' milk often carried more DDT than health laws permitted in cow's milk.

Countries began to ban not only DDT but other long-lived, broad-spectrum killers such as endrin, aldrin and dieldrin which are all chlorinated hydrocarbons which do not break down. Bio-assays of soil samples in the United States, after the application of heptachlor, dieldrin and aldrin showed a 100 percent mortality of all organisms – a totally lifeless soil. Tests in South Africa showed DDT, out of all the chlorinated hydrocarbons, had the greatest residuality – up to 20 per cent still being deadly two years later. In Europe, because soil metabolism in temperate

Crop spraying

regions is slower, 79 per cent of DDT remained active after three years. Dieldrin was the second longest lived.

The chemical firms warned that by banning these "wonder chemicals" the world's crop yields would crash and mass starvation would follow. Governments went ahead and banned them, and famine did not follow – at least not through rampaging insects. What was shameful was that many of the companies, particularly those in West Germany and the United States, after their governments banned their products, switched their sales teams to Africa and sold in vast tonnages the most dangerous of the insecticides – those that were deemed too dangerous to use even in sophisticated farming operations in the West. The sales continue even today. *Environmental Matters,* a British industrial information newsletter, quoted the British Chemical Industries Association as saying that in many cases a country of manufacture does not use a particular pesticide because it has neither the crop, nor the pest. DDT, for example, is the best way to quickly eradicate the malarial mosquito, but neither Europe nor North America has this problem. If malaria did arise in southern Europe as a result of the greenhouse effect (and it might) would Europe resort to DDT? I believe it would.

In March 1990, according to a report in the *Weekly Mail* by Eddie Koch who was quoting Greenpeace activist Jim Vallette, the Mobay corporation of Missouri sent 40 drums of an organophosphate,Tokuthion, to South Africa where it was used to spray fruit against insect pests. The US Environmental Protection Agency had banned the sale of the toxin in America. Three months later Mobay was fined the equivalent of R120 000 for exporting insecticides to the non-English Third World with warnings written only in English.

Few people would advocate scrapping all insecticides, herbicides and fungicides – indeed, without agricultural chemicals the world's harvest would be severely depleted. But agricultural chemicals need careful and educated handling and invariably they are handed over to either untrained or inadequately trained people. A common practice in South Africa is for farmers to wash down spraying equipment in the nearest river. One frequently sees African women carrying water in drums that previously contained deadly chemicals. The tins are marked

"Poison" and the user is instructed in large letters: "puncture after use", but a 20 litre drum is a valuable utensil in rural areas. According to the World Health Organisation there are 2 million cases of pesticide poisoning worldwide each year. Nearly all the cases are in the Third World.

A very worrying aspect is the way farmers, who can be more ignorant of nature than many townsmen, will misuse poisons. In the Magaliesberg they place poison-injected oranges in the veld for baboons to pick up. What if a child comes along? They are unable to think that far ahead. The new journal *Bushcall* - issued by the Bophuthatswana National Parks Board - in its first edition in 1990, carried an item about a northern Transvaal game farmer whose neighbour used Temik (aldicarb), an insecticide, to lace water holes in the hope of killing vultures whom they suspect of stock killing. At such a water hole, near Tshipise Lodge, the game farmer found a dead impala, waterbuck, red hartebeest, ostrich and tawny eagle.

In South Africa there are many hundreds of different agricultural poisons in use. When *The Star,* in March 1989, asked the Department of Agriculture whether it was still using BHC (benzine hexachloride) on locust swarms - a widely banned chemical which was in fact officially banned in South Africa too - a spokesman said it had been, but now all stocks had been used up. The fact that BHC had been used by the Government was in contradiction of its own policy. The spokesman added: "We are now using other agricultural poisons - diazinon and fenitrothion - which could be more harmful to the environment." These two compounds affect the central nervous system if ingested through the skin or lungs. The picture accompanying the article showed three men spraying land - none wore gloves or masks. The shame of it was that there was probably no need to use any insecticide at all.

There are other ways of halting the build-up of insects: one can fool insect pests by rotating crops. A potato crop this year might start attracting Colorado beetles, but if wheat is planted the following season the Colorado beetles starve to death. Crop rotation also reduces dependence on fertilisers by allowing natural chemicals, taken out by a potato crop for example, to build up again while, say, a wheat crop is growing.

*Locust swarm.
Source* The Argus

Research is progressing to develop strains of crops which are resistant to pests and diseases.

When it comes to insect pests the most intriguing of all is the locust. More and more scientists now believe they should be left alone, because it's cheaper. The last two big outbreaks in South Africa – in 1985 and 1986 – cost the taxpayer R48 million in poisons. It worked out at R45 a hectare, 10 times more than the average annual income from a hectare. It was the most expensive locust-control operation in South African history and mostly benefited only the pesticide manufacturer.

The truth is that after 80 years of spraying locusts with more and more expensive pesticides the swarms are as bad as ever. It is, therefore, hardly surprising that some authorities are now questioning the wisdom of it all. It has been said that farmers themselves are creating the ideal conditions for locusts. Certainly this is what happened with the "locust bird", or quelea finch, a tiny red-billed bird which today swarms in incredible numbers. In natural veld one sees small clouds, like locust swarms, looking for grass seed. They do no damage and they are never far from water and thus were, historically, never widely distributed. But as farmers grew grain, year after year in the same region, and built dams, they created the ideal habitat and the bird population exploded. Today aircraft are used to bomb the birds with contact poisons when they roost at sunset.

At an SA Institute of Ecologists conference in the McGregor Museum in Kimberley in 1987, Dr Phillip Hockey of the University of Cape Town pointed out that it was an offence for farmers not to report the presence of locusts on their land, and that farmers had no say in whether insecticides were then used on their properties, even if the chemicals made their crops unmarketable. Yet many farmers conduct their farming so efficiently that they can absorb the shock of a swarm of locusts, and even welcome the frass, the nitrogen-rich droppings left by the insects.

In the locust wars in the Karoo in the second half of the 1980s, the Government gave special permission for stocks of the banned BHC – a broad spectrum killer – to be used against locusts. A spokesman later explained that the BHC had been in storage since 1981 so it seemed a good idea to get rid of it. Dr Mike Mentis, professor of ecology at the Witwatersrand University commented: "By the same token

Spraying for locusts.
Source The Argus

would the Government allow doctors to use up old stocks of thalidomide?" (Thalidomide, an effective anti-nausea medicine, was banned in the 1960s after being found responsible for deforming babies in the womb.) No monitoring was done to discover the environmental impact of spraying the 6 649 tons of BHC on the veld, and the chemical industry itself had little incentive to research all the possible side-effects of such poisons. Hockey underscored the new disquiet about the attitude of farmers and officials towards locusts. He pointed out how the main locust outbreaks had occurred in the Karoo where one in five farmers said the impact of locusts on normal veld is negligible. Grazing is not seriously affected, and well-managed mixed farms can ride the consequences. In fact the resultant frass which speckles the ground accelerates nutrient cycling in the soil and could even increase its productivity. The locusts killed by chemicals between 1985 and 1987 would have supplied about 2,26 millions tons of frass – the equivalent of 14 700 tons of nitrogen fertiliser worth, then, between R18 million and R20 million.

"Clearly," says Hockey, "spraying operations have not solved the locust problem. Outbreaks still occur." It emerged that the regularity of outbreaks is today exactly the same as 90 years ago when there were no chemical sprays. Before 1907 outbreaks typically lasted about 13 years, with periods between each outbreak of 11 years. Chemical spraying was first tried in 1907, and by 1920 large changes in locust behaviour were apparent. Outbreak periods now began to last six to seven years with quiet periods lasting seven to eight years. The pattern by 1988 was two years of locust plagues and two years without them.

Stanley crane

A side effect was that the natural enemies of locusts have been wiped out. Jackals and foxes helped check locust outbreaks by wolfing them down in the hopper stage. But farmers, often appallingly ignorant of natural history, shot and poisoned them in numbers. Hockey noted how locust plagues seem to stimulate predator birthrates, including bird predators. He suggested that biological controls may be cheaper and more effective than chemical controls. One way of reducing a build-up was very simple indeed – avoid planting locust-attracting crops year after year.

One problem is that after all these years, after all these

millions spent on poisons, we still know very little about locusts. Only recently was it discovered, for instance, that the ordinary, inoffensive little grasshopper is one and the same animal. Something makes it turn into a monster. As Hocking observed: the R48 million spent on BHC in the 1985 and 1986 campaign was R48 million more than we spent on research.

Another problem chemical has been 2,4-D, a powerful herbicide used by Natal cane farmers. It is known to have a low mammalian toxicity. But vegetable farmers down wind of canefields began complaining in the late 1980s that their vegetables were dying from what appeared to be 2,4-D. Professor C P Nel of Pretoria University examined their crops and told an investigation that the damage could only have been caused by toxic herbicide. The vegetable farmers failed to gain a Supreme Court injunction against 17 chemical companies marketing the herbicide. The court held that the farmers should have acted against the users, not the manufacturers. The legal costs were enormous and the farmers were to pay. This would have meant some of them losing their farms. The legal representative of the chemical firms offered a deal: the industry would pay the costs if the farmers advertised in certain newspapers and magazines that they had changed their minds and that they now favoured the hormone herbicides, and if the farmers signed an agreement that they would never again campaign against herbicides. The deal also required Mark Laing, a University of Natal researcher, to stop his research into harmful hormone herbicides. The farmers and Laing refused. The greens group, Earthlife, exposed the deal and, soon after, Shell, one of the 17, withdrew its hormone herbicides and dissociated itself from the demand on the farmers. Earthlife is now trying to get worldwide action against multinational chemical companies marketing dangerous biocides in Africa.

The matter remains unresolved but the weight of evidence points to the fact that cane farmers, despite their claims that 2,4-D is fairly harmless, are using an unnecessarily powerful chemical which, in South Africa's warm climate, easily turns to a gas which can float way off course. Kevin Lovell, a plant pathologist at Natal University, demonstrated how as little as 400 million millionths of a gram of 2,4-D, per litre of air, applied to a lettuce for six hours, would reduce growth by a third. Annual losses according to some farmers were as high as 60 per cent. Bristol University researchers, testing equally infinitesimal quantities also found quite scary results. Mark Laing of Natal University suggests that such a volatile chemical is entirely unsuitable for use in areas where mixed crops are grown. There is also the question of what such chemicals do to humans and the truth is that far too little is known on this score and that which is known is cause for grave concern. Laing is correct in calling for an independent body to protect the public's interest.

South Africa certainly has a more liberal view of powerful poisons than other industrial nations. DDT is still used in hospitals to kill mosquitoes; Lindane (banned in most countries), is used to protect timber stocks; dieldrin (supplied by the Dutch who outlaw the stuff in their own country) has been sent from South Africa to Botswana for spraying on the Okavango Delta to kill off tsetse fly. The West Germans managed to sell Botswana quantities of endosulphan - a broad spectrum killer banned in West Germany - for the same purposes. The manufacturers told the media that endosulphan was so specific, if applied in the right doses, that it would not harm a housefly. In the event it did not do much harm to the tsetse fly either. But it contaminated the whole web of life in this once pristine region.

Tsetse fly

The trouble with chemicals is that their effects are sometimes so insidious they become apparent only after it is too late. And the chemical industry and the big agribiz concerns which use chemicals on a large scale, are so powerful that they can quickly mobilise their public relations people and, if necessary, their lawyers, and overwhelm or intimidate those who protest.

The chemical industry is fortunate that the Government of South Africa does not lay down standards regarding water quality in so far as chemical contamination is concerned and that very little testing for residuality is done. The day will come however, when a more concerned public will demand a more sensible attitude towards water standards and then the chemical industry may have to do some rethinking.

Kirkpatrick Sale in his landmark environmental book, *Human Scale,* (1980), said:

The average American ate 2 lbs of chemical additives in food in 1960 and 10 lb in 1978. Most of these additives were put there not to preserve shelf life and retard spoilage, as it is usually claimed; more than 90 percent of the additives (both by weight and by value) were there to deceive – that is, to make agribiz produce look, taste, feel and nourish more than the real thing.

Fertilisers – getting more from less

Monocultures, apart from causing pest populations to explode, also tend to suck from the soil specific nutrients which then have to be replaced artificially by applying chemical fertilisers. Just as the need for pesticides encouraged a big and aggressive industry so did the need for artificial fertilisers. And here again, the marketing side has sometimes been guilty of overkill. The world has been using more and more fertiliser to produce the same yield. According to Kirkpatrick Sale, in 1940, for a given area, the US used 11 tons; 30 years later it was using 57 tons, and by 1975 it was using 95 tons – all to produce the same amount of food. Nowadays there are signs that it is using much less – and still obtaining good yields.

Plants cannot distinguish between natural and artificial fertilisers. But fertilisers themselves are not enough to sustain crops. In the old days – around mid-century in Britain – farmers still practised crop rotation on a wide scale. Pests were less of a problem (because they had no time to build up) and fertilisers were not so necessary. When my family moved up from London to the Staffordshire/Warwickshire border at the outset of World War II, we children revelled in the sight and smell of the freshly ploughed field at the bottom of our garden. The plough was drawn by two huge shire horses (great fertiliser manufacturers in themselves!) and the farmer would plant potatoes one year, wheat the next and clover, lupins and grass the third. He would then graze cattle. Thus the leguminous plants would replace the soil's nitrogen and feed the cattle. And the cattle, of course, would produce dung which would also replenish the nitrogen. The cattle pads plus ploughing in the grass ready for next season's crop improved the soil's tilth or structure.

Along came agribiz, as opposed to agriculture. The banks, for instance, moved into farming. The fact that nature cannot guarantee to produce 4 per cent growth per annum did not concern big business. It could boost yields artificially and, at the first sign of soil exhaustion, it could cut out in that area and cut in somewhere else. Agribiz was able to grow maize year after year pumping in nitrogen to replenish that which was being used up by the cereal. The roots provided a snug home for all sorts of organisms that thrived on maize – so agribiz began to spray poisons. But "chemical farming" is unsustainable. The soils get lighter and lighter and thus more and more erodable.

If a crop in South Africa fails the farmer can go off to what is ironically called the Land Bank, and obtain financial relief. South Africa's agricultural debt in 1990 reached R14 billion.

What is happening in Iowa, in America's corn belt, is an indication of what is likely to happen in South Africa. In 1989 farmers reduced their applications of fertilisers by 8 per cent. In 1990 it was expected to drop by at least another 2 per cent and maybe even 10 per cent. Yet crop yields remained the same. *The Wall Street Journal* (30 May 1990) reported that farmers' views started to shift after surveys began showing widespread contamination of water. Iowa City health authorities warned mothers not to use town water for baby formulas. In 1987 Iowa had applied a tax on nitrogen fertiliser, after finding residues in borehole water. The state also now makes farmers pass a test to prove they know how to apply chemicals safely.

Three out of four Iowa farmers said they had come to realise they had been using too much fertiliser, insecticide and weedkiller and they were becoming concerned about their own safety in applying chemicals. One farmer, Ron Dumphy, using a kit devised by Iowa State University, tested his own soil – normally the chemical firms would do this for the farmers and then advise them on what they need – and found he needed only half the usual amount of fertiliser. He still won the local maize yield contest. University of Nebraska researchers believe the US could cut fertiliser use by 10 per cent without experiencing a drop in production.

Sorghum

More and more farmers in America are switching from maize to soybeans or alfafa (nitrogen-producing legumes) and then back to maize. The switch to legumes not only fixes nitrogen in the soil but it starves out any maize pests that might be building up.

16 Variety, the spice of life

> The continent ages quickly once we come.
>
> Ernest Hemingway.

THE road to Draghoender from Prieska is a long road, especially when the sun is high and white and you are in a badly sprung pony cart and grinding the fine red dust between your teeth. And even more so when you are sharing the road with a plodding herd of migrating springbok.

The herd that T B Davie saw in 1896 was said to be strung out "over 138 miles and, in places, was 15 miles wide". One suspects "the 138 miles" (220 kilometres) only because it is a little too precise under the circumstances but there can be no doubt that these sporadic treks by millions of springbok did extend over considerable distances as the animals tripped along like sheep. As Davie drove his cart among them they moved aside, displaying resignation rather than fear.

They had trekked for days in an almost lemming-like way. They passed down the streets of dorps where the locals, to save bullets, clubbed them with rifle butts and sticks. Everywhere the middens of skins and skeletons grew and trees were festooned with biltong. The buck carried in their midst stray sheep and goats, and even cattle and bontebok. And when they reached a fence the buck in the front ranks were forced through by the weight of those behind and in this way thousands of *trekbokke*, entangled in fences, were cut to pieces by the sharp little hooves of the masses. When they came to dongas, and the front ranks tried to turn, the unstoppable tide of brown antelope pushed them in until their bodies filled the gullies and the herd, like an ant swarm, was able to pass over them. Nobody has ever satisfactorily explained where they were going or what was their fate but it is generally assumed overpopulation and grazing pressure triggered the migrations and that they were going to their deaths in the dry desert of the west.

Those who saw the 1896 springbok migration were witnessing the end of an era, for the buck never massed again. The once uncluttered landscape became criss-crossed with fences and the divided herds became easy meat. The worldwide, nineteenth century overkill which annihilated the bison of the Great Plains of America, the saiga antelope of the Steppes, and the great tuskers of Africa, also resulted in the disappearance of the springbok from many localities.

The century that began with South Africa's golden hinterland packed with 30 species of antelope, fat herds of quagga and zebra, herds of giraffe as many as 50 strong, grey convoys of elephants; the century that began with the booming of the male ostriches and the roar of the big yellow Cape lion, ended with desultory rifle fire. Man had picked the great plains clean.

South Africa is an extraordinary country with an extraordinary variety of creatures, nurtured on a landscape so singularly lacking in fertile flood plains that it has broken the spirit and the hearts of countless farmers who never really got to understanding it. Yet, despite the impoverished soils, the decomposed granite and the ancient aeolian sands of the sun-baked plateau, nature had worked out an understanding: come drought or times of great rains, the vast grasslands carried the optimal number of animals. Twentieth century man has been cruelly robbed of those great spectacles but it is possible that twenty-first century man will recreate them. Already there may be more wild animals in South Africa now, at the end of the twentieth century, than there were at the beginning.

The big five and others

My wife and I were staying in a house at Trafalgar Beach on Natal's South Coast one winter and I was watching a pair of tambourine doves on the lawn. As I watched through binoculars, a pair of red duiker stepped into my line of vision from the strip of forest which covers the dunes along Trafalgar Beach. I raised my binoculars above the forest canopy to the surf: there I saw a pod of dolphins showing off in the rollers. Beyond them I saw the spouting of southern right whales. It was a little demonstration of the unique South African experience and of its power to evoke a state of speechless wonder. In 1990 I had another demonstration of this incredible variety when I attended the tenth anniversary of Sabi Sabi private game reserve. In the space of 24 hours I saw "the big five" – elephant, rhino, buffalo, lion and leopard.

Austin Roberts, cataloguer of South Africa's treasury of wildlife, listed more than 400 kinds of mammals. But he was inclined to be a rather pedantic "splitter", making half a dozen subspecies where other taxonomists might only recognise one or two. Nevertheless South Africa's variety of mammals (279 species at least) – is greater than North and South America combined and far greater than Eurasia.

The biggest . . .

South Africa, with 1 per cent of the world's land surface, has 10 per cent of its bird and plant species and much more than that of its large mammal species. It has the world's largest land mammal (the African elephant), the world's tallest (giraffe), the world's fastest (cheetah), the world's smallest (the shrew – several kinds including one whose body is the size of a fingertip); it has the biggest reptile (the leatherback turtle); it has the world's largest antelope (eland). It has seven kinds of cat – the lion, leopard, cheetah, caracal (lynx), serval, African wild cat and black-footed (or small-spotted) cat. In dog-like species it has the Cape hunting dog, various jackals, foxes and hyenas, including the rare brown hyena.

The smallest . . .

Its birdlife is no less extraordinary: when Carl Linnaeus was describing the kingfisher of Europe there were 10 waiting to be described by science in South Africa. While in Europe they talk of "the swallow", here we have more than a dozen. While in Europe or America most people never see an eagle, here we have several species. It is the same with herons (10 species), storks (9), pigeons and doves (14), cuckoos (12), owls (12) . . . an almost tedious variety amounting to nearly 900 species and including the world's biggest bird, the ostrich, which betrays not a wince when it lays its eggs standing up and watches them clatter on to the pile already laid. South Africa possesses the world's largest flying bird too, the kori bustard, or gompou, which weighs up to 19,5 kilograms.

Butterflies too – South Africa has more than 800 species.

The fastest . . .

The coast teems with marine life. Annually several new species of fish are brought to the J L B Smith Institute of Ichthyology in Grahamstown for classification. South Africa has 2 200 species of fish around its coast, as well as 28 kinds of dolphins and small whales such as the beaked whales, and eight of the giant baleen whales including the biggest animal that has ever lived, the 100 ton blue whale.

The tallest . . .

Endangered wildlife

Sadly, so many animals are today on the list of endangered species and even those we perceive to be common are not really so: I doubt there are more than 2 300 lions running wild in South Africa or more than 600 cheetah. Brown hyena number around 400 – about the same as the Cape hunting dog. Even the giraffe is more conspicuous than numerous, numbering between 4 000 or 5 000. Elephant fluctuate around 8 500 but have to be regularly culled in Kruger Park where 8 000 of them live.

But, in recent years, there has been much good news. The black rhino, reduced in Africa from 70 000 to fewer than 3 500 in a few years, numbers 385 in Natal and 160 in Kruger Park. Kruger, where the black rhino had been extinct since the 1930s, had received 60 rhino from Natal in the 1960s and 1970s. Potentially the park can accommodate 3 500 black rhino – as many as exist on Earth. Pilanesberg National Park in Bophuthatswana has 42 (from 28 donated by Natal) and aims at having 120, and there are two dozen scattered in other reserves. The white rhino (actually there is no colour difference; the "white" comes from Dutch "weid" and refers to its wide mouth), down to between 40 and 60 early this century (all in Natal) now numbers 2 500 in South Africa and maybe 1 500 in the rest of Southern Africa – again, entirely due to donations and sales from Natal Parks Board, whose rhino management programme became a model for Africa.

One of the most remarkable recoveries was that of the black wildebeest, the prancing gnu with a blond mane which came so perilously near extinction in mid-century through overhunting and which now numbers many thousands.

The only known extinctions in Africa have been in South Africa, the blue buck being the most notable one. This buck (*Hippotragus leucophaea*), a close relative of the sable, disappeared early in the nineteenth century from its habitat in the southern Cape. Only four very poorly mounted specimens of this animal exist – in the museums of Paris, Leyden, Stockholm and Vienna. The only souvenir of this strange buck in South Africa is a pair of horns (very similar to a roan's) in the Albany Museum, Grahamstown. The blue buck was said to be a "velvet blue in life" – the colour dulled after death. Another extinction was the quagga (*Equus quagga*) whose Hottentot name, *kwagga*, was an imitation of its call. The last one died on 12 August 1883 in the Royal Zoological Gardens in Amsterdam and is now in the museum there. It is a good specimen – the only one in existence. The South African Museum in Cape Town has a mounted specimen of a very young quagga calf. Some authorities believe the quagga might have been a southern

Black wildebeest

Blue buck

race of Burchell's zebra (*Equus burchellii*) and attempts are being made to "breed it back" by crossing individual Burchell's zebras which most closely resemble the quagga, an animal which bore stripes only on the mantle. The third extinction was that of the Cape lion. Only one good museum specimen exists – in the British Museum. This particular specimen was shot in the 1830s near Colesberg. Its body length appears to have been longer than the existing lion and the animal had a fuller mane and a yellower coat.

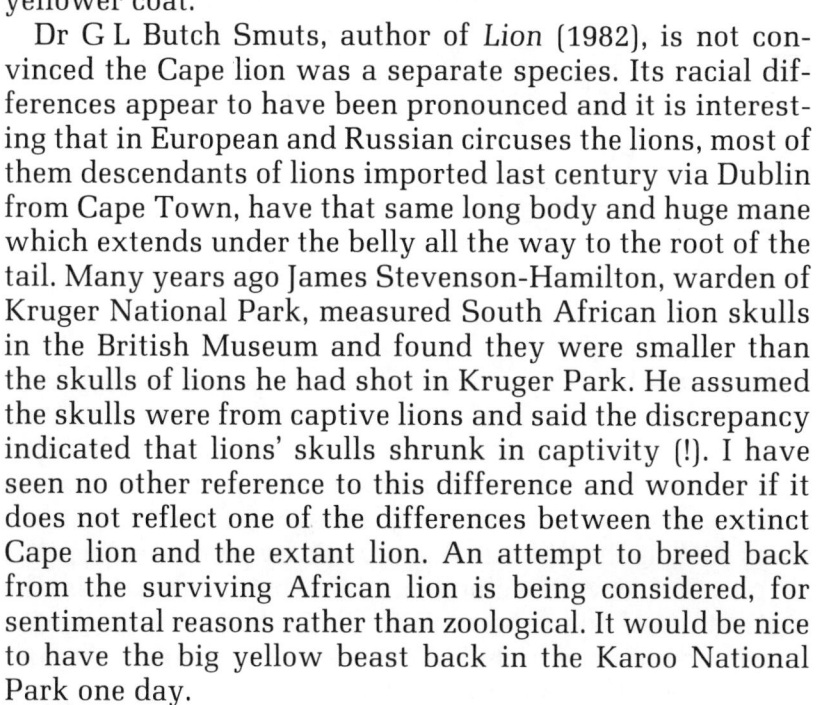

Quagga

Dr G L Butch Smuts, author of *Lion* (1982), is not convinced the Cape lion was a separate species. Its racial differences appear to have been pronounced and it is interesting that in European and Russian circuses the lions, most of them descendants of lions imported last century via Dublin from Cape Town, have that same long body and huge mane which extends under the belly all the way to the root of the tail. Many years ago James Stevenson-Hamilton, warden of Kruger National Park, measured South African lion skulls in the British Museum and found they were smaller than the skulls of lions he had shot in Kruger Park. He assumed the skulls were from captive lions and said the discrepancy indicated that lions' skulls shrunk in captivity (!). I have seen no other reference to this difference and wonder if it does not reflect one of the differences between the extinct Cape lion and the extant lion. An attempt to breed back from the surviving African lion is being considered, for sentimental reasons rather than zoological. It would be nice to have the big yellow beast back in the Karoo National Park one day.

State lottery

At present all major species of animals in South Africa, despite culling and an increase in hunting, are on the increase. This is because of the increase in the numbers of game farms and even national parks in the last 10 years. Tourism and hunting are both lucrative industries and, of South Africa's annual 1 million or so visitors, most are drawn here by the country's wildlife. South Africans themselves are keen on nature and to get on to one of the hiking trails in national parks, such as the Otter Trail along the Cape coast or one of the Kruger Park trails, is a form of state lottery – one has to book a year ahead just to get one's name into a hat. If you are chosen you pay in full – a year in advance.

There are several other trails, some with overnight huts, run by the Directorate of Forestry, by provincial nature conservation departments, by non-government organisations such as the Wildlife Society and by private enterprise. A pleasant new development in urban planning is the institution of suburban trails along formerly neglected stream courses which have now been cleaned up and landscaped. This hierarchy of natural areas – from suburban river trails to national parks – is important. Taking the Transvaal as an example, the suburban river trails around Greater Johannesburg act as filters protecting the next category of natural area – the out-of-town beauty spots, such as Hartbeespoort, from being overwhelmed by people seeking somewhere to picnic or walk. Hartbeespoort Dam, a delightful resort area, by providing a variety of picnic areas for people who like to enjoy the outdoors with lots of people around them, filters the masses from the adjacent Magaliesberg mountains whose trails are few and fragile. The resort areas along the Magaliesberg, in the Waterberg, or at Loskop and the Suikerbosrand, fulfil the recreational needs of thousands who might otherwise seek out and overwhelm Kruger Park or the Zululand and Natal reserves.

South Africa now has 17 national parks, most of which are really too small to deserve the title. The only two large parks are the Kruger National Park (almost 20 000 square kilometres) and the Kalahari Gemsbok National Park which is roughly half the size. There is a new park in the Karoo which, in years to come, will probably be expanded and an unusual and beautiful new national park at Saldanah Bay noted for its great variety of coastal bird species and expansive arid landscapes which, in spring, become a brilliant sea of flowers. Another new park, not yet proclaimed, is the Richtersveld, a wild region of bizarre rock formations and hot little valleys just south of the Orange River's giant meander before it reaches the Atlantic.

Following a heated public reaction in 1979 over news that Iscor, the iron and steel corporation, had been allowed to prospect for coking coal in Kruger Park in violation of the National Parks Act the Government amended the Act. Iscor had already deemed it prudent to withdraw. Although, under the new Act, all the old parks, such as Kruger, remained inviolate (they cannot be mined or even explored for minerals), all new parks are open for mineral

Pelicans at St Lucia

exploitation. In the strict international sense of the term "national parks" the new parks cannot be considered as such because they are not inviolate. But neither are America's or Britain's.

Only 2 per cent of South Africa is set aside as national parks protected by the National Parks Act. A similar amount is set aside as provincial and municipal reserves including reserves in the independent homelands. Provincially and municipally run game reserves can be deproclaimed almost at will but it would need a two-thirds majority in Parliament to deproclaim a national park.

The South African public in the last 20 years has become very defensive of its parks and 10 years after Iscor's ill-fated attempt to mine coking coal in Kruger Park's Pafuri area (right up in the scenic north) a similar move by Richards Bay Minerals to mine titanium in the hills next to St Lucia Game Reserve met with an even bigger public petition – 15 times bigger. But, because this beautiful estuary is a provincial reserve (under the Natal Provincial Administration), its fate remains in the balance.

Another emotional but unignorable outburst, this time by "animal lovers" more than conservationists, followed news that the Minister of Environment had given a Taiwanese businessman permission to club to death 30 500 west coast seals. All the businessman wanted was the testicles of the bulls which he intended drying and selling as an aphrodisiac in the East. That would have constituted, in Western eyes at least, a bizarre and frivolous waste of animal life. He later agreed to use the whole carcass and this, said the Minister, was why the deal had been agreed to. But there seemed no guarantee that he would not in fact throw the carcass away. Many in the conservation lobby backed the idea of seal harvesting, in principle, on the grounds that conservation is the wise use of natural resources. It was interesting analysing why so many people were horrified at the thought of seal clubbing even though it was far more humane than the methods used in slaughtering farm animals which are trucked great distances to line up at some abattoir. Why do people not campaign about cruelty to pigs? Nobel laureate Konrad Lorens had the answer in 1943. He produced a paper which suggested that large eyes (relative to the area of face), a shortened protruding forehead, coupled with large head size relative to body size;

short, thick extremities; a rounded body with soft, elastic surfaces, and round protruding cheeks evoked in adults an emotional "nurturing response". Indeed wildlife campaigners have found it easier to "save" the big, hairy and cuddly than to save something like the Cape vulture or molesnake.

There was a noticeable shift in attitude by the wildlife lobby in 1990 where the more intelligently interested public began to realise that wildlife conservation, on its own, was a non-starter in the "new South Africa". Many were severely embarrassed when it appeared (erroneously) that a campaign to save the black rhino had netted R4,2 million. It seemed so obscene when one realised there were destitute families living in the veld with no roof over their heads.

Fortunately the Wildlife Society had, for some years, involved black people in conservation science and awareness – in fact it had a couple of very learned black lecturers in the field. But the conservation lobby in general was only just awakening to the fact that wildlife reserves might be anomalous in the new order of things. They were beginning to realise they had better demonstrate to rural black people that game reserves were beneficial not only to the mainly white tourist, some of whom brought in foreign exchange, but to people living around the game reserve fence. In truth these neighbours had been almost calculatedly overlooked in the past. A Kruger Park official had spelt it out at an Endangered Wildlife Trust symposium in Sandton in 1988 when he said the park owed nothing to the people over the fence and that it did not have to apologise to anybody for the way it was conserving wildlife. He was right and wrong at the same time. Natal and Bophuthatswana had recognised the need to directly involve the neighbouring villagers and ensure they benefited directly from any game reserve in that they received meat after a cull, and were able to get thatch and wood. Some reserves now establish woodlots around the perimeter for fuel. They were also at pains to let the locals know that game reserves and tourism were the best "cash crop" available in the drought prone bushveld and that they brought further benefits by providing jobs and by providing a market for local businesses and services.

At about this time, South Africa's independent neighbours

were emerging from a long period of non-development under Marxism and were beginning to realise that if they could only rebuild their game reserve camps and rebuild their wildlife populations they could begin attracting much needed tourist dollars, marks, pounds and yen. Despite the 20 year trough in Africa's economy nowhere were the big national parks deproclaimed. Indeed many black rangers lost their lives defending the reserves.

Jenny Macgregor, researcher at the Africa Institute, writing in the institute's journal *African Insight*, mentioned how conservation was often assumed to be a "modern" concept introduced to Africa by expatriate experts and (here she quotes John McCracken) "unrelated to the perspectives of African producers who were believed to be interested only in the short term exploitation of natural resources." Macgregor says:

> *In fact many precolonial communities for whom the hunting and gathering of wild products was a traditional way of life, had developed institutions, often religious in character, designed to enforce restraint in their handling of the environment. In order to ensure their own survival and that of the soils, plants and creatures which they needed in order to live and which formed a basic part of their rural existence, these people developed a deep awareness of these products and their interrelationships and ecology. The African elephant has been hunted by the men of Africa – but only to fulfil their needs ... In some cultures the elephant was venerated as a mythical character and hunting was conducted according to strict tribal customs.*

This inborn understanding of nature which still exists in millions of people is something we discussed in Chapter One. Sabi Sabi, a large private game reserve on the edge of Kruger Park, used to send groups of tourists out with a white game ranger and a black tracker, the latter sitting at the front of the Landrover pointing out spoor and using a well-trained eye to spot game. The directors soon realised that the trackers' knowledge of the bush was of enormous fascination to visitors and was more than complementary to the more scientific and technical knowledge of the game rangers. In the mid-1980s Sabi Sabi began promoting trackers (those who could speak English) to the rank of rangers. One of them became deputy chief ranger. The practice is now widespread in South Africa.

In November 1990, Stan Sangweni of the ANC delivered an "ANC discussion paper on an Environmental Policy for a new South Africa" at the University of the Witwatersrand and he devoted some time to wildlife. He attached importance to the "heritage" argument as a reason to conserve wildlife. This surprised some of the whites at the conference who perceived that black people had "no soul" when it came to wildlife and that they saw buck as merely edibles.

According to some rather arbitrary rule of thumb the World Conservation Union (IUCN) recommended that a country should strive to have 10 per cent of its land set aside as inviolate national parks. The 10 per cent is not really practicable in most developed countries. Britain claims 40 per cent of its area is covered by national parks but their national parks are often developed (ploughed, paved, built upon) to such an extent that South Africa might legitimately claim the entire Karoo as a national park. In the United States, national parks are, relative to the size of the USA, very small. They cover only 3 per cent in the lower 48 states and have been allowed to become so overcrowded and overdeveloped from the point of view of camp sites and tourist facilities that some are more like resorts. It is probably too late for South Africa to achieve the IUCN's 10 per cent, but what the country has is of exceptionally high quality, perhaps the highest quality in the world from the points of view of accessibility, tourist facilities and variety. Kruger Park is the size of Wales but never has more than 8 000 visitors. And I have no doubt that as tourism increases and South Africans become more educated and, therefore, more interested in their own country's natural history, so more natural areas will be conserved and marginal farming areas returned to nature and restocked with wildlife.

Mike Cohen of the Department of Environment Affairs points out that the World Conservation Union's recommendation that all countries conserve at least 10 per cent of their territory, has a scientific base. It is theorised that if 10 per cent of an ecosystem is protected then approximately 50 per cent of the species in that ecosystem will ultimately survive. He has a better idea:

> *I believe that we will have achieved adequate conservation when 100 percent of South Africa is under some form of conservation management. I am not pleading for a large nature reserve, but for a system where all development will be based on sound conservation principles.*

Dr Cohen says that for too long South Africa has been viewing conservation as an isolated issue and that people believe conservation is simply a matter of fencing something off. A country has reached maturity, he says, when nature conservation is taken for granted because people realise that their future depends on the health, viability and diversity of the natural veld.

> *One way of visualising the variety of protected areas is to see them on a spectrum, one end of which comprises wild resources that are maintained undisturbed. Here the main function is the maintenance of ecological diversity and representative ecosystems free from human interference. Protection is fairly strict. These areas should range from wilderness in the true sense through national parks, provincial nature reserves to areas where all the resources can be used on a sustained basis. At the other end of the spectrum we should have scenic highways, nature parks on the outskirts of cities, urban parks and green belts within the urban complex providing vital movement routes for some wild species as well as abatement of air and visual pollution. They offer recreation to the public and protect some natural amenity.*

Mike Cohen's office in Pretoria runs the South African Natural Heritage Programme which encourages land owners on whose land there are places of conservation significance – let's say a habitat on which some endangered

Variety, the spice of life

"... we will have achieved adequate conservation when 100 per cent of South Africa is under some form of conservation management."

species is found, or, perhaps, a fine piece of native woodland – to apply for it to be listed as a Natural Heritage Area. The French-based switchgear company, Telemechanique of Midrand, backs the programme by annually awarding cash sums to any such areas in need of financial assistance. One farmer, for example, notified Mike Cohen of a cave containing two very rare species of bat, but the man was too poor even to drive to town to discuss it. He said his cows often entered the cave and disturbed the bats. Telemechanique financed a fence around the site. So far about 150 sites have been identified but eventually it is hoped many hundreds more, in rural and in urban areas, will be preserved thus forming chains of protected areas along which animals and plants can migrate.

A problem the Department of Environment would like to solve is the way an urban region, such as the Witwatersrand, forms a impenetrable barrier to many animals which, under natural conditions, would move across. The Witwatersrand with its long line of mine dumps and dense line of towns and cities forms a huge barrier between the Magaliesberg range to the north and the Suikerbosrand and Klipriviersberg ranges to the south. Cohen is currently working on an idea he calls "patch parks" in which he envisages incorporating municipal bird sanctuaries, derelict land maybe, and even ecologically viable private gardens eventually forming natural stepping stones for birds and mammals to move across.

National parks

Some claim that KwaZulu had the first "national park" in the world. Shaka, in the 1820s, established an area on the confluence of the Black and the White Umfolozi rivers as a reserve which could be hunted only every five years when his impis were allowed in to kill what they liked. It was a crude form of wildlife management. The laws were tough: poachers would have their skulls crushed with a single blow of a knobkerrie. I suspect there were earlier "reserves" of this nature, especially in the Far East.

It was President Paul Kruger, the puritanical leader of the Transvaal Republic, who founded the first formal national park. This was the Pongola Game Reserve east of Piet Retief in 1894. It was deproclaimed at the insistence of farmers in 1921 and it took them five short years to shoot out the game and wreck the land. Kruger fought for two years to have the *Raadsaal* proclaim the Sabie Game Reserve on the Sabie River in 1898. Kruger's move was quite out of keeping with the times and the thought of protecting wild animals from hunting must have puzzled many. Hunting was considered a noble sport and Victorian aristocrats and Boers alike revelled in it.

The hunting urge in the white man was quite strange. It was as if, because Europe was largely sterilised by mid-nineteenth century, the European was working off some pent up inner frustration. Captain William Cornwallis Harris spoke of wild animals as "the enemy" and in the 1830s, mainly in the central Transvaal, poured quantities of lead into the flanks of anything he saw. In an eight-month hunting trip he took 18 000 slugs and carried extra ingots of lead in case he ran out. Thirty years later (1860) Prince Alfred, 16-year-old son of Queen Victoria, took part in what must have been the most shameful hunt in South African history. On the farm Bainsvlei west of Bloemfontein the local people had spent weeks driving game from all around until it was herded on to the farm. The Prince rode with two riders loading for him. He and other mounted hunters blasted away from point blank range until they were soaked in blood. The women, watching from the stoep, are said to have been thrilled by it all. Even a hit counted as a "good show". Countless animals died and even more limped off to die later on.

Kruger National Park, more or less in its present shape, was formalised in 1926. It is today almost 20 000 square kilometres in extent, making it one of the largest reserves in the world. It is entirely fenced. At some future date it is expected that Mozambique, which abuts Kruger's eastern flank, will proclaim a reserve of similar size. Talks between the two countries concerned began in earnest in the late 1980s. Another forthcoming move will be to take down the veterinary fence which divides Kruger from the large privately owned neighbouring reserves on its western flank. Thus Kruger Park could become part of a 50 000 square kilometre reserve – the biggest in the world. It will make wildlife management far easier.

Although Kruger Park is safe from deproclamation, various administrations have left their mark upon it: it has an airport inside its boundaries, though the warden,

Salomon Joubert, has reduced the number of aircraft movements. Kruger Park's main camps have tended to become larger and less rustic, and less personal too. Skukuza, "the capital" of Kruger Park, is now a sprawling well-lit complex which, fortunately, is right on the edge of the park. On the other hand there has to be some trade-off if more tourists are to be admitted and, after all, Kruger is a vital part of South Africa's tourist package. The park's policy is to allow no more than 4 000 to sleep overnight in huts and bungalows and 4 000 to sleep in caravans and tents. The administration is now going for additional smaller, unfenced camps hidden deep in the bush and has encouraged private individuals and companies to finance them, the deal being that for 10 months of the year the public can book them.

The park has developed conference centres – three so far – with luxurious accommodation. One wonders whether such centres are appropriate in national parks. Kruger's newest camp, Narina, on the banks of the Lower Sabie, is specifically for conferences, which means business people, who are not there to enjoy wildlife, will take up valuable accommodation. This type of facility should surely be left to private enterprise in the reserves abutting Kruger.

In 1931 the Kalahari Gemsbok National Park (9 500 square kilometres) in the northern Cape was proclaimed along with Addo Elephant National Park and the Bontebok National Park. The Kalahari, whose undulating arid landscape supports herds of gemsbok, thousands of springbok and large predators, abuts an even larger game reserve on the other side of the Nossob River, in Botswana. It is one of the world's growing number of "binational parks" – or "peace parks" as Jim Thorsell of the IUCN calls them. Its roads, which mainly follow the river beds, are soon to be fully tarred to keep the dust down, something which many purists will find difficult to accept.

Tsitsikamma Coastal National Park comprises a strip of land 75 kilometres long and extending 800 metres out to sea along the most exciting shoreline in South Africa. It incorporates the Otter Trail, a five-day hiking trail which hugs the rocky coastline as well as passing through lush coastal forest and through fynbos on the top of cliffs.

The "homelands" – those tribal regions which have opted for a form of political independence from South Africa –

claim national park status for some of their reserves. According to most criteria they deserve this status. In fact the third largest national park belongs to one of the homelands – Kangwane National Park – which occupies 60 square kilometres on the Swaziland border.

Bophuthatswana has the fourth largest national park – Pilanesberg National Park (55 square kilometres) which, being only two hours from Johannesburg, is extremely popular. In 1980 the circular park, nestling in the worn-down stump of a volcano, comprised mostly exhausted farmland where a few duiker and smaller mammals survived. The local people were moved outside the encircling mountains and wildlife was re-introduced. Now Pilanesberg has almost everything except lions. Pilanesberg National Park pioneered a number of ideas which are now becoming standard in national parks and reserves. It was established by private enterprise, via the SA Nature Foundation, which poured millions of rands (donated mostly by big South African companies) into the reserve as a goodwill gesture to the then new Bophuthatswana nation. The SANF has done an enormous amount towards establishing new reserves and expanding existing reserves right up to the Zambezi Basin. The government of Bophuthatswana, committed to proving to the people it had moved from Pilanesberg that they had a tangible stake in the park (which is mainly enjoyed by white tourists), made a number of bold moves: it introduced big game hunting in one section of the park. The hunting area is out of sight and out of earshot of the main area and serves as a management device in that it lucratively looks after the necessity to cull. One safari of two weeks' duration brings in more money than a whole year's revenue from game-viewing tourists. Mounting the trophies has become a local industry and the meat from the hunt "goes over the fence", at cost price. Meat from hunting and culling now produces more protein than Pilanesberg ever did as a cattle area. The park allows local people to collect thatch grass and has established woodlots for fuel around the perimeter. It has also created maximum job opportunities for locals. Today one sees black families motoring round the park or as passengers in hired combis – an entirely new phenomenon.

Natal Parks Board, which has about 50 provincially proclaimed reserves, including the world's most famous rhino sanctuary, the Umfolozi-Hluhluwe Game Reserve, was established in 1947. It has, in recent years, handed over some of its reserves to the KwaZulu government whose Natural Resources Board is now under the directorship of Nick Steele, a "white Zulu" who was formerly one of Natal Parks Board's more famous game rangers. Serving under Ian Player, Steele was one of the small team who, in the 1960s, by trial and error, developed a technology for immobilising and then moving rhino to other reserves, even as far up Africa as Kenya. As the white rhino flourished in their new areas the species moved from being in the category of "endangered" to being considered safe.

Natal Parks Board has also opened up a hunting area, a 4 200 hectare thornveld region just outside Mkuzi game reserve. The luxury camp there caters for hunting parties in the winter months and game-viewing tourists in the summer.

Ian Player, with the backing of the Natal Parks Board, founded the wilderness trail movement in South Africa in the 1960s. He inaugurated trails for young people who had shown leadership ability at school. Part of the idea was, and still is, that each child, at one stage in the few days on trail, had to go off alone (a Zulu tracker would be able to find them should they get lost) and sit and contemplate. It was remarkable how many children, black and white, said it was the first time they had ever been truly alone in their lives. They would return before sundown to the companionship and security of the campfire and would be encouraged to relate their thoughts. Many said, long afterwards, that the experience changed their lives. An equally memorable experience for children (and adults who do similar trails) is the couple of hours "watch" they have to do at night. The African night is never still, and neither is one's imagination when staring into the night in the middle of lion country. Player's trails ensured that future leaders were won over to the side of nature conservation and, as they filled the positions of top professionals, company directors and politicians, he calculated they would back the conservation cause. Today, Player – son of a Johannesburg gold miner – is a member of the Natal Parks Board and a world-renowned figure in the international wilderness movement. It was thanks to him that South Africa's first "wilderness area" – in the Umfolozi Valley –

was proclaimed. Player claims that, in the strict sense of the word, Scotland has more true wilderness than South Africa. Wilderness denotes a place where the only signs of people are footprints. A single hut, or even a distant pole, would reduce the status of a wilderness area. By my reckoning South Africa has only one place left where one can get more than 10 kilometres from a road or railway and that is in the northern Cape.

Rocco Knobel, retired director of the National Parks Board said in a speech in 1971:

> We have to accept that our generation is probably the last that will have the opportunity of setting aside any place of superior scenic beauty, spacious refuges for wildlife, or nature reserves of any significant size or grandeur.

Few nations have such splendid opportunities. The growth of international tourism may spur South Africa into creating more reserves. Already marginal farmland in the Lowveld of the Transvaal and Natal is being converted into game farms for hunting or game viewing. The Addo Elephant National Park in the eastern Cape has been doubled in size. KwaZulu, having taken over Ndumu in northern Zululand – a wetland reserve containing 5 per cent of the world's known bird species – has added to it the Tembe National Park, noted for its fine sandveld and elephants. The Karoo National Park is being constantly added to.

But the greatest prize of all is the potential international park which can be formed by joining Kruger Park to a park of similar size next door in Mozambique. This binational park could then become the nucleus of a conglomeration of contiguous national parks and reserves beginning at St Lucia estuary in the South, then north through the reserves of Zululand and Maputo, through Xinave (a huge former safari hunting region east of the Kruger complex), up to Gorongoza, west through the Chimanimani Mountains to Gona re Zhou. Eventually, along the Zambezi and Limpopo valleys, connections can be made to Whange, the Okavango and the desert parks of the south-west.

In September 1990 SARCCUS (Southern African Regional Council for the Conservation and Utilisation of the Soil), a non political body to provide opportunities for co-operation in soil conservation, nature conservation and so on, met in Namibia to discuss the possibilities. South Africa agreed to assist Mozambique in establishing a park down the side of Kruger Park. Surplus animals such as elephant and buffalo which are culled in Kruger Park could, in future, spill over into Mozambique's new park. Southern Africa could end up with the greatest tourist attraction in the world: a region of unparallelled wildlife viewing, prime bird-watching, big game hunting (the only place in Africa where one can hunt the big five), big game fishing, underwater exploring, a colourful cultural diversity, spectacular scenery and long sandy beaches.

Jim Thorsell has been helping countries in Southern Africa make the first moves towards establishing binational parks: South Africa and Botswana have, for some years, been more or less running their respective Kalahari Gemsbok National Parks (both countries have a park by this name) as one. They straddle an international border. Another likely one straddles the Lesotho/South African border. Thorsell is also working on prospective binational parks straddling the borders of the former "Communist Bloc" in Eastern Europe. As in Southern Africa, hostile political relationships have left some beautiful and wild no-man's-land areas along a lot of formerly tense frontiers.

The flora

There is another dimension to South Africa's natural treasury: its plantlife. According to Dr Ledger of the Endangered Wildlife Trust, Southern Africa has 23 200 species of plants of which 18 560 are endemic to the region. This makes it "the richest region in the world in terms of species to area, and 1,7 times richer in these terms than Brazil". The Cape Peninsula, an area the size of the Isle of Wight, has more species than the whole of Great Britain. These are mainly fynbos species - proteas, ericas (heaths) and everlasting daisies.

In a high hollow in the south-west Cape's Hottentots Holland mountains, east of False Bay, one can still see the wagon tracks gouged into the sandstone during the eighteenth and nineteenth centuries by the Dutch, British and French settlers. This is in the Gandoupas, the pass of the eland, which in summer is ablaze with wild flowers. There are 300 varieties of ericas alone - three-fifths of the world total. I wrote in Mountain Odyssey (with David Coulson in 1983):

> In January the mountainsides are delicately tinted with the pink varieties: Erica corifolia, Erica longifolia and Erica savilea, with just a finishing touch of scarlet Erica curviflora here and there. In many places along the 40 km long Hottentots Holland range is South Africa's national flower, the basin-sized king protea – Protea cynaroides – very showy, with its heavy red bloom topped with fluff, and never far away is its nearest rival, Protea magnifica – two of the most spectacular blooms in nature.

Proteas are synonymous with South Africa and of Africa's 120 species a quarter are found in the Hottentots Holland.

Botanists divide the world into six floral kingdoms, of which the Cape Floral Kingdom is by far the tiniest, being only 0,04 per cent of the Earth's land surface. But it is also the richest, with more than 8 500 species of mostly fynbos (literally "fine bush") of which 6 000 are found nowhere else. Many are endangered and one or two, for years considered extinct, have recently cropped up in new areas. It might well be that some are left-overs from a previous mini-ice age and are up against the limits of their habitat requirements.

Further north, in Namaqualand, in what is for most of the year dry mountain scrubland, the spring rains bring a wonderland of flowering plants. These Namaqualand daisies form vast meadows of brilliant yellow, or deep red, or pale blue. Sometimes the landscape appears to be covered in snow, so close are white daisies packed together. Sometimes the landscape looks paint-spattered.

The threats

The biggest threat to South Africa's remaining wild places is ill-considered development. It seems that the public is engaged in a never-ending battle, usually with the Government itself, regarding what parts of South Africa should be held sacrosanct.

Forestry, a normally laudable industry, has been allowed to swamp the character of many once beautiful areas. The eastern Transvaal has been smothered with pines and blue gums to the point that its character has been transformed into that of Canada or Australia. There are almost no areas left which bear witness to the old Jock of the Bushveld country. The Woodbush Forest Reserve, the last big native forest remnant left inland in South Africa, is badly infested by pine and gum and the Government's own pine plantations pack right up against the indigenous trees.

In the 1970s Government foresters planted pine trees in the high dunes of the Eastern Shores of St Lucia. They even planted in the wetlands to dry them out. The pines severely reduced the supply of fresh water which used to continually seep from the dunes to dilute the St Lucia Estuary's incoming seawater. Meanwhile another Government department allowed the destruction of giant sycamore fig trees along the Mkuzi River which fed the top end of Lake St Lucia. Eighteen logjams blocked the river. Another department, this time Water Affairs dammed the Hluhluwe to please a handful of farmers and so interrupted another freshwater source. St Lucia, a tidal estuary, became three times saltier than the sea. Its reed beds died; its once prolific birdlife disappeared; its crocodiles, encrusted with salt, became too buoyant to dive for fish. Tourism slumped. There was nobody in Government who was responsible or who cared. In 1990, although the Mkuzi was by now uncorked and the lake recovered, the dunes came under pressure again, this time from Richards Bay Minerals (50 per cent owned by Britain's Rio Tinto Zinc) which claims that as pines are spoiling the dunes anyway, they might as well be mined for their titanium. The Government's Department of Environment seemed about to agree when a massive wave of public indignation made it think again. The Department then demanded that the mining company carry out an environmental impact analysis. A decision on the fate of St Lucia was then left to the Cabinet.

There are many examples of the Government's and industry's insensitivity when it comes to prime scenic and tourist regions. In the 1960s the Transvaal Rubber Company built a warehouse on top of Howick Falls in Natal; about that time Palaborwa Mining company was allowed to build a copper refinery on the edge of Kruger Park. Today its heavily smoking chimney stack can be seen on the horizon from not only Kruger Park but from Klaserie Game Reserve and many other prime bushveld areas. The plume from this stack sometimes spreads 40 kilometres across the bushveld. The refinery has been a serious

Palaborwa

polluter for years but there are few data on the effects of its fall-out even though it has been known to have killed cattle poisoned by copper-contaminated grass.

Highway engineers have done enormous and usually quite avoidable damage to important scenic areas. The older professional engineers are often totally unable to see why aesthetics should matter as long as the view looks good from the road-user's point of view. When the highway through Du Toits Kloof Pass – the one that leads to South Africa's longest road tunnel – was designed, the environmental impact was ignored up until the last moment. Even then the Department of Transport was not prepared to pay for an environmental impact assessment. The conscience-stricken contractors who wanted an EIA to be done, footed the bill themselves but were threatened with penalties if their studies held up construction.

Part of the problem was that civil engineers, at least until recently, were taught nothing of aesthetics. Their job was to "break the wilderness" and every fresh piece of wild country penetrated by a road was a triumph. A few, such as Eric Hall, city engineer for Johannesburg, rebelled. He earned enormous respect from the public when, for instance, it became necessary to erect a large reservoir on the side of scenic Linksfield Ridge. He insisted on extra funds to hide the reservoir and, what would normally have been an eyesore, is now a pleasant botanical area. Hall was the main architect of the environmental impact assessment clauses in the new environmental legislation. But he was one of only a few. The newer generation of civil engineers are far more aware.

Eskom, over the last decade, has adopted a strict policy regarding aesthetics and will go to considerable expense to design pylon routes which have the least impact. This is a change from the old days: in the 1960s it placed a pylon servitude straight through Kruger Park. Eskom, in the 1970s, was challenged by ornithologists for its policy of shooting Southern Africa's unique Cape vultures, one of the world's rarer birds. The vultures would perch on the cross members of pylons and their excreta would run down the insulators, sometimes causing flash overs which would black out large areas. These huge birds also tended to touch the conductors on take off thus shorting the supply. Even martial eagles were shot because their huge and untidy nests would sometimes leave loose sticks to dangle and, perhaps, touch a conductor and black out a neighbourhood – an event which could cost hundreds of thousands of rands in lost production and other problems. John Ledger, an entomologist who was better known for his interest in ornithology, working through the Vulture Study Group which he helped establish, approached Eskom and explained the ecological importance of vultures and eagles. Eskom appointed a standing committee of mostly engineers and invited Dr Ledger to join it. The engineers redesigned their pylons and retrofitted the old ones with special vulture perches. It worked perfectly. As for the eagle nests, linesmen now carry secateurs for tidying up any loose ends.

The future

Who really needs wildlife? After all there are between 10 and 30 million species of different living organisms in the world, from protozoa to Californian redwoods, from aardvarks to zebras. Science has studied, or at last given identities to only 1,4 million species. So who would really miss a few hundred thousand if they were to disappear? Who really needs the blue whale, or black rhino, or Lake St Lucia?

Brian Huntley in his *Biotic diversity in Southern Africa* (1990) says that although the figures are debatable there is one unarguable fact: "We are currently losing species at least 1 000 times faster than normal evolutionary rates." He believes the situation is becoming critical and says that as many as 100 species a day are being wiped out. Nearly all of them would be unremarkable to look at yet many of them might have more ecological importance than, say, the tiger or rhino. Indeed, even the most phlegmatic person would feel uneasy if he heard that the last wild tiger had died in the wilds – yet tell him that the Madagascan periwinkle had died out and he'd not raise an eyebrow. Yet that diminutive little creeper has yielded two drugs which have revolutionised the treatment of leukaemia. About a third of all medicines have been derived from plants and fungi.

As I have pointed out elsewhere, biodiversity is the essence of this planet's living system. Variety is the spice of life. It also has economic importance: if a certain type of bee or butterfly (butterflies are the second most important pollinators after the bee) were to be extinguished it could take with it many species of plants. Donella Meadows, professor of environmental and policy studies at Dartmouth College, was quoted in the *Los Angeles Times* as saying:

> Biodiversity performs environmental services beyond price. How would you like the job of pollinating all trillion or so apple blossoms in New York State some sunny afternoon in late May? It's conceivable maybe that you could invent a machine to do it, but inconceivable that the machine could work as elegantly as the honey bee, much less make honey on the side.

She makes a useful analogy: if you want to destroy a people so thoroughly that they had no chance of recovering you would burn their libraries and kill their intellectuals. By reducing biodiversity we are doing just that – destroying nature's knowledge which is filed away in the DNA inside living cells. A single plant cell can carry genes capable of producing 400 000 different traits. Meadows says that biologist E O Wilson worked out that the amount of information in a house mouse, if printed out, would fill all 15 editions of Encyclopaedia Britannica published since 1768.

The disappearance of just one organism could begin a chain reaction that could rob man of, perhaps, the secret of prolonged youth – I am not being fanciful – or it could begin a chain of reactions that could lead to the rapid demise of man. A classic example of this chain reaction effect comes from the western Cape, where many farmers believe all snakes are poisonous. Thus they killed off the harmless mole snake. Mole snakes kill by constricting their prey which are mainly rodents. So the rodent population grew and the grain crop suffered. The farmers then used poison to kill the rodents. Seagulls began dying because they were scavenging the dead rodents. Trawlers then began noticing a higher percentage of diseased fish in their catches – because seagulls were no longer picking off the slow, sick fish.

Paul Ehrlich and his wife Anne, in their challenging book *Extinction* (1982), asked readers to imagine walking towards an aircraft on which they are about to travel and seeing a man prizing rivets out of the wing. The man, working for "Growthmania Airways" explains his boss has found that they can get two dollars a rivet. But, you cry, how about the wing? It might fall off! The man reassures you that the manufacturer has probably made the wing very much stronger than was really necessary and that in any case he has removed lots of rivets before and the wing has not fallen off. As a matter of fact, says the man, he is also going to fly in the plane. Mad? Of course. But is it any different to what we are doing in reducing the number of species on whose existence and variety the planet's living system depends? Huntley points out that the rivet poppers are depleting the earth's rivets – its different species – at the rate of 100 a day. The extinction rate far exceeds that of 65 million years ago when some cataclysm – perhaps a meteorite striking the Earth – wiped out the dinosaurs which had ruled the world for 120 million years. (Man has been around a mere 2 million years and already he may be in trouble.)

Only the economics of tourism will ensure the survival of places such as Kruger Park. In 1989 tourism earned R4 000 million, of which almost half was in foreign exchange. By about the turn of the century tourism should eclipse the gold industry as South Africa's main money earner.

The ngos (non-governmental organisations) are playing vital roles. The Wilderness Leadership Foundation, founded in South Africa by Ian Player, has taken hundreds of young people into the bush. So has the most tireless wilderness trail leader of all, Clive Walker, who founded effective non-government organisations such as the Endangered Wildlife Trust and the Wilderness Education Trust. More and more industrialists are now backing wildlife initiatives. In fact, were it not for the Sugar Association which, in the 1960s, gave tens of thousands of rands to Player's wilderness concept, it would have been stillborn. Eskom, AECI, SA Breweries, Sappi, Mondi, the packaging industry – all of which have, in no small measure, contributed to South Africa's environmental problems – have been generous in their support of wildlife projects.

Wildlife conservation has had a lowly status in Government eyes. The official attitude to poaching says a great deal: if a man gets through the fence to kill a buck he is considered to be a criminal and if he used a gun or a vehicle in the exercise both can be confiscated. In fact such people are treated with a harshness that is quite out of place. Yet the Department of Environment is puzzlingly lenient with the big time crooks – mostly Taiwanese – who are involved in the international rhino horn and elephant ivory racket. They have been equally soft on Taiwanese caught illegally fishing off the coast. In fact a poor man caught creeping home at night with a few crayfish for supper can expect a far greater penalty than a man caught with a trawler full of illegally caught fish or a man caught with a crate of rhino horn.

The question of whether it is moral or wise to allow trade in elephant ivory and rhino horn has loomed large in South Africa in recent years, especially as South Africa is a conduit for illegal ivory and horn, collected in Central Africa and Angola, and destined for the Far East. Poachers are prepared to kill and be killed as rangers try to protect Africa's last 600 000 elephants (there were 1,3 million five or six years ago) and 3 000 black rhino. Under the CITES agreement (Convention on International Trade in Endangered Species) international trade in ivory and horn has been stopped. There is some controversy regarding the wisdom of this. South Africa, short of elephant habitat, is compelled to cull elephants. The ivory produced by these operations supported an ivory carving industry and brought R7 million a year for conservation. In Zimbabwe it fetched R12 million. In fact between Zimbabwe's Whange National Park and Botswana's Okavango Delta, 70 000 elephant roam. That is a very big resource to have frozen. Hundreds of rhino horns have also been accumulating as rhino have died or been killed in fights over the years or caches of poached horn have been confiscated. The ban on rhino horn dates back many years but it did nothing to stop the killing. If anything it increased it because, as the horn became more difficult to buy, the price went up. On the other hand the more recent ban on ivory does seem to be working and ivory jewellery has gone out of fashion along with leopard skin coats.

Many governments are now employing shoot-on-sight tactics in confronting poachers in the field. One can hardly blame them. The poachers are armed with rapid firing rifles. What is reprehensible is that despite all this death and destruction, when the big time crooks are caught by the police, the courts fine them a few hundred rands.

The most effective wildlife body on the non-government side in South Africa is unquestionably the South African Nature Foundation, which is affiliated to the World Wide Fund for Nature (WWF) in Switzerland. It was established by Anton Rupert, the tobacco tycoon, in 1968 at the request of Prince Bernhard of the Netherlands who headed the WWF. In 22 years the SANF has raised more than R70 million from big business and this has helped fund 280 conservation projects throughout the Southern African region. It has created five national parks, paid for the expansion of 30 reserves, established three university chairs and many research projects, funded major efforts which have helped save the black rhino, roan antelope, wattled crane, jackass penguin and many more threatened species and, through an old colleague, Rob Soutter, has established an effective and widespread education campaign. The SANF is now headed by John Hanks, a Cambridge man who 20 years ago went out to the Luangwa Valley in Zambia to do research for his doctorate. Under Dr Hanks, a former professor at Natal University and head of the Natural Resources Institute there, the SANF's objectives have been refocused. They now include preserving genetic, species and ecosystem diversity; ensuring the sustainable use of renewable natural resources and fighting wasteful consumption.

Private land owners and ngos are today liaising much more closely with official bodies. Hans Grobler of Natal Parks Board points out that their importance has been underestimated. Writing in *Natal*, newsletter of the Natal Parks Board, (1990), he said:

> *Species such as the bontebok, black wildebeest and the Cape mountain zebra may well have been extinct by now were it not for certain individuals who protected them on their land. There are still more oribi on privately-owned land today than in formally protected areas. It will in fact never be possible for the formal conservation authorities to give effective protection to all wildlife species or areas of nature conservation significance.*

Dr Grobler points out that ngos such as the Wildlife Society are also managing game reserves and that there are now professionally-run non-government reserves, particularly in the Transvaal, large enough to maintain breeding populations of rhino, elephant, buffalo and the big cats. A fifth of South Africa's white rhino are in private reserves.

The farmers of Natal pioneered an interesting and important new idea – nature conservancies: in the Balgowan area in August 1978 private land owners with contiguous farms pooled their efforts and their resources to combat poaching. The Natal Parks Board guided their efforts. Dr Grobler says:

> Subsequently, many other landowners followed their example and today there are over 100 conservancies in Natal with 1 250 individual members covering an area in excess of 850 000 hectares. Conservancy game guards are trained by the Natal Parks Board and now number over 350. Conservancies have also spread to other provinces in South Africa and have been highly successful. There are 16 conservancies in the Free State (one of 300 000 hectares), three in the Transvaal and 14 in the Cape, with additional ones proposed for all four provinces.
>
> Natal Parks Board provides game at a reduced price, free management advice and management plans on request, to conservancies.
>
> What does this mean in real terms to nature conservation? If we can use the Natal example, the conservancies (850 000 hectares), biosphere reserves (24 583), private nature reserves and game farms (c. 50 000) and the Natal Parks Board holdings (627 240) add up to 1 551 823 hectares, which is 28 percent of terrestrial Natal. This does not include the conservation areas of KwaZulu nor some of the Department of Forestry conservation holdings.

Hans Grobler comes to the same conclusion as Mike Cohen of the Department of Environment Affairs: eventually have 100 per cent of the province (and the country) "under some form of conservation for the wise use of our natural resources".

17 Population: The wild card

> It is worth mentioning some of the "wild card" surprises which could dramatically change the course of events in southern Africa... The regional impact of AIDS is an unknown quantity at present. The data base is too small to start writing doomsday scenarios.
>
> Brian Huntley, Roy Siegfried and Clem Sunter, SA Environments into the 21st Century.

WHEN Queen Victoria ascended the throne of England – we are not talking of ancient history here – there were 1 000 million people on Earth. It had taken mankind two million years to attain that figure. But it took only another 100 years to reach a second billion. That, in itself, is alarming enough. But 30 years later (1960) the human population reached its third billion and barely 15 years later it reached 4 billion. It now stands at well over 5 billion. If the world population of any animal of this size had exploded in this fashion mankind would have been unified in a campaign to bomb it out of existence.

But there is another side to the phenomenon of human population growth. In fact there are many sides.

AIDS is very much the wild card. And when Huntley and his associates wrote the lines which head this chapter the data base concerning the disease was indeed small, and the thought that was arising in the minds of demographers was too appalling to articulate. In fact when, towards the end of 1990, I began this chapter, I decided to tack the "AIDS thing" on the end. My mind refused to grasp the potential scale of the pandemic.

But we have to face up to the unavoidable truth: that possibly as many as a quarter of people living in South Africa today may die from AIDS – unless some miracle happens. The simple truth is that there is no cure for AIDS and the disease is growing in Africa as well as in the poverty-stricken urban areas in the Americas, at an inexorable rate. It appears to be decreasing only where the population is educated and where the virus is confined to homosexuals and those who share syringes for drug taking. In Africa AIDS has become a heterosexual disease. That is what makes it the most terrifying disease to hit mankind since the bubonic plague of the Middle Ages.

The only good news in the unfolding tragedy is that AIDS can be avoided by intelligent people. Most of the dead will be those who did not understand, until it was too late, what AIDS was. The Medical Research Council, in a 1990 survey of four black Cape Town schools, discovered that two-thirds did not know AIDS was incurable. Eighty per cent of these cited condoms as being effective but a fifth of them admitted they did not know what a condom was. Significantly, 96,2 per cent of all the children wanted information, preferably on video.

The thin data base to which Huntley *et al* refer has hardened in the year since they wrote their book. Too clearly it is revealing that the number of HIV-infected people is rapidly growing and that beginning around the turn of the century the death rate will, quite suddenly, climb to a few hundred thousand a year. Within two or three years of that happening, South Africa will probably have witnessed the deaths of 10 million people.

Incredibly, at the Population Development Programme conference in Johannesburg in November 1990, neither the State President, who opened it, nor any of the speakers in their formal presentations, even so much as mentioned AIDS. Educators were saying nothing on the issue. According to Malcolm Steinberg of the Medical Research Council: "The education authorities are locked into curricular change, which is very, very slow - and we are running out of time day by day." The SA Broadcasting Corporation steadfastly refused to carry advertisements for condoms, a device that can save millions of lives. These contraceptives would, at the same time, usefully reduce casual conception which is rife in urban areas. Yet it is the contraceptive aspect that puts black men off - making women pregnant is seen as proof of their virility. Even young sexually active black girls are suspicious of condoms. The MRC survey quoted one as saying: "When you use a condom it means you don't like him and you don't trust each other." Many girls felt that they had no say in whether to use a condom.

It is difficult not to read into the current situation a certain feeling of inevitability. I believe that a reason why the international community is not very concerned about AIDS in Africa, and why many South Africans are not really concerned, is that they see it as some sort of natural retribution. For a long time many people have been wondering how nature would reduce soaring human growth. Would it be mass starvation? Would it be a third world war? Who would have thought of a virus, transmitted through sexual intercourse, which seeks out and destroys man's defences against all diseases? Worse, it actually mutates so fast that by the time a vaccine can be developed the virus has changed its shape and so the vaccine would be useless. Here is nature culling humans just as it culls any organism whose growth rate becomes a threat. There is also the thought that the human species has become so weakened by the effects of overpopulation, by homosexuality, by drug abuse and by environmental pollution that, like the seals and dolphins who are suddenly dying by the tens of thousands of a mysterious disease in the polluted northern seas, man too is now succumbing to a natural culling operation.

I believe that, as a result of AIDS, South Africa's population will level out at 50 million people. Most of the dead will be black. The economic and social consequences for South Africa will be enormous and, as economist, Andre Spier, wrote in his manual for decision-makers, *Facing AIDS* (1990), we have to begin planning now for a public health disaster.

There are certain contradictions in the AIDS scenario which I am tempted to cling to in the hope of being able to say that this cruel scenario may not come about. The World Health Organisation, for example, said in 1990 that it expected about 5 million to die, worldwide, around the turn of the century. This would make AIDS one of man's rarer diseases. Diarrhoea is killing almost three times that number even now. But then, reading subsequent WHO reports in which Zimbabwe claims only one or two new AIDS cases and Zaire not much more – it is difficult to base much credence on WHO's projections. (In March 1991, Zimbabwe's new Minister of Health announced there had been a cover-up. He said 27,5 per cent of Zimbabwe's working population was infected by HIV.)

The United Nations Population Fund announced in May 1989 that it expected the world population to settle at 14 billion – an increase of 4 billion on its previous guess. It did not bring AIDS into its accounting. Even with AIDS, which, because of its nature should burn itself out fairly rapidly once the number of fatalities has peaked, the world population will continue to increase, though at a declining rate. It seems likely that the world population will peak at a lower figure than the UN supposes but even if it merely doubles it is a distressing scenario when you take into account that we cannot feed the 5,2 billion we have today. Of the world's present population, 70 per cent live in the largely underfed Third World and that is where the population explosion is taking place. And that is also where AIDS is most rife.

The population explosion

There are, according to the UN Environmental Programme (1990) 1,7 million children under the age of 15 in the world, of which 1,4 million live in the developing world. In other words there is a tremendous reserve of fertility building up. But the picture might not be as grim as it appears. Mostafa Tolba, executive director of UNEP, in the foreword to *Children and the Environment* (1990), says:

> During the 1990s, a larger number of children will be born than in any decade before – or later. As education spreads and living standards improve, human fertility is declining in most of the world's countries. The swelling numbers of children and youth already born will have families of their own, but their increase is projected to cease to balance declining fertility at about the end of this decade. World population will be growing, at slower and slower rates, and barring catastrophe, never again will such a high percentage of that population be children.

To put the current global population of 5 000 million into some sort of perspective: if the entire world population were put into the United States, the population density would be only about 60 per cent higher than in present-day England – and England is hardly overcrowded. Its landscape is still 80 per cent rural. The Earth itself is hardly crowded. The problems crop up with the distribution. The places where populations are growing fastest are, too often, the places where food supplies are running out. The biology of it all is fairly straightforward. Put a population under stress and it will reproduce like mad. A salmon produces millions of eggs to compensate for the millions of eggs and fry that will be snapped up by predators. Birds lay far fewer eggs. An eagle, high in a tree, is confident with laying one or two eggs at a time because its offspring have such an excellent chance of survival. But not all birds can afford to be that confident: the guinea fowl which lays its eggs on the ground where they are vulnerable to jackals, snakes, leguaans, mongooses and other predators, lays a dozen and more. As many as 50 have been found in one nest.

In the same way, human beings tend to breed more when faced with the probability that their offspring will die at an early age. (I wonder, in fact, whether, as a result of the

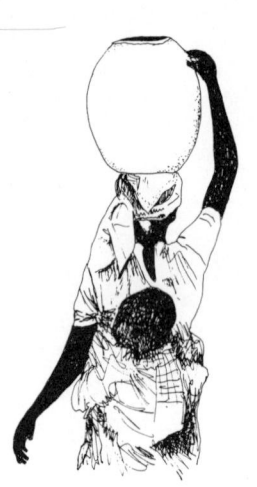

AIDS pandemic, there will not be a compensatory leap in fertility in the post-AIDS world.) In the Third World 14 million children a year die from diarrhoea alone. But United Nations Children's Fund data show that once a community has primary health care, and parents have an assurance that their offspring will reach maturity, they have fewer children: a drop in the child death rate leads to a drop in the birth rate. This is demonstrated in Soweto, an entirely black section of greater Johannesburg whose birth rate, according to a Family Planning Association survey in the early 1980s, was dropping towards that of the white suburbs.

Eleanor Preston White of Natal University, speaking at the International Conference on Population Development in Pretoria in 1988, outlined two other reasons why, with the exception of well-developed urban areas, black couples have large families.

> Most black people in South Africa do not have access to adequate non-family-based social security. Instead, they very wisely, hope to rely on their children's earnings to support them in old age and illness. The more children, furthermore, the more likely it is that at least one will have a job.

The SA Council for Population Development – a private sector initiative – said in a 1990 pamphlet that there would be 8 million unemployed by 2000 and 10 million children under the age of 15 who would be coming on to the jobs market later. It believed that prosperity – an 8 per cent annual economic growth rate – would enable the country to educate and house all its people. It felt that that was the secret to reducing the size of families. The prospects of that sort of economic growth rate seemed very remote indeed. The council suggested that family planning instruction should be part of staff training programmes. Yet it is worth trying even though the cultural block against contraception is widespread in black Africa. Resistance to birth control methods might not be immutable. Preston White mentioned how the Roman Catholic Church has adamantly resisted contraception, yet nowadays practising Catholics in the United States (and in South Africa) have only two children on average. "Anthropologists now believe that culture is potentially extremely flexible," said Preston White.

Source The Star

Mainland China, badly frightened by its own rate of population growth – one-fifth of the world population lives in China – has managed to bring its birth rate tumbling, albeit by using some quite draconian measures. A couple which has a second child in Shanghai (population 12 million) can be fined three times their annual income. In most regions of China the 1990 fines were 10 per cent. Such laws are inhuman and are causing widespread infanticide. But they illustrate how desperate some countries' situations are. Recent surveys in China indicate that women with a tertiary education have an average of just over two babies each while illiterate women average between four and five each. It was also found that rural women with a primary education averaged more than four babies while their urban counterparts had fewer than three.

Africa, as a continent, is the emptiest (discounting Antarctica). Its population is only two-thirds of India's yet it has almost 10 times more land. All the same, a great chunk of Africa is smothered by the Sahara, by the Sahel (which provides a very marginal human habitat), by the Kalahari/ Namib deserts and by the central rain forest. For whatever reasons, much of Africa has poor potential as far as sustaining large numbers of humans is concerned.

In the mid 1960s it seemed that the "green revolution" would save the world. The green revolution came about through the development of some important new hybrid crops including a strain of wheat, for example, that had a short stalk and an enlarged ear, and a vigorous new type of short-stemmed rice. India, a country which had experienced frequent famines, became a net food exporter. But the success of the green revolution depended on irrigation schemes, pumps, fertilisers and pesticides. These usually needed government funding, which masked their true costs, and they also required mechanical skills which, in some regions, did not exist. Many schemes collapsed permanently when pumps broke down and nobody knew how to repair them or parts could not be found. In South Africa, which is somewhere between being a "developed" and a "developing nation" the global trend is reflected: South Africa's annual rate of increase in food production came down from 7 per cent in the 1960s to 3,1 per cent in the 1970s. According to the Institute for Futures Research at Stellenbosch the rate of increase from 1980 to 2000 is likely to be only 2,4 per cent – that means food production is just about keeping pace with population growth. South Africa, including the "independent states", had about 36 million people in 1988 (our censuses have been very unreliable) and will have about 45 million in 2000. Urbanisation will have slowed the birth rate considerably by then and AIDS itself is likely to begin its culling process.

While biotechnology, which is mostly concerned with the manipulation of genes to produce new strains of, say, drought or pest-resistant plants, will continue to help feed the world, its advances have not been as dramatic as some scientists hoped. Genetic engineering seemed to hold far more promise 20 years ago, when we knew little about it, than it does today. In fact the grasses (which include cereals) are particularly difficult when it comes to gene manipulation and many scientists who, 20 years ago, spoke of turning deserts into wheatfields, were biotechnologists rather than botanists. Botanists, who had a more holistic view, were, and still are, sceptical about just how far one can manipulate nature. We are doing a little better with animal biotechnology because we are more familiar with animal cells and know much more about them. But, as Paul Ehrlich said, the battle to feed mankind is over. We lost. Certainly science is falling behind.

In a World Bank report (November 1980) it was said that rice, the world's most important staple food, was just keeping pace with population growth. And according to the International Rice Research Institute, each year 80 to 100 million more rice consumers are born. Klaus Lampe, director general of the institute said that by the year 2020, "the earth will have 8 billion people of whom 4,3 billion will be rice consumers. He was doubtful whether the crop could keep up, especially as the high-yielding green revolution varieties had peaked in 1985 and irrigation was falling from favour.

In South Africa, as in the rest of the world, biotechnology is slowing down as universities run short of public funds. The Government is keen for private enterprise to take over the funding of research establishments and, of course, private enterprise, in doing so, is understandably setting research priorities which are biased towards applied research projects with a promise of quick returns. Academic research is grinding to a halt. This is tragic because it is mostly serendipity – chance discoveries in the laboratory or field – which have brought mankind its most useful scientific discoveries.

In a nutshell, with all our agricultural technology and experience the world situation is that farmers are having to feed 88 million more people a year with 24 billion fewer tons of topsoil (Worldwatch Institute, September 1989). In any event, under present circumstances, more food means more people and, at the end of the road the inevitability of empty rice bowls, empty putu pots and death. China, in the eighteenth century, trebled its population after introducing maize and potatoes. The results were tragic. China has experienced since then some of the most terrible famines in history. It will be futile growing more food without a concomitant slowing down of the human birth rate.

A colleague of mine, Ramsay Milne, *The Star*'s New York man, told me the following story of a journey from Calcutta to Bombay on a troop train at the end of the second World War.

We were told we would be fed en route and, when we stopped at the first station we were each handed a packet of army sandwiches. But on the platform were swarms of starving people clawing at the train and pleading for food. We handed our packets through the windows and were horrified to see how they were torn to shreds as desperately hungry people fought for them. At the next station where sandwiches were given to us we separated the layers and handed them out to people. By the third food stop we were ourselves hungry and some men slunk into corners of the carriages to eat, but, knowing there were people an arm's length away starving to death, the men could not swallow. So they gave their sandwiches away again. But as the long journey progressed we had to eat and we began to rationalise, telling ourselves how our meagre rations were not going to solve India's problem.

When Ramsay Milne told me this story in the 1970s the United States was exporting millions of tons of wheat a year to Asia and Africa. A lot of the wheat coming to Africa was "charity wheat" to help starving regions. These regions had high death rates and higher birth rates and the parallel between Milne's sandwiches and the charity wheat was very compelling. Countries can only survive when their population growth is in equilibrium with their environmental income.

Ominously "the world's bread basket" – the North American Prairies – is nowhere near as productive as it used to be. Rising costs of farming and falling crop prices have caused many millions of hectares to be taken out of production. There is also the likelihood that the greenhouse effect will disrupt the present pattern of the world's grain belts.

The urban contraceptive

The world's birth rate is slowing down and a major reason is the gradual urbanisation of the globe. Urbanisation is the most benign and effective method of bringing the human population towards a steady state. The influx of squatters which is throwing South African cities into a mild panic is a good sign rather than a bad sign. It is relieving some of the strain on the rural food-growing areas and it is making it easier to provide the masses with housing and primary health care and, ultimately, jobs. Of the three it is primary health care which is the factor which will do most to reduce population. Primary health care increases children's survival rates, and although this produces a temporary increase in the population growth rate, it quite rapidly reduces it. It is the story of the salmon and the eagle.

This is just as well for South Africa: the UN assesses that each person needs 0,4 hectare of arable land to grow his or her food and in 1990 South Africa had only marginally better than that - 0,5 hectare per person. By the end of the century it will be down to considerably below the UN recommendation.

Professor Wilfred Mallows, South Africa's first professor of town and regional planning (at the University of the Witwatersrand), in delivering the inaugural Nola Green Memorial Lecture in Johannesburg on 25 May 1988, examined the growing crisis on the Witwatersrand as migrants poured into the cities. He looked on the bright side - at how cities brought a higher degree of civilisation and, above all, how they curbed population growth.

Mallows said the world's great cities had grown, not from their own natural increase, but mostly from influx from rural areas or from other countries where conditions were inferior. Their development brings two other benefits: vastly increased productivity and more leisure time. At the same time there is a need to train the newly urbanised - "to re-educate them" - so that they can be absorbed into city life as quickly as possible. Mallows suggested this could take a generation. His view that it would take a generation may have been too pessimistic. South Africa's black population already has an industrial and urban heritage. Before the *difacane,* when elements of the Zulu nation erupted from the coastal belt and laid to waste the black civilisations of the interior, there were centuries' old Iron Age settlements, especially in the Transvaal, and some were of enormous size. Large villages have been unearthed with solid dry stone walls and even sliding doors which locked - dating back three and more centuries. The doors slid into cavity walls and a peg, driven through a hole in the inside wall, stopped the door being pulled back from outside. I have watched the excavation of huts with a form of central heating, rather along the lines used by the Navajo in America. In these old South African settlements hot rocks were taken from the fire outside and placed in an earthenware pot recessed into the hard floor of the hut. When they cooled they were taken back to the fire and exchanged for hot ones. Urbanisation does not represent quite the culture shock that some imagine.

The 20th Century - an era of crowds

Mallows says that the bigger a city the bigger pull it exerts "and the greater, wider and deeper its demand for labour of all kinds." But, inevitably, there is a delay of several years before rural migrants settle in and that means a large number of urban poor. As the poor become educated and productive, so the metropolitan area's growing pains begin to lessen. The fact remains that urban expansion, which has created our present standard of living, would not be possible without this immigration. Mallows sees the critical point in a nation's development as being the time it reaches 50 per cent urbanisation – "the point of no return". At about 90 per cent urbanisation a country's population growth levels off to zero and may drop to negative growth. South Africa is just over 50 per cent urbanised.

The countries best able to feed themselves are not necessarily the ones which have the most farmland. They are invariably the ones which are most urbanised and industrialised. Japan, with 122 million people, can feed only 55 million of its people from its own resources but it is well fed because it can trade industrial goods for food. Britain, with 52 million people, can feed only half that number but, like Japan, it can trade its industrial output, very profitably, for food. In fact Britain, at a squeeze, could feed itself. During World War II it began farming higher into its hills and, the most useful move of all, it encouraged a "Dig for Victory" campaign to persuade people to grow their own vegetables. Urban dwellers took over "allotments", small plots the size of a room, sometimes on freshly bombed sites which were dug up and planted with vegetables. Cities can do a lot to feed themselves. In *Children and the Environment* Unep officials tell how, in the township known as Jerusalem near Bogota in Colombia the inhabitants have no land and little money to buy food ...

> But more and more families are harvesting crops on their rooftops, using the hydroponics technique. Hydroponics allows them to grow plants rapidly using fertiliser and a little water. Tito Lopez claims that hydroponic methods have increased his family income by 15 percent and "probably improved our diet by 30 percent. Before we ate only cabbage, onions, bananas, rice and flour. Now we also have Swiss chard, radishes, lettuce, tomatoes, celery and carrots."

> Many of Bogota's poor families are now raising food at a third of its market cost, while producing 20 times more per square metre than traditional agriculture ... The simplified hydroponics scheme has been developed by an ngo (non-government organisation) which specialises in low cost technology.

A similar ngo, GROW, has had success in Johannesburg's poorer areas showing people how to grow an entire family's vegetable needs on a plot the size of a door using household rubbish as compost. Such measures are an integral part of urban upliftment, education and primary health care and will help curb the population explosion.

Huntley, Siegfried and Sunter estimate that urban populations in Africa are growing at 5,1 per cent a year which gives a population doubling time of 14 years. In South Africa they believe there will be 35 million people in the cities by the century's end and estimate the current influx rate at 750 000 a year. To cope with the housing backlog South Africa must build 1 000 new houses a day. This is a perfectly attainable target providing healthy economic development is restored in South Africa.

Huntley believes there are 3 million squatters in South Africa (1989) and compares Durban with Mexico City in terms of its rate of expansion. The point is arguable: it has been said that Durban is now South Africa's biggest metropolitan area in terms of people. A much quoted figure is that Greater Durban has a population of 4 million. Yet a 1989 survey by Tongaat-Hulett Properties showed that the population between Ballito Bay on the North Coast and Amanzimtoti (south of Durban) and inland to Cato Ridge was 2,2 million. Soweto's population, frequently given as being over 2 million (in fact Mallows put it at 2 million) may be fewer than 1 million (1990). A census conducted by Witwatersrand University demographers in 1989 – it was held on a Sunday when most people were at home and was backed by an aerial survey which accurately counted the houses and shacks and multiplied by 10 – arrived at fewer than 1 million.

Whatever the figures, South Africa's population is not disastrously high and, given a firm agricultural policy, it could, even in 20 and 30 years' time, easily be fed from its own resources.

Bearing in mind the lack of accurate raw data, and particularly the enigma of AIDS, it is impossible to say at what level South Africa's population will peak. It seems most unlikely it will reach the 80 million forecast a few years back. My guess is that it will not reach even 70 million before dropping back to 50 million. The white population is already at ZPG (zero population growth) and the Indian and coloured populations are nearing that.

The aids pandemic

The AIDS pandemic, as I have said, is likely to be devastating. There is no cure in sight and the disease is penetrating the human population with appalling efficiency. According to some scenarios it is likely to kill at least 10 million South Africans now living and possibly double that figure after the turn of the century. The bulk of the victims will be urban blacks. The most important fact is that most of these millions have not yet caught the virus. In other words, with a concerted campaign championed by black leaders, the disaster could largely be avoided.

AIDS (an acronym for acquired immune deficiency syndrome) begins as a viral infection – the virus being the human immunodeficiency virus (HIV) – which is spread by normal sexual intercourse; through anal sex; from mother to baby; through infected blood as well as through the use of contaminated syringes. HIV can leave people predisposed towards dying of tuberculosis and other common diseases and thus they may not be listed as having ever been HIV-positive. Of those who get HIV, 90 per cent end up with AIDS, which is always fatal. AIDS kills through a variety of means from a form of pneumonia, tuberculosis, thrush, chronic diarrhoea, rare tumours, blood disorders, brain and central nervous system disorders. The average period between infection by HIV and the onset of AIDS appears to be seven years in the case of blood transfusion accidents, and 11 years in the case of homosexual men. Some authorities believe people may carry a HIV infection for 20 years before AIDS manifests itself. But once AIDS is diagnosed it is fatal within eight months to two years.

There is no evidence that the virus which causes AIDS can be transmitted by kissing, cuddling, shaking hands, telephones, lavatory seats, sharing cups or bed linen, swimming pools or coughs and sneezes and mosquitoes. A study of 90 children whose parents had AIDS showed none of the children had HIV infection.

A University of Natal economics research fellow, Alan Whitehead, investigating AIDS for the Development Bank in 1990, estimated that the full impact of the AIDS pandemic, as far as South Africa was concerned, was likely to make itself felt only in 1995 when alarming numbers of HIV-positive people were likely to be identified. By then, though, it will be too late to stop a catastrophe. Treating an AIDS victim is likely to cost at least R15 000 a person and, because of loss of productivity, each person will represent a R60 000 economic loss. If effective action is taken in time by the Government, it would be possible to increase the doubling time of the spread of the virus from nine months to 15 months. The latter is the best we can hope for and will mean 3 million HIV positive people in the year 2000. So, at some stage, within seven to 11 years, 2,7 million of these 3 million will die. But in the years they carry the disease they will probably infect many others.

If the 1990 trend is allowed to continue then more than 4 million will die immediately after the turn of the century and 12 million would, by then, have the virus and would die later. Interpreting Whitehead's figures, present trends indicate that the equivalent of 40 per cent of South Africa's 1990 population could die from AIDS. Taking the best case scenario I cannot see fewer than 10 million deaths.

AIDS in South Africa is growing far more rapidly than it is in the industrialised north where AIDS is mainly affecting the homosexual population. In Britain AIDS has declined because, one assumes, it was essentially a homosexual disease in that country and homosexuals are now more cautious. In the United States it appeared to be declining in 1989 when it was considered a mostly white homosexual problem, but in 1990 it began to assume ominous proportions among heterosexual black and hispanic urban populations. In South Africa it is also spreading mainly among black heterosexuals. Indeed, that is the pattern across Africa and the Caribbean. In South Africa, according to Whitehead, about six in every 100 sexually active blacks will be infected by HIV at the end of 1991 and 18 in every 100 by the end of 1992. Whitehead is being conservative here. On a nine month doubling scale well over a fifth of all blacks could have the virus by then.

Andre Spier, who with a team spent two years addressing the South African situation, wrote in a summary of his business "action" manual, Facing AIDS:

> *African AIDS is mainly spread by heterosexual intercourse since homosexuality and intravenous drug use (the two most common causes in the West) are not widespread. Therefore, all sexually active people, which is most of the adult population, are at risk. Official reporting of AIDS in Africa, due to many compelling reasons, one of them being to a simple statistics gathering mechanism, is believed to be only 10 percent of the real number of cases. The real figure should be 500 000 or more (full blown AIDS cases) which corresponds to some 25 to 50 million HIV-infected people who will develop AIDS in the years to come. This amounts to an overall infection rate of 10 to 20 per cent of the total adult population.*

South Africa, said Spier, was, at the time, not as badly affected. But he said most evidence points to it reaching that state by 1995. HIV-infection could reach 500 000 by the end of 1991 and between five and 10 million by the turn of the century. More than 90 per cent of those infected will progress to full-blown AIDS.

> *This progression of AIDS follows a curve which starts to rise slowly, then grows explosively, only to flatten off, once the pool of people which can become infected, diminishes. Nobody knows what the future figures are going to be, but the number will be substantial and highly destructive to the whole of society.*

> *Over 300 000 people dying of AIDS in the year 2000 is more than double the number of hospital beds presently available.*

There are some hard questions which even the thorough Spier felt obliged not to articulate: what happens beyond 2000? Where will we bury so many million victims in so short a time? And in view of the fact that most will have to die in their own beds (there will be no hospital beds for most of them) will we witness scenes reminiscent of the Black Death when burial parties went around stopping at homes to collect the dead? Why aren't we thoroughly alarmed? I don't know the answers. I am simply asking the questions.

The Panos Institute in London, an information and policy studies unit, put out an authoritative dossier in 1990, *The 3rd Epidemic,* which was published in association with the Norwegian Red Cross. It quoted Jonathan Mann, the medical doctor who founded the World Health Organisation's global AIDS programme. Mann said the "first epidemic" was the undetected spread of HIV beginning, unnoticed, sometime in the 1950s and 1960s and which galloped across the world in the 1970s – still unsuspected, infecting the United States, Haiti, Africa and Europe.

The "second epidemic" was the steady rise of AIDS cases. Tracing the disease backwards WHO suspects as many as 5 million have already died from AIDS but that the causes were mistakenly put down as pneumonia and so on. The third disease isolated by Mann is:

> Unlike the first two in that it is a social, rather than medical infection: the denial, blame, stigmatisation, prejudice and discrimination which the fear of AIDS brings out in individuals and societies. Today these three epidemics are still mounting. We must expect them to continue to do so for some decades yet, until a curative drug and a vaccine can be made widely and cheaply available. Meanwhile each country and community to which HIV spreads will have to continue to deal with the first epidemic and hidden infection, the second epidemic of AIDS illness and death, and the third epidemic of social and political reaction. The third epidemic is a challenge to our compassion, our judgement and our humanity. It poses difficult dilemmas at every level of society.

The Panos Institute lists a few examples: the British schoolboy, a haemophiliac, who developed AIDS from infected donor blood. He was shunned by friends and neighbours, rejected by his school and died aged 10; a man in Papua New Guinea who was tossed out of his village to die with nobody to look after him; a French employee who learned of his HIV-positive status only when his employer posted it on the notice board to warn his colleagues; the parents of a 16-year-old Bombay prostitute who refused to accept her back. She committed suicide in police custody.

18 The built environment

*What is life if, full of care,
We have no time to stand and stare?*

W H Davies

THE growth of cities is a natural process and the agglomeration of cities and towns into metropolitan regions is also a natural and unstoppable progression of events. So is the development of megalopolises – the sort of concentration of metropolitan areas which is evolving as greater Johannesburg and Pretoria expand towards each other.

At the beginning of this century, four-fifths of Europe's population lived in small towns and villages. Now four-fifths live in dense urban areas. We are witnessing in Europe the maturing of a crescent of urbanisation in an almost, but not quite, unbroken urban belt from Amsterdam to Rome. Britain, the most urbanised country in Europe – nine out of 10 Britons live in cities – provides an interesting case study for South Africa because Britain, much smaller in area than the Transvaal, has 50 per cent more people than South Africa, yet its landscape is 80 per cent countryside. And how rural is urban Europe! This has been achieved without resorting to packing people into highrise buildings and it provides a reassurance that high density urbanisation, the final destiny of man, need not be feared. More than anything, Europe demonstrates that large cities can be places of beauty and tranquillity as well as stimulation.

Physicists have a "steady state universe" theory which proposes that the universe, with its solar systems and galaxies, is in a condition of dynamic equilibrium. Much the same can be said of a country when it reaches maturity and its urban birth and recruitment rate equals the urban mortality rate. Many of Europe's maximally urbanised nations have achieved that blissful state called "ZPG" (zero population growth). This is when nations can begin to plan, and re-arrange the furniture, with achievable visions of the future, because they know how many people they are catering for. South Africa reached the halfway stage towards becoming fully urbanised, during the 1980s – by 1990 it was about 57 per cent urbanised – and thus came to what Wilfred Mallows calls "the point of no return." From here on we will move rapidly in the direction that post Industrial Revolution Europe took. It is from Europe, according to Mallows, that we must take our lessons. We can learn little from sub-Saharan Africa simply because no country is anywhere near as urbanised as South Africa, nor as educated and nor as industrialised. Zambia is the next most urbanised, at 36 per cent.

Double storey shack in Alexandra township, Johannesburg.
Source The Star

Mallows warns:

Of all the thresholds [towards urbanising] the most critical is clearly 50 per cent – that is when, for the first time, the balance between country and city shifts towards the city. It is a point of no return and the moment of the greatest trauma when conflict is most violent, decisions most divisive and uncertainty and doubt universal. South Africa stands on this Great Divide. It is the fundamental reason for our tensions, conflicts and violent cross-currents.

Mallows says Britain reached 50 per cent about 1860, at which stage its population was about the same as South Africa's now. Greater London was the same size as Johannesburg/Soweto. In fact London's working class East End was uncannily similar to Soweto. Mallows quoted

Walter Besent's description of the East End of London in 1870. The description could well be of 1990 Soweto:

It is a city full of churches and places of worship, but there are no cathedrals. It has elementary schools but no private or high schools, no colleges or higher education and no university. There are no fashionable quarters. People, shops, houses, conveyances are all stamped with the unmistakable seal of the working class. Perhaps the strangest thing of all in this city of 2 million people, there are no hotels. This means, of course, there are no visitors.

Designing cities

In the late 1950s I did a couple of weeks' stint as crime reporter and was sent to a Hillbrow flat where a young woman had gassed herself. She left a note to her parents, in a small Karoo town, saying she was lonely. I wondered how a 21 year old, living on the fifth floor of a large block of flats, with 200 people above and 200 below, and 40 000 more in the surrounding flats, could have been lonely. She worked in a typist pool in downtown Johannesburg and to get there she would have had to walk along one of South Africa's busiest streets and ride on a crowded bus. Yet she was lonely.

I only really understood what it was all about when, in 1974, Robert Ardrey gave a lecture at the University of the Witwatersrand in which he asked his audience: "What are the three things a human needs most?"

The first and most fundamental need, he said, was "security". Most First World people have security; they have a roof over their heads and know they will have food tomorrow. Once one has security, said Ardrey, you are in danger of becoming bored. So the second thing we need is "stimulation". Most of us, he said, have stimulation because we are educated and read, or watch television and can argue intellectually. So, for somebody who has security and stimulation, what is the third and final prerequisite to a stable urban community?

"What is it," Ardrey asked his audience, "that so many city dwellers lack?" We all scratched our heads. "Identity!" he said.

I began to realise why Hell's Angels dress so conspicuously and are so calculatedly noisy; why skinheads and punks dress the way they do. They yearn to be noticed, to be identified. It helps explain why the young woman from the Karoo was so lonely. Imagine for a moment if she had become ill, collapsed perhaps, on a pavement in her home town. Passers by would have immediately gone to her assistance because, either they would have known her or, if she had been a stranger, they would have wanted to help. Small town people are like that. They all have identity, and strangers are soon given one. But had this young woman collapsed on a busy metropolitan street, almost anywhere in the world, most people would have crossed over the street to avoid becoming involved; some might even have stepped over her.

Loneliness, particularly among the elderly (who tend to get abandoned in cities) is, very often, an environmental condition and just one of the many stresses of modern city life. The fault lies in urban design.

I knew an elderly man in Parktown, Johannesburg who was suffering from what one could only describe as "terminal loneliness". He was originally from the Mediterranean and had become a rich man living in a large Johannesburg house. It was a typical suburban house in that it faced away from the jacaranda-lined street which was designed basically for fast traffic. Thousands of Johannesburg homes turn their backs on the street and therefore the community, and wall themselves off, mainly because most suburban streets are inhuman, and over-engineered noiseways. Suburban mothers live in fear of their children, or the family dog, going outside the gate. A good suburb, to be accessible to cars, does not have to be criss-crossed by dangerous roads. There is no need to encourage fast driving in suburbia.

The old man of Parktown was a widower and alone. All he wanted was to die and, after a period of miserable existence, he did just that, having sat daily in an armchair facing his empty back garden where the swing under the tree had not swung for years because his children and grandchildren now lived their own lives in distant suburbs. This break up of the extended family is one of the unfortunate side effects of the car-based society which has enabled people to live long distances out of town. The extended family was important, probably vital, to social stability: three generations lived in close proximity and shared each other's tragedies and triumphs: granny babysat the children, the old passed down their stories, knowledge and wisdom and the young tried to shock the old (and usually succeeded). It was all an important part of human development. There is no alternative college of values. Today the elderly have become abandoned, divorce has become the norm, discipline among the young has broken down.

I sat with the old man one afternoon and tried to imagine what he would have been doing back home in his Mediterranean village, and then I realised how important, not only this "identity" thing was, but the role of the street. The old man would have spent his dotage sitting on a chair outside his house, or on his stoep, looking up and down the street. Passers-by would have all known him – they might not have liked him but they would have known him – and they would have greeted him out of respect. Like most old characters he would have been a human landmark, an historical reference point for the community, and people would have inquired after his health. He would, no doubt, have been critical of the young and noted how many boyfriends the girl down the road had, but that is the prerogative of the aged. The young would still have recognised him in some way – a wave, a nod. Even by scurrying past, pretending they hadn't seen him, they would have afforded the old man a certain quiet satisfaction.

Can a city rehumanise itself? I believe it can. In Holland planners are restricting traffic access into suburban streets by half blocking them with large planters so that vehicles entering the street have to slow down to negotiate them. The streets themselves have been redesigned and the roadway is no longer shaped purely for the convenience of cars, instead it winds its way among strategically placed trees or planters. The surface texture is changed so that motorists recognise they are no longer on a tarred road specifically for cars. In fact only those who live in the road are inclined to enter it. The street now becomes an extension to the area's public open space and it becomes pleasant for houses to face on to the street. Children can kick a ball around, and meet after school. This introduces a further positive aspect: security against crime. With many houses facing into the street there is usually somebody looking out, making it difficult for a stranger, or a potential housebreaker let us say, to move around undetected. The *woonerf,* as these streets are called, is the antithesis of a Johannesburg suburban street which is generally totally screened off by high walls.

People are the most important thing in a city. They *are* the city. The problem is that the design of modern cities such as Johannesburg, has been heavily influenced by engineers whose education, until very recently, singularly avoided the "soft sciences". I once stood with a particularly respected engineer looking down from a high building at Johannesburg, its marshalling yards, its crowded, fast-moving motorways and its compressed jumble of skyscrapers. Nowhere could I see public open space or relieving greenery. The engineer said: "Now that's what a city is all about." Is it? I wondered afterwards what he was looking at and I fear it was the traffic streams and soaring motorways. He was, I surmise, saying to himself: "Just look at all that engineering!" Engineers, until recently, were not taught about human needs except in the most material terms. Most South African engineers consider it an absurd notion that a street should be an extension to suburban living space, or that traffic noise is avoidable, or that the problem of "where will the children play?" has anything to do with engineering.

Many cities, the world over, have become dehumanised in the twentieth century, partly because of the preoccupation with the car and the assumption, by engineers, that the car must be able to travel fast and have the right to use peak hour rat-runs through suburbia.

There are a multitude of serious problems: the urgent need for more land to be designated and serviced for the new urban arrivals, the desperate squatters; the need for electricity for that 70 per cent of people (mostly in black townships) who have not yet got it; there is noise stress, crime, joblessness, vagrancy, litter, frustrated youth, the neglected old, the neglected young, the latchkey kids - children of working mothers who have the front door key strung around their necks so they can let themselves into the flat or house after school to sit alone until somebody comes home. There are gross environmental inadequacies and inequalities, yet, as urban society reacts negatively under the strain, we have tended to call in sociologists, psychologists, psychiatrists and criminologists to help people adjust to the environment. This has been a terrible mistake. We cannot possibly change people. We have to change the cities.

Town planners who, technically, are professional environmentalists, should be fixing the priorities. Civil engineers say that town planners and the others in the planning professions (civil engineers, surveyors, architects, water engineers, etc) should be part of a team. It would still require, to my mind, that the planner heads the team. Engineering is a tool, nothing more.

One of the things we can do to is to break up the larger cities into more human scale, politically autonomous, areas. The ideal size of a town is, according to Kirkpatrick Sale, 70 000 to 100 000. With that population a place has all the skills necessary to run a town. Consider how small were the towns of Europe when they built their beautiful cathedrals, using local talent for the stone masonry, the stained glass windows, tiles, wood carving ... Even today Canterbury, Salisbury, Rheims and Rouen, with their magnificent cathedrals and ornate buildings, are relatively small cities.

London, with its 8,5 million people, works quite well because although it has three times Johannesburg's population, it is divided into 32 boroughs, each of which jealously guards its individual small town character. Places such as Hamstead Heath, are essentially villages with typical village streets of small shops whose proprietors know the names of many of their customers. Yet each has a powerful say within the umbrella metropolitan council, concerning the alignment of its own roads, the density and height of its buildings and the preservation of its open space and heritage buildings. By contrast, Johannesburg is one city governed by more than 50 councillors, few of whom have a really holistic vision of their city and most of whom have only a scant knowledge of suburbs on the other side of town. I met a powerful councillor who lived in a poor suburb who actively disliked the northern suburbs - yet he made decisions affecting those people.

One of the worst aspects of urban planning in the Transvaal is that a small group of faceless retired Pretoria men are empowered to reverse town and city council decisions. These men are the Townships Board. If a developer wants to build an office complex where only residential houses are permitted, and he is turned down by the municipal council, he may go above the council's head and ask the Townships Board. The likelihood is that the board will overrule the council (it does so by holding a public hearing and then advising the Minister of Local Government of its view and the Minister acts accordingly). The chairman of the board, asked by *The Star* to name the men in the board, refused. He claimed it was not in the public interest for people to know their names or what their expertise was. It turned out that a retired policeman, a former mayor of a platteland dorp, and a magistrate - all ratepayers of Pretoria and with no allegiance or answerability to the towns whose plans they could reverse - were presiding over multi-million rand planning decisions in Johannesburg. While an appeals board is desirable it should be answerable to those it affects, and it should be composed of people elected from the municipality itself and be under, perhaps, a retired judge.

The pronounced lack of human scale in South African cities has led to a situation where suburban people are constantly fighting indifferent and often shockingly ignorant authorities. One of the most effective and spirited fighters against this state of affairs is Flo Bird of Parktown, Johannesburg. She helped found the Parktown Association, which is a pressure group established to save the historic suburb from being slowly demolished by a city council whose hardline establishment, aided and abetted by an even more hardline Transvaal Provincial Council, wanted to erase every vestige of British colonial architecture. Mansions from the rip-roaring gold rush days were demolished and replaced by featureless, bare concrete structures such as the Johannesburg Hospital and Teachers Training College. Architect Conrad Berge, a respected urban critic, said: "I am not against them knocking down nice old buildings. It is just that they do not replace them with nice new buildings."

The National Monuments Council was practically powerless to help through lack of money. The state's allocation to the NMC for buying up historical homes and sites speaks for itself: in 1987 and 1988 it gave around R1 million annually. In 1989, nothing. In 1980 about R800 000 and in 1990, R795 000. "This is the only money made available by the State for the preservation of the entire man-made heritage of South Africa," said Flo Bird. She points out the sponsors and donors who are willing to assist with national monuments receive no tax benefits, "yet if you sponsor an international rugby tour you get a 98 per cent rebate. The taxpayer foots the bill."

There is no doubt that the city that has cared least about its heritage in the past 40 years has been Johannesburg. The big question now, says Herbert Prins of the department of architecture at the University of the Witwatersrand, is whether the government of the "new South Africa" will display more interest in preserving what little is left of the colonial architecture than did the present administration. Prins tends to answer his own question by observing how independent black Africa, apart from Africanising place names (Salisbury became Harare, for instance) and moving colonialist statues to less prominent places, left the grand old buildings and homes standing. Landmarks, especially old landmarks, are very important to a city. And after two or three generations, any negative or controversial attachments that some buildings might have had, tend to become less emotive. Who would tear down Rome's Colosseum even though it was built by a cruelly oppressive regime which threw humans to lions as a spectator sport? Landmark buildings become comforting because of their familiarity and they provide a sense of place, a point of reference for strangers, and impart a sense of permanence when, perhaps, all about them is being redeveloped.

Open spaces

Although much of what has been discussed so far has been to do with South Africa's "First World" cities, the principles are relevant to the country's future cities which will tend to be a mix of First and Third World in flavour, rather like Lisbon, San Paulo or, God preserve us, Lima. But unless there is enormous progress economically and, of course, politically, we are likely to condemn ourselves to developing cities which resemble the worst of South America's.

It is vital in tomorrow's cities that people, who will be living in greater and greater densities, have adequate open space. Every urban dweller needs to have access to space, to grassy places, to walks, to places where children can run around and make a noise. And in South Africa these need to be defined now. One of the least expensive but maximally

A cloud burst turns Johannesburg's Braamfontein Spruit into a raging torrent. Source The Star

rewarding ways to provide this is to establish what are known as river trails. In the recent past suburban streams in cities on the central plateau were almost automatically canalised to drain summer stormwater from the urban areas as fast as possible. As the urban areas became more paved and more built up, so runoff increased. Natural runoff in South Africa is about 7 per cent but this rises to 90 per cent in urban areas. Thus, urban and suburban streams have become strips of neglected land drained by ugly sluices into which people dump garden refuse, obsolete kitchenware, supermarket trolleys and even car hulks. Houses walled themselves off from streams in much the same way as they walled themselves off from the street. Engineers have now come to realise that it is not a good idea to canalise streams because this merely increases water velocity and passes the problem downstream where banks become washed away and more concrete channelling is then called for. It is now considered sound practice to slow down, rather than speed up, runoff from urban areas. Dams and artificial pans are now used to take up the shock of stormwater and any surplus can be diverted to flood sports fields or carparks. The stream banks themselves have been cleared of rubbish and opened up as walking and riding trails.

The prototype urban river trail in South Africa was along the 32 kilometre long Braamfontein Spruit which runs from Hillbrow, Johannesburg, through the city's northern suburbs and on through Randburg and Sandton. Its story is an example of that environmental dictum, "Think globally, act locally." The trail was initiated by neighbourhood effort and illustrated how useful newspapers can be when it comes to public action. In 1971 The Star's environmental campaign CARE mapped the stream, whose name, let alone its geography, was hardly known, and suggested the public to "put the sparkle back into the Braamfontein Spruit". The river was, in most parts, overgrown by wattles and rank growth of kikuyu grass. It was filled with junk. The Zoo Lake Lions Club offered to organise the clean up of a specific section of the stream and so provide a model area. The area was so choked with vegetation that the stream had not been visible for years. The newspaper appealed for people to come to the area, in Victory Park, one Saturday morning in March, 1973. The area was many hectares in size and totally overgrown. Four hundred volunteers arrived at 8 am – so did several Johannesburg council officials and councillors. The council, having realised the public really had the bit between its teeth, had already mowed the grass (for the first time in years) and had begun cutting down blue gums and wattles. A local waste company had put out several 6 cubic metre buckets in which people could place the rubbish. The Mayor arrived in a formal suit and in his Rolls Royce – and, getting caught up in the spirit of the thing, spent the morning helping drag car hulks from the water. The Boy Scouts built a bridge over the stream which saved kilometres of walking for people pushing wheelbarrows. A local cool drink manufacturer sent in a truck load of drinks and, towards evening, a brewery sent a load of beer. By dusk the stream course had been exposed and many were surprised at its beauty: white water rushed through a now exposed ancient granite outcrop and, the biggest surprise of all, there were willows growing along the river bank which had been hidden from view by large black wattle trees. That evening braaivleis fires glowed along the newly cleared 300 metres of stream and families grilled meat under the stars. Today the example set by those 400 people has spread all along the stream, which now boasts its own corps of "mounties" – scarlet uniformed rangers mounted on horses who operate from Sandton. The River Rangers are partly financed by Sandton Council and partly by private enterprise. Copses of indigenous trees are springing up, planted ceremoniously on Arbor days, and many new species of birds – rameron pigeons, grey loeries, plum coloured starlings and woodland kingfishers – are making their way up the valley from the distant bush country.

Several more streams along the Witwatersrand and elsewhere have since been cleared and landscaped.

Using the same do-it-yourself approach, South Africa's sometimes drab black areas can be greatly uplifted. Japhta Lekgetho, Soweto's tireless environmental campaigner, inspired thousands of young people to help clear up waste ground in the huge township. The grounds of his environmental information and education centre are on a cleared section of the Klip Spruit now lawned down to the water's edge. Lekgetho, a former geography master, began his campaigning after the 1976 riots in Soweto in which frustrated youths went on the rampage. Among the government buildings they destroyed were the beer halls whose revenues had been used to finance Soweto's meagre infrastructure. The beer halls were never rebuilt and, within a few months of the riots, local youths were voluntarily clearing away the ruins and grassing the empty sites for play parks. A playground equipment manufacturer, impressed by what had been done, donated and erected equipment.

Environmental improvement is very often a voluntary thing – at least until the politicians notice the public's enthusiasm and then they will usually throw their weight behind it.

The human scale

What is it that makes some cities great and other cities unpleasant?

There is no set formula or shape for an ideal city but there are free lessons to be had. For instance, people in Johannesburg tend to walk faster than people in Paris, or Rome, or Munich. A German survey found that pedestrians in streets with heavy traffic walked almost twice as fast as people walking in a "pedestrianised" street from which traffic had been barred. In streets unstressed by traffic people were relaxed and looked into shop windows more, and bought more. Look how, when one visits an historical European city, one tends to walk around for the sheer pleasure of walking. It is a more enjoyable experience because, for a start, the street scenes tend to be human in scale and there is so much "pedestrian experience", as town planners like to say. By contrast, many modern city streets such as one finds in New York, Detroit or Johannesburg, tend to be canyons formed by oppressively high and rather uninteresting buildings. Old cities, having grown "organically", little by little over centuries, are designed for humans rather than vehicles. Traffic, in the more relaxed cities of Europe, has learned to cope with the labyrinthian streets. Indeed, more and more cities are barring traffic from their central streets because of noise, vibration and fumes. Old cities provide attractive street scenes while modern city streets tend to be dominated by unsynchronised, self-centred buildings each trying to shout down its neighbours and each a monument to some corporate image.

Helmut Jahn, the Chicago architect who designed the blue glass tent-shaped Anglo American Corporation's building in Diagonal Street, Johannesburg, when asked if, in retrospect, he thought his building was a bit out of keeping in this rather quaint area said: "When I design a building it is a statement in itself."

Ironically one can see reflected in Jahn's building's glazed frontage the last of Johannesburg's Victorian street scenes - a row of 1890s Indian-owned shops in Diagonal Street - saved from a mining house developer only after a last-minute public protest.

Streets in older cities tend to have vistas. Indeed vistas are jealously preserved. In contrast the streets in modern grid iron cities such as Johannesburg have no vistas. They reach boringly into infinity. In Cape Town, whose Table Mountain provides a magnificent vista, a motorway tangle

Heritage architecture

smothers the view from the harbour end of the city centre. One of the motorways has been abandoned in mid air, a monument to engineer-oriented planning. Older city streets, not having been designed by engineers using rulers and worrying about traffic flow, have interesting bends so that there is an air of anticipation as to what might lie beyond the curve.

Street trees can help "lift" an otherwise dull street. Johannesburg has few streets lined with trees, which is why Commissioner Street looks like Jeppe Street and they both look like Von Wielligh – although the city is now redressing that deficiency.

Just as I believe the sign of a good suburban environment is when a dog can sleep in the middle of the road without getting run over, so I believe the sign of an environmentally healthy city centre is when people stroll, hands behind back, looking about them. Modern cities fail to inspire. They are devoid of wonder and their architecture, if it can be described as such, is more suited to graveyards. It is soaring and arrogant. The old cities, and one catches glimpses of what I mean in Pretoria's Church Square and in sections of Cape Town (and all over Europe), have an architecture which is meant mostly to please the eye. One stops and stares in admiration and sometimes ecstasy. The Romans had a simple urban design rule: they never allowed bare concrete – there had to be "detail to excite the eye."

Pompeii – the Roman city buried by a Vesuvius eruption in AD 79 – did not allow wheeled traffic, such as carts and chariots, into its business centre where the banks and the shops were. The area was cordoned off with stone blocks across the street. This was apparently a common practice in ancient cities. While most people will agree that humans like congestion – the sort of bustling congestion one experiences in a marketplace – nobody enjoys competing with traffic. An interesting difference between Paris and Johannesburg is that in Paris, which has twice as many people and six times as many cars, there is less conflict between traffic and people and traffic noise is less noticeable. This is because Johannesburg's traffic is squeezed between high rise buildings whose flat facades amplify the traffic's din and reflect it back into the street. Paris's main streets are wider and buildings are rarely more than two or three storeys so the traffic noise goes over the top and is lost in the air. The sound waves which do not escape over the roof tops are scattered by the ornate architecture, the cornices, the pediments and recessed doors and windows, as well as the large numbers of bulky horse chestnut trees, London planes and oaks. Paris also scores by giving generous space to pedestrians. As do London and Rome. In Johannesburg almost half the city centre is covered by tar – none of it rates-producing. In fact all of it rates-*demanding*. Paris and London are about 25 per cent tarred. Tokyo is less than 10 per cent paved, but then Tokyo is a traffic nightmare.

Traffic congestion was partly responsible for causing Johannesburg's central business district (CBD) to cease growing in the 1970s. Eloff Street, once known as the "Golden Mile", was abandoned by shoppers and shopkeepers alike. Cars had priority over people and the street became a noisy, fume-filled canyon in which it was impossible to chat on the pavement. There were no trees. The upper floors along Eloff Street became derelict and then shopkeepers began to pull out. At about the time Eloff Street died off, the city of Minniapolis in Minnesota (USA) was having a similar problem with its main street which had much in common with Eloff Street. But there the authorities acted. For just over $1 million, they were able to disguise the harsh geometry of the street by winding a serpentine busway along it. They abolished cars. They introduced different textures underfoot and planted trees so that the pedestrian related to the leafy canopy overhead and no longer to the buildings towering above the street. Novel street furniture was introduced. They called the result Nicolett Mall and it became reinstated as Minneapolis's favourite downtown meeting place. The retail business was rejuvenated and produced rates which could be used to further enhance downtown Minneapolis. Buskers introduced music and artists showed off their work.

Nigel Mandy, founder and chairman of the Johannesburg Central Business District Association (CBDA), tried to persuade the city council to try a similar approach with

Eloff Street, the initial attempt to close it to traffic failed, despite a lighthearted attempt to promote it. Source The Star

Eloff Street but the very conservative management committee insisted that people came to the city only to do business, "so why waste money?". The prolonged tussle that took place between Mandy's CBDA and the doleful city fathers revealed what was wrong with city design in South Africa – there was simply no imagination. The council begrudgingly decided to close the street to traffic between 10 am and 2 pm daily. People persisted in walking on the pavement – unless (as Mandy said) somebody shook a charity collection box under their noses – and the city council commented, half in triumph, that, patently, malls don't work in Johannesburg. Slowly the politicians understood, and finally they abolished cars in Eloff Street and introduced a serpentine busway and planted stinkwood trees and put in colourful bus shelters. The noise was still bad because of Johannesburg's noisy diesel buses and the narrow nature of the street and its high buildings. All the same, shopkeepers reported a 20 per cent greater turnover. Eloff Street still lacks the human touch – principally because the city council, not wanting people to relax under the shade of the trees "for security reasons", provides no seats and has designed the street plant boxes in such a way their edges are too sharp for sitting on.

The contrast between other major cities and Johannesburg when it came to attitudes towards people has been most pronounced. For years Johannesburg's council (most of those involved have now gone) ensured that the three park lawns in the city centre – three is all there is – had their sprinklers turned on just before lunch time to ensure the grass was too wet for city workers to sit or lie on. Public space had absolutely no priority in planning. When, in 1985 Nigel Mandy, Pat Corbin of the Chamber of Commerce, and I met the mayor in front of the city hall to discuss ideas for re-instating the public square which used to be there the mayor was enthusiastic. But the management committee turned the idea down because it was against public gathering places in principle; it did not want to encourage people to gather. Thus a particularly weird type of political neurosis was dictating an inhuman city centre design. The new and younger council which took over has re-instated the square.

Little wonder that, apart from the completion of the huge Carlton Centre shopping and office complex in 1972, the city centre retail component did not expand at all for more than a decade. Most of its major departmental stores closed or moved out to the suburban shopping centres. But this outward movement was not unique to Johannesburg. Worldwide people were reacting to the frustrations of downtown, the agony of finding parking, the eternal conflict between cars and pedestrians. Many abandoned the old city centre as a shopping and working area. New suburban centres were built and centred on malls, often underground and hermetically sealed against urban noise and fumes. They were almost theatrical market places whose shops opened up on to music-filled "streets". South Africa might have the finest climate in the world but it still builds totally enclosed malls, like Toronto, and surrenders its God-given sunny outdoors to traffic and parking. You'll find more outdoor cafes in the towns of climatically unreliable Europe than you'll find in almost perpetually sunny South Africa.

As the old guard Johannesburg city councillors bowed out, their damage done, a last ditch attempt was made to improve the environment of Johannesburg CBD. The old council had, in fact, bowed to pressure and created a very attractive mall along a formerly unattractive Smal Street, but their motivation was partly because of security reasons. Architect and planner Jimmy Watson had for years been pushing the idea of turning the rather boring and little-used street, which had no shops in some blocks (just the sides of warehouses), into a two-storey mall of small shops. His plan was passed mainly because the council had become concerned about muggings in the quiet street, which linked the city's two biggest hotels, and part of the mall deal was a private security corps. The mall worked a treat, but until there are more reasons for coming to town the city centre will remain the sort of place where the last person home after 6 pm switches the lights off. The central business district, its once bustling theatre land long closed, and having few reasons for people to visit it other than to work, is closed 12 hours in every 24 and most of the weekend. All that infrastructure, all those services, and they are used for the equivalent of only six months a year. Cities, like nature, thrive on variety and Johannesburg's CBD is typical of many modern cities in having none.

In the autumn of 1991 the council opened a revamped

Library Gardens, which used to be Market Square, as part of the "Civic Spine", a project intended to give the city a softer centre. Nearby, the First National Bank was completing some classic-style blocks. Trees were appearing. But all that was really happening was that Johannesburg was becoming a huge office park. People still tended to walk fast and, significantly, Nigel Mandy, chairman of the Johannesburg's Central Business District Association and world renowned as an exponent of the importance of city centres, had long ago moved his office 20 kilometres out of town to work in the surburb of a neighbouring town.

King Car

The battle against being suffocated by cars is slowly being faced: in Cape Town and Durban the councils have introduced informal public transport so that people do not need their cars in town. Durban has a particularly colourful system in which people travel in open "mynahs", motorised sulkies named after the ubiquitous India mynah bird. Durban has closed off many streets and now more and more pavement cafés are appearing, and instead of demolishing its obsolete Victorian railway station and railway workshops it converted them into a yuppie market place of small-scale shops and eating places. Cape Town has reconverted a former market square – Green Market Square, which had become a tarred carpark – back into a cobbled market square. The busy market has encouraged many small-scale and one-person businesses. Most cities in South Africa, now that the Department of Transport is selling off railway land and obsolete docklands in central areas, have great opportunities to depart from being purely functional areas to becoming places which fulfil recreational and other needs.

City planners have realised that they must come to grips with the traffic dilemma. Too many cars can kill a city, yet too many restrictions on cars can also kill a city. Somehow ways have to be found to supply public transport that is comfortable, fast and, above all, regular. Johannesburg has tended to run its public transport more for the benefit of the operator than the passenger and as a consequence bus travel has a poor public image. All the same, three-quarters of Johannesburg's workers use public transport: half of those working in the CBD come by train from the East and

OPPOSITE *This was once the stately suburb of Parktown, Johannesburg.*
Source *The Star*

The built environment

West Rand and from Soweto; a quarter come by bus and combi taxi. It is mostly Hobson's choice because apartheid, until it collapsed in the late '80s, forced all workers who were not white to live on the edge of town.

It is the quarter who come by car who are the most demanding in terms of space and municipal and State expenditure. The problem is, again, worldwide and the only solutions seem to be expensive ones. Underground trains, according to a World Bank survey, are usually far too expensive to build and operate for developing countries and, in any event, as soon as motorists perceive an easing of downtown traffic congestion they go back to using their cars. Almost nowhere have underground rapid rail systems actually cured congestion but, by allowing more people to reach the city centre, they have allowed city cores to accommodate more office bulk and so generate more rates. In developing countries, buses with reserved buslanes seem a more appropriate answer. On the other hand light rail is not much more expensive and is a great deal quieter. The most expensive option of all would be to build more highways, for they not only destroy rate-producing land but they are expensive to construct and even more expensive to maintain. And, unless they have tollgates, which is not feasible in urban areas, they bring in no revenue at all.

The third Arab oil crisis in 1990 gave fresh impetus to ending dependence on imported oil. South Africa, with an abundance of cheap coal, is capable of fuel self-sufficiency. It already produces most of its own petrol and it could easily run electrified public transport systems. But first it must get more city workers out of their cars. Marcia C Lowe, author of a Worldwatch Report in 1990 on *Alternatives to the Automobile: Transport for Livable Cities* says that the cleanest type of transport is an electric rail system while the dirtiest is the car. As for comfort, the car has stretched the peak hour in some cities to 12 hours (in Seoul) and even 14 (Rio de Janeiro). In most parts of South Africa the rush hour is still only one hour long. They are easily avoided. I personally drive 20 kilometres into my downtown office every day and I have never been caught in a serious traffic jam. All those who sit in the traffic queues around 8 am are willing volunteers. Thus introducing big bold public transport systems into South African cities is unlikely to prise motorists from their cars. An exception is the busy route from Soweto to Johannesburg, where congestion lasts two or three hours as combi taxis take over from a notoriously uncomfortable utility bus service and from a train service which is picked over by some of the most bloodthirsty criminals in the world.

For economic reasons alone it is important that South Africa avoids the traffic trap which has ensnared so many overseas cities. London, for instance, opened up yet another ring road in 1988 – the 190 kilometre long M25 – and within weeks broke the world record for traffic jams as traffic

Three road authorities were involved in building these roads through Roodepoort – the central government, the province and the municipality. Source The Star

backed up for 53 kilometres. The problem appeared to be that interchanges were too close together (roughly 6 kilometre intervals) and, therefore, people were using this expressway as an intersuburban road. The M25 was designed, not for that, but for allowing trunk road traffic to avoid going through London. It is amazing that traffic engineers, with all their computer models and impact studies, can be caught so completely by surprise. The same is happening to Greater Johannesburg's ring road. It was meant to allow traffic using the N1 from the Limpopo to Cape Town to skirt Johannesburg. Instead it is mainly used as an inter town link by the towns ringing Johannesburg. And as more and more housing developments are encouraged to spring up along it so more and more people demand more ramps on to it. Traffic densities are becoming a problem, especially as the speed, 120 kilometres per hour, is so inappropriate for a six-lane highway on which traffic is constantly changing lanes. There is now talk of building an "outer-outer ring road" and so the treadmill rolls on. Highways beget cars. Cars beget highways. Real human needs are dependent on neither.

The world's 400 million private cars form "the world's largest source of air pollution" according to Lowe. There are, according to another Worldwatch Institute report, 1,3 billion motor-driven vehicles in the world. In her indictment of cars she says that wherever cars have been taken out of a city street, commercial trade has picked up 25 per cent. Yet the car has been allowed to dominate town planning.

Lowe has a sensible solution: make motorists pay the true costs of using a car. The costs of roads alone, if the commuting motorist were forced to contribute his fair share, would frighten him or her into joining a bus queue. The Worldwatch report even mentioned the unmentionable: penalising firms which give out company cars, free petrol and free parking. In the US some civil service units have begun charging for parking and this has been enough to persuade many civil servants to share or "pool" their cars and so reduce their monthly costs.

In Japan certain levels of employees, if they use public transport, have their fares paid in full by their employer. On the bullet trains, which can do 240 kilometres per hour, a three-month season ticket costs $8 600 for those living

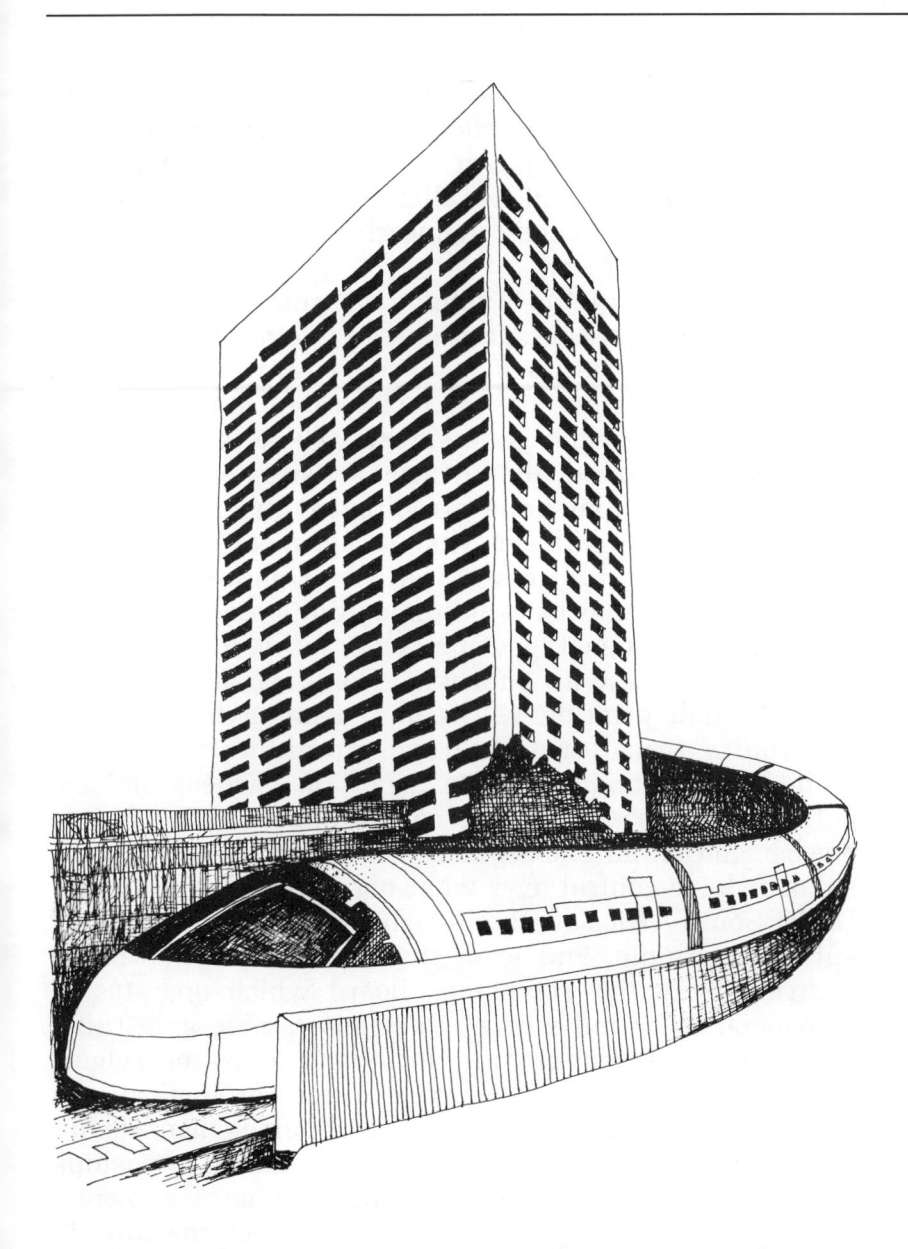

120 kilometres out of town and the journey takes 50 minutes each way. Passengers are guaranteed a seat. But again the costs represent an unintelligent social investment. As in Europe, where ultra-high speed trains are becoming the vogue in France and Germany, they serve only a narrow band of yuppie workers who are also not paying the true costs of this form of travel. The general public good is not served. Indeed the loss of amenity caused by these ultra-fast rail routes as they cut through towns

and villages makes it a serious pollutant. (I must confess to being prejudiced against high speed in surface transport. The world must slow down, not speed up. International flights are one thing but travelling from home to the office does not need this frenetic engineering. It creates problems, it does not solve them.)

One solution to the dilemma of public and private commuting is to encourage people to live near where they work, which sometimes means encouraging business houses and certain types of factories to move into the suburbs. Strict zoning is a neurosis. There is no sensible reason to demand that all industries are situated in one area while all residential units are situated in another. This trend of mixing office parks (sometimes office parks incorporating public restaurants and shops and even theatres) with suburbs is becoming quite marked around Johannesburg. Some types of manufacturing industries are quite compatible with suburbia. There is nothing wrong with a small printing works or a fashion house or an electronics firm down the road, providing they fit in architecturally and providing they have gardens and are not reliant on heavy transport coming and going. But before one can go that far one has to be sure that the people of the suburbs have control over what happens in their suburb. Under South Africa's rather Russian planning bureaucracy suburban people, and even their local council, can be overridden by the Townships Board which operates at Provincial level and which is not answerable politically. The reason why suburban associations sometimes vigorously fight off attempts to build offices or institutional headquarters in the suburbs is because there is then a temptation for politicians and developers – and the townships boards – to see the suburb as a future zone for offices only. This serves little purpose other than to wreck the suburb. Parktown, Johannesburg was a beautiful residential suburb, then a small clinic was allowed to open. Then another. This was fine as far as most people were concerned. Then an office was allowed. And another. This forced up land values and thus high rates began to force people to sell their homes. The prices were attractive too. Today one sees a mass of offices and streets and pavements overrun with cars, showing that no advantage was gained as far as reducing the commuting problem was concerned.

With careful and democratic local control there can be a happy medium.

Electronics, eventually, will also weaken dependence on commuting. More and more people are now able to work from home and communicate with their office in town by way of personal computers. They need to go into town only, say, twice a week for meetings.

Noise pollution

Suburban life does not go back much more than 100 years. That was about when the well-sprung horse-carriage enabled the wealthier to live a little way out of town, away from flies and the noisy taverns. The electric tram enabled the clerks and professionals to follow suit. But it was the car that really boosted the trend. In Johannesburg the new car-generated suburbs at first reached outwards only as far as 10 kilometres from the city centre. But this created a problem: as the suburbs grew and arterial roads increased in number and heavier and heavier streams of cars daily travelled to and fro so the city centre became choked and the older, inner ring suburbs became threatened by sluggish traffic corridors.

The engineers' answer to the traffic snarl-up was more highways. So, in the 1960s, motorways began radiating even further out of town and that produced a second stage of suburbanisation. Now these new suburbanites *really* needed cars. As suburbs leapfrogged suburbs, and as the new affluence led to larger grounds, so the dream of a good public transport system, although it had really been a very vague sort of dream, became even less attainable. The suburbs were too distant and the houses too thinly spread for them to be served economically by buses. As Conrad Berge put it: "The engineers hadn't solved the traffic problem, they'd merely smeared it around." The motorways created even thicker traffic streams converging on city centres. Central compression increased. The older, inner ring suburbs suffered badly as motorways now cut through them.

There were no laws requiring civil engineers to consider noise problems. There still aren't. Johannesburg and Pretoria formulated anti-noise bylaws many years ago but excluded traffic noise! The Environmental Conservation Act 1989 empowers local authorities to combat noise providing they are capable of enforcing them. None does. There are even fines of up to R20 000 or two years in prison allowed for in the Act but there is not the remotest chance of anybody being heavily fined. There are no standards established as to what is noise and there are no measuring instruments that would stand up in a court of law.

The Department of Transport built the N1 motorway through Sandton and Randburg and gave it a ribbed concrete non-skid surface. The noise destroyed people's lives and caused a drop in rateable values. No attempts were made to recess the road into the landscape (the original plan called for this) or to build noise screens. Indeed, the man responsible for the design blamed people for building houses in the vicinity. At a CSIR conference on noise I criticised the design and incurred the wrath of a Department of Transport delegate who shouted: "What do you want? A quiet highway or a safe one?" I said: "Both!" and argued that engineers can provide both. In Canada the laws against noise are such that highway engineers are not allowed to bring noise levels above the existing background levels. If they do they have to pay whatever it takes to reduce the noise for surrounding homes. Thus a multi-lane urban highway in Montreal did not raise suburban noise levels one decibel. In Seattle, a recessed motorway was still found to be unacceptably noisy and the municipality had to roof it over. This not only solved the noise problem but it gave the areas a new linear park.

It is almost impossible to achieve dead silence – nil decibels. The rustle of leaves would produce 15 decibels. I measured the noise level in my study at 11 pm when it appeared dead silent and it was 28 decibels. A public library would be about 35 and a quiet suburb would have a background level of 45 decibels, as would a general office. A busy highway would be 80 decibels, so would the top deck of a bus. At 85 prolonged exposure would permanently damage the ears. In industry the laws are that workers must wear protective ear muffs or they will not be eligible for workmen's compensation should they go deaf. At 100 decibels you would not be able to hear yourself scream. The average disco would be around 95 to 100 decibels and even higher, which leads to most disc jockeys becoming deaf in later life. A jetliner at take off hits 120 decibels, which is near the threshold of pain.

Noise is a very serious pollutant. Several studies have found that in areas where there are intermittent high noise levels, such as in the region of highways and airports, there are greater numbers of miscarriages and stress-related illnesses, including cancers. People living near highways may, intellectually, get used to noisy trucks passing during the night but they never adjust physiologically. Experiments have shown that every time a noisy vehicle passes, their blood vessels dilate – a sign of stress. A serious stress factor in surburbia can be barking dogs. In fact this form of noise pollution is the one about which municipalities receive the most complaints. Johannesburg has prosecuted dog owners and even ordered the removal of dogs. Some suburbs, such as Parkhurst, Johannesburg have as many as 20 dogs – watchdogs mostly – to a hectare. Indeed they call the place Barkhurst.

Generally speaking, the fight against noise is being lost in the cities. Yet it is a serious urban problem which has answers: pneumatic drills and "pavement crackers" can be muffled, so can diesel engines; highways can be designed to reflect traffic noise back into the traffic. One of South Africa's greatest indictments of the standards of civil engineers when it comes to highway planning, and attention to environmental impacts, is the concrete highway (the N1) which I mentioned earlier. It arcs across the top of Greater Johannesburg and its notorious high-pitched noise, mainly from tyres, penetrates deep into the suburbs, devaluing many hundreds of homes and affecting the health of thousands of people. In a Department of Health journal *(Salus)* in 1990 the following paragraph appeared in connection with this particular highway:

> *Although this type of noise pollution is quite pervasive, it is more harmful at the psychological than the physiological level. Excessive exposure to loud noise, on the other hand, causes damage to the ear itself.*

One gets the feeling that the anonymous writer views psychological damage as less important than damage to the ear. Many would disagree. There is a way of halving the highway's noise – lower the speed limit from 120 kilometres per hour to 80 kilometres per hour through the built up sections. This would also mean the non-skid ribbing could be tarred over because skidding would be less likely at the lower speed. When I suggested this to an engineer from the Department of Transport he was incredulous. He said motorways were built for speed. Anyway, he said, he lived near a highway himself and the noise never bothered him. I thought of telling him about the Greek philosopher who observed that the more intelligent one was the more sensitive one became to noise. I refrained only because I could not remember the philosopher and the official would never have understood anyway.

Inside-out cities

In the 1980s the new far-flung suburbs which had been created by the motorways began to coalesce into autonomous towns. They were stuck like flies on a spider's web made up of arterial roads – a web which had only strands radiating from the centre. The new towns were beginning to do more and more trade with one another and people living in one new town began finding work, or schools, or favoured shopping centres, in the next. Suddenly new traffic streams began to cut across the established radial pattern. Rat runs developed between the houses of the very people who had moved out of the core city to escape just this. Old-fashioned engineers who still greatly influenced municipal councils had an answer: more arterials. This time they would cut across the radial lines of the old highways. But the public had had enough. The new towns were peopled by young professionals, architects, town planners, engineers, doctors, lawyers and others. Women too were far more educated than their mothers and far more vocal on public issues. They resisted the engineering "solution". Cars, they said, had done enough damage. The time had come for other solutions.

Other solutions? In September 1990, the London *Sunday Times*, after talking to all the experts they could find, offered a blueprint for saving London from traffic thrombosis. London's traffic chaos is annually causing around 8 000 businesses to move out of town. The newspaper advocated special permits (a toll system of sorts) for cars entering the city, the abolition of the company car in the next budget, a radical increase in parking fines, the banning of commercial loading and offloading between 8 am and 8 pm, and the controlling of rat runs through residential areas by using speed humps and squeeze points. But the keystone to the system would be a vast upgrade of public transport with priority lanes for buses and automatic priority at traffic lights. The bus driver could activate the lights from his cab as he approached. They also suggested "superbuses" with the regularity of trains and extra comforts. I mention the newspaper's suggestions only because we are looking at the city of London which has tried everything and which already has a tube train system which is the envy of most cities. London's dilemma is a warning to us.

The squatters

There were, in 1990, probably about 7 million squatters, or let's rather say "new urban dwellers", in South African cities – all without proper homes. Sadly the country was caught totally unprepared. In the past, influx control laws (an integral part of apartheid) had physically restrained black people from living in cities and when influx controls were lifted in the 1980s the human flood began. It will continue, says the Urban Foundation's Ann Bernstein, until South Africa's eight biggest cities move from accommodating 12 million to accommodating 32 million, a level she believes will be reached in about 2010.

In the battle to house as many people as possible, as quickly as possible, officials have gone back to drawing plans for Soweto-style grid iron settlements and laying out tiny square plots along each road. Each plot would need a fence and a gate, and a house in the middle. Each road, apart from maintenance, would need surfacing, storm water drains, water pipes, sewer pipes, electric cables; each house would need its individual water, electricity and sewerage connection. The sprawl is maximal so service costs, including transport costs, are guaranteed to be maximal. All this for the poorest urban dwellers of all! Architect Heinz Hachler who has designed many sub-economic schemes and who takes the unusual step of interviewing squatters to find out how they prefer to live, suggested a better way. He said it would be more sensible to cluster the houses so that each cluster formed a small communal village whose homes need no fences, no gates, only one road and only one common sewer, water and power line. His scheme accommodates far more people than can be accommodated in the grid iron approach and leaves three-quarters of the site empty for playgrounds and other uses such as allotments (for growing vegetables), as well as for the future expansion of the cluster. Roads would be reduced by two-thirds and this would cut capital costs for each dwelling unit.

19 Waste: Space Age or Garb-Age

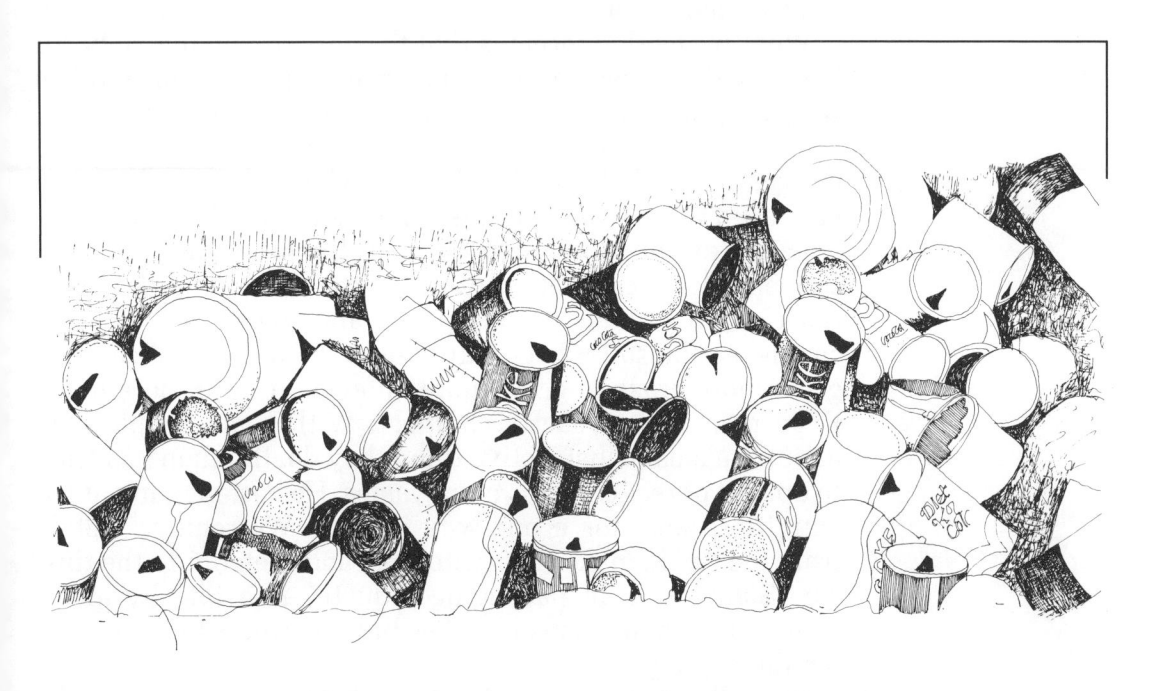

Waste not, want not.

Old proverb

MAN is standing between a dwindling heap of the usable and an ever-increasing heap of the unusable. I forget who said that but whoever it was, was wrong. Somebody else said that today's rubbish tips are tomorrow's mines. That's more like it.

What we tend to forget is that the only reason life on Earth has lasted all these millions of years is because of nature's recycling scheme. There is no such thing as waste in nature. Everything is recycled, including our breath: we inhale oxygen and exhale carbon dioxide which plants take up to give off oxygen ... Rain falls, collects in puddles and in the oceans, evaporates into the air, forms clouds whose condensed water falls as rain. Or the lion which kills the buck and then adds its droppings, and, eventually, its own carcass to the soil where nature uses the body's nutrients to grow more grass to grow more antelope to feed more lions. Even man makes useful compost. With some people it is about the most constructive thing they do. But man has tried to opt out of recycling his own wastes. He has, in many of his activities, gone for a one-way system. We remove metals from the earth, make them into tins, and then dump the tins. The South African packaging industry is a bit shy about exactly how many cans it makes but you can bet it is around 5 million a day.

We will not, in this chapter, look at the waste dumps in the sky: the millions of tons of sulphur and carbon, etc, which are all quite usable but mostly represent an irretrievable loss of natural resources. Nor will we deal with the millions of tons of substances which find their way into the rivers and the sea. We will skip the 2 000 million tons of mine waste too because that is dealt with elsewhere. This chapter looks only at what the man in the street calls refuse and litter.

In fact let's get litter out of the way too. It is a cosmetic problem which can be solved relatively easily. Switzerland can show us how. If you drop even a match in the streets of a Swiss city a passer-by may well pick it up and give it back to you; then you want to curl up into a foetal position until night falls when you can crawl home. Litterbugs are uncouth – like people who spit on the pavement. If the police catch you littering in any one of 100 cities in the world they will treat you like a common criminal. In South Africa the authorities mostly stamp their feet. Driving out of Nelspruit once, on the new and landscaped highway to Johannesburg,

I saw a well-dressed woman in an expensive car toss a drink can out of her window. I do not believe one can educate that sort of person except by fining them. In contrast, a woman on an American highway threw a tissue out of her window and then noticed a traffic officer on a motorcycle tailing her. After some distance he pulled her over and said: "Ma'am, you threw litter on to the highway back there. You have the choice: a fine of $500 or go back and pick it up."

The municipality of Johannesburg alone spent R25 million in 1990 picking up after people. Gys du Plessis, head of solid waste management in Johannesburg, says that while it costs R90 a ton to dispose of rubbish retrieved from litter bins it costs R900 a ton to dispose of each ton of litter strewn on the streets. There are better things on which to spend that sort of money. The Keep South Africa Beautiful Association, in the early part of the 1980s, instituted the "Clean Community System" in which it advises and aids municipalities to fight litter. In the United States it was found that for every $1 spent on such anti-litter campaigns (which include "educating" either directly through schools or through posters and imaginative promotions), $10 was saved because of the excellent response. In some communities litter was cut 80 per cent. All the same, many of these campaigns are backed by tough fines.

It would be a simple matter to announce that large fines will be imposed after a period of, say, six months of intensive educational campaigning. Our problem is that we would have to exercise an extraordinary discretion. Giel Niewehout who, a few years back, ran Randburg's imaginative and effective cleansing branch, said: "There is the problem of the new urban people. They buy a carton of sorghum beer, drink it and drop it when it is empty. This is not because people are sloppy, it is because they are confronted with a situation which is unique in their experience. In a rural village nothing is wasted. Scraps are fed to the chickens, empty containers, of which there would be few, become utensils, paper and other combustibles become fuel." Squatters, who may be uneducated, are, even in their grinding poverty, clean in their habits. I have witnessed it in South Africa, Mauritius and Brazil – shack dwellers carefully sweeping the space in and around their dwellings. People, generally, have a desire to live in clean surroundings.

At the same time it is easy to understand why municipalities are loathe to accost litterbugs in the street. There is a distinct threat of physical harm. The worst-littered areas of cities are often the most crime-ridden and inspectors would have to act in squads to be effective and safe. That would make it very expensive.

The packaging industry has, from time to time, made attempts to defend itself against being blamed for the litter problem. Quite rightly. After all, it is not the industry which litters any more than Sheffield's knife manufacturers are into throat-slitting. But sometimes the packaging industry can be misleading. In the mid 1970s *The Star*'s CARE campaign did a roadside survey near Witbank and found that bottles and tins constituted 80 per cent of the items of litter picked up from the grass at the roadside. It is noticeable, wherever one goes, that tins, non-returnable bottles and plastic material are the most conspicuous items in the Earth's overburden of litter. This is partly because paper packaging tends to dissolve in the rain and break down in the sun. But bottles, like diamonds, "are for ever". Tins, too, can last centuries. A year after the CARE survey, the Council for Scientific and Industrial Research published a survey revealing exactly the opposite. It found newspapers to be the worst litter component and cans and bottles rated only 7 or 8 per cent. Having organised the CARE survey I was at first nonplussed. Then I discovered that the survey was paid for, and the data were supplied by the packaging industry itself. The method used was ingenious: items of litter were measured in A4 units: thus three beer cans would cover the space of one A4 sheet of paper. So a beer can would be rated as one-third of a litter unit. But a newspaper (*The Star* published 120 pages a day in those days), spread out, would measure 720 times more than a beer can! The survey was conducted in the rainless Highveld winter when paper decomposition was minimal. And the areas to be surveyed were cleared two weeks before the survey to ensure there was no build-up of cans and bottles and no time for paper to break down into the soil.

Conservationists have had some robust and, I like to think, mutually educative battles with the packaging industry which, through its front organisations, Keep South Africa Beautiful, Keep Johannesburg Beautiful and others, has done, and spent, a great deal on getting the public to be more litter conscious. At the same time it has achieved its main objective, outlined at a series of closed meetings in 1972 (when a campaign called Keep South Africa Tidy was launched), to fight off attempts to impose deposits on containers. This alliance of packaging and beverage companies has a big stake in the throw-away society. The more bottles thrown away, the more bottles the industry can sell. The same goes for cans.

On the very day *The Star* announced its environmental awareness campaign, CARE, (March 1971), Leighton Slater, the then chairman of the Argus Company which owned the newspaper, received by hand delivery a long letter from an executive of a major packaging firm beginning "Dear Leighton . . ." It fulsomely praised the paper's initiative and asked to see the man behind the campaign – which happened to be me. Slater sent the letter down to me saying I was in no way bound to see the writer whom he knew only vaguely through golf. All the same, I went. The director's opening

School children clean up a suburban walking trail. Source The Star

remarks gave an inkling of what I was up against. He said, after a perfunctory greeting: "Tell me, from where does your newspaper get its income?" To which I replied: "Mainly from advertising." He said: "Right! And the packaging industry is a very big advertiser indeed. Don't you forget that!" I published a verbatim report of our exchange next day and after that we struck up a straight-talking relationship which lasted many years.

The fact remains, deposits on bottles and cans are an effective way of ensuring they are recycled. A colleague, Graham Ferreira, placed quart beer bottles, returnable Coca-Cola bottles, beer cans and "dumpies" (non-returnable bottles) in a pile in a Cape Town park. Within an hour the returnables were gone.

The packaging industry has spent millions on propaganda, some of it unbelievably naive, aimed at giving the impression that returnable containers will cost the public dearly and will demolish jobs. A statement by the Packaging Council of South Africa said that "restrictive containers measures" (they cannot bring themselves to say that dread word, "deposits") will lead to the closing of plants, lost jobs and higher prices which, it never fails to add, "will be passed on to the consumer". It further warns that returnable bottles require 15 times more water to clean than a new bottle would need in the manufacturing stage.

The packaging industry's policy has been to argue the merits of packaging. It points out how pre-packaging now makes it impossible for shopkeepers to mix stale and fresh produce; how it has solved the problem of short-weight, unhygienic handling and has helped guarantee quality and standard weight. All this is true but the "usefulness" and consumer convenience of a commodity did nothing to save CFCs from being axed, or DDT. Nobody will deny the enormous convenience of packaging, but that does not excuse us from continuing to find ways to reduce waste. Part of the clean up has to be some sort of curb on this throw-away cult. We make it far too easy. Zimbabwe puts South Africa to shame when it comes to cleanliness, because Zimbabwe allows only returnable bottles. Malawi, too, is cleaner, for the same reason. Deposits have not always reduced litter in the more affluent Western nations but wherever there are lots of poor, there you will find no returnable containers lying around.

A Greek survey came up with the following useful information: a bus ticket takes a month to biodegrade, cotton takes five months, a wool sock a year, a bamboo pole three years, a wooden stake three years and an aluminium can 500 years. I imagine a cool drink bottle would take 5 000 years, maybe more.

Dumps: tomorrow's mines

Dumps can be interesting places. One day, when I went to a Johannesburg tip to dump an old but good quality washing machine which was giving us more trouble than it was worth, I met a solid waste management academic from the University of the Witwatersrand whom I knew. He looked with shining eyes at the washing machine. "Don't dump it," he said. "Stick it down here." Years later I heard the machine, which he fixed, was still going strong. In New Zealand some rather genteel neighbours of ours, hearing we needed a chair, suggested we go to the tip and offered to accompany us after work. I was amazed to see scores of well-dressed people strolling round the perimeter of the tip like connoisseurs at an antique fair. They were even looking into the boots of cars belonging to people who had come to dump stuff, and were taking items before they could be unloaded. Professor Andre Rabie, the environmental law expert at Stellenbosch University told me how he and his wife, when they were impoverished post-graduate students in Germany in the 1970s, furnished their flat and found toys for their child, from discarded items. The Germans, he explained, have a quite refined method of dumping unwanted household items. Some cities issue an annual list of streets, each with a date next to it. Each suburban street is allocated one day a year on which people can dump absolutely anything they like. If you get there early you can pick up all sorts of treasures which need a lick of paint, or some patient glueing or a couple of screws. At the end of the day the municipality takes away the leftovers.

According to Jacqueline Myburgh, in her recycling handbook published by the Wildlife Society, *Once is Not Enough* (1990), South Africans generate about 24 million tons of domestic rubbish a year and, by the end of the century, the Pretoria-Witwatersrand-Vaal complex alone will be producing 15 million tons. Recycling, said Myburgh, conserves resources, reduces the need to import, usually requires less energy than producing goods from raw materials, saves smothering land under rubbish tips, creates labour intensive operations, beats inflation, gives charities a chance to make money (by setting up receiving depots) and reduces pollution.

Man is consuming colossal amounts of natural resources, often quite frivolously. A Worldwatch Institute study (1990) found "that the average American consumes most of his or her own weight in basic fuels, minerals, and agricultural and forest products". It added: "Despite phenomenal growth in their consumption of goods Americans are no more satisfied with life now than they were in 1957". The researcher, Alan Durning, believed that a change of values will ultimately be needed "both for personal fulfillment and to keep human demands from exhausting the Earth."

Already the world is scrambling around looking, mostly in vain, for more deposits of all manner of minerals. Consol, the South African glass-making giant, is so desperate for silica for making throw-away bottles, that it felt compelled to pre-empt the proclamation of the Magaliesberg mountains as a nature reserve by carving into one of its most conspicuous mountains. Thus did Consol establish its right to mine there for all time. By the same token the world is so short of oil that, as I am writing, it is surveying the colossal damage of the Iraqi war which cost thousands of young lives. The war would not have happened if Iraq produced orange juice. And, short of oil though South Africa is, it continues to make billions of throw-away plastic containers (from oil and coal)

Scrapped cars in Frankfurt, Germany. Source Deutsche Presse-Agentur

as well as other plastic packaging material, which are then dumped. Not even the potential energy locked within these materials is used as fuel.

Waste is morally bad. If the world were to use no natural resources at all for 25 years, those living would still have to make do with only half of what we have today, because the world's population will be doubled by then. There is a school of thought which says it is ridiculous to save stuff for the unborn because they will find new materials just as we have. So, they argue, why stint on using up metal and oil? Look how the Club of Rome, in its *Limits to Growth* report in 1974, predicted that certain common-or-garden commodities would soon run out. Copper was an example. Yet today a shoebox full of sand can be turned into fibre-optics capable of transmitting electronically as much information as 1 000 tons of copper wire did a decade a ago. On the other hand there is no sense in squandering material in the way First World populations do. The upper income earners, black and white, of South Africa's cities consume, and throw away, about as much as the average American. While the average South African produces almost 1 kilogram of rubbish a day, the average Johannesburger dumps close to 2 kilograms a day. The amount of refuse is growing by 4 per cent a year, which will eventually place an impossible strain on the country's 234 municipal dumps, nearly all of which already have problems. A survey carried out by William Hattingh of the Pretoria Technikon revealed that half the dumps were causing some kind of water pollution, half had problems with air pollution, a third posed threats to public health and three-quarters were an aesthetic problem. A quarter of the tips had a combination of all these problems.

There is a school of thought which looks upon refuse tips as mines. It sees them as valuable for the retrieval of recyclable material; as a source of energy for power stations which can mix refuse with conventional fuel (166 power stations do this in the United States), and, thirdly, as a source of biogas which can substitute even for petrol. This school says that as long as domestic waste reaches the dump it can be economically sorted and recycled. If this approach could be made to work on an economical basis it might well be a better way of retrieving glass, metal and plastic than the cash deposit system. But it will probably need some central agency to provide the capital for the plants.

Recycling

When in 1972 Neil Armstrong, the first man on the moon, came to South Africa he explained how his home town, Franklin, Ohio, had just hit on a novel approach to municipal waste. Armstrong, a professional engineer, had become something of an environmental evangelist since his moon odyssey and was enthusiastic about his home town's achievement. Franklin is not a big town – it had only 10 000 inhabitants at the time. One of its councillors was Joe Baxter, Jnr, a paper mill engineer. Baxter suggested solving the town's refuse problem by initially pulping it. There was some self-interest too: 60 per cent of the refuse was paper. Franklin received a $2 million grant for the experiment from the Solid Waste Office in Washington and in May 1971 the plant was constructed. By August it was processing not only 50 tons of rubbish a day from Franklin, but rubbish from neighbouring towns who were paying Franklin to take their stuff. The rubbish was dumped onto a conveyor belt which carried it up to a huge spinning drum (a 3,6 metre wide centrifuge called a Hydrapulper). Here recycled water was mixed with the refuse. All pulpable and easily granulated material was converted into a slurry by high speed cutters (as in a liquidiser), and all non-friable material, such as cans, was ejected by centrifugal force through openings in the sides of the vessel. From there they fell down a chute where magnets plucked out the metal for selling back to the steel mills.

The slurry, containing food wastes, paper, glass, plastic, rubber, rags, bones, grass and leaves – was then pumped into a liquid cyclone which removed heavier components, again by spinning them off centrifugally. Eighty per cent was glass, which went back to the glass manufacturers. The rest was pumped into another machine (Fibreclaim) and the paper fibres extracted. The residue was dewatered and incinerated. Every 50 tons of refuse yielded 9 tons of paper fibre, 3,3 tons of broken glass, 3,3 tons of ferrous metals and 500 kilograms of aluminium. The operation, which was then working only one shift a day (because quantities were so small) was already profitable (if one deducts the capital cost) and, in addition, it saved valuable space.

In the winter of 1991 Johannesburg was due to start up one of the world's most advanced recycling plants and, instead of going to Government for funding, it invited private enterprise and, surprisingly, received 10 tenders. A Pretoria company won the right to retrieve from incoming trucks at Robinson Deep tip, paper, glass, metal, plastics and jute. The jute component was from the nearby municipal produce market. Out of the total 1 500 tons of rubbish a day the operation is geared to intercept for recycling 400 tons a day. Much of the rest is biodegradable (it will rot in time). Johannesburg stands to score not only from a royalty but from the fact that the operation gives Robinson Deep three more years of life. This means a huge saving in transport and fuel because the dump is only 3 kilometres from the city centre. Few cities are as lucky as that. Robinson Deep tip has been going since 1930 and will last at least another 15 years. It is rich in another useful commodity – biogas. (This we look at later.)

Only a tiny percentage of South Africa's municipal waste stream was being recycled by 1990 but at least it was ahead of Britain which was recycling only 1,5 per cent. The European Community was considering measures to step up the amount all round. West Germany was doing best: 10 per cent. The State of Pennsylvania in the United States in 1990 passed legislation requiring all towns with a population over

Old car tyres present both a problem and an opportunity

10 000 to sort their refuse into different commodities in 1991. It was concerned that the number of refuse sites had come down from more than 1 000 in the 1970s to fewer than 20. The US Environmental Protection Agency requires that by 1992 a quarter of America's refuse must be recycled.

Not that Johannesburg was the only town recycling its wastes. In 1990 Randburg leased its refuse tip to a private firm which set up a recycling facility and, within a year, hoped to be operating a profitable recycling enterprise. The operator expected to employ 100 unskilled workers to hand sort glass, tin, plastic and metals from domestic refuse. The Robinson Deep operation, which is many times bigger, is much more automated and employs 60. Randburg's project was designed to use even "wet refuse" – food wastes mostly – which would be turned into compost for sale to the public. Even builders' rubble would be crushed and screened into sand for re-use.

Attempts to persuade householders to separate their rubbish into different bins – glass in one, metal in the other, plastic in a third and wet refuse in a fourth, have been tried with usually disappointing results in many parts of the world. While recycling is obviously a part solution to the ever-growing mountains of trash, it is not the ideal one. The ideal one was suggested by Chris Albertyn of the South African green group, Earthlife: "Make less trash in the first place."

PLASTICS. Plastics are the most controversial and the most versatile of packaging materials. They have proved a great convenience in the First *and* the Third World. In the case of the former it has been a boon in packaging; in the Third World it has served more mundane but quite essential services such as water pipes, dam linings, water containers and, for squatters, shelter. But, in the First World its image is fading. Its image has been partly damaged by industry's own attitude: the world is filled with cheap plastic toys and other geegaws seemingly designed to last a day. Millions of cubic metres of toys made in Hong Kong and Taiwan are piling up on rubbish dumps. Thus plastic has a "trashy" image.

Rubbish dumps, despite the packaging industry's claims that plastics represent only 7 per cent of refuse, by weight, are becoming almost solid plastic, mostly because most other materials break down. William Rathje, a US "garbologist", in evidence to a senate sub-committee on waste in 1990, stated "plastics take up only between 9 and 12 per cent of the volume (of refuse tips)". How he arrived at such a conclusion beats me. In 1989 the European Community's total solid waste was 2,2 billion tons a year, of which 4 per cent was domestic waste. Only 7 per cent of the domestic waste was plastic and only 0,28 of the total annual waste was plastic –

but because plastic is long lived, the dumps contained one-third plastic by volume. Europe is now looking to biodegradable plastics as the solution.

At the Mitchell's Plain tip in the Cape, where graders make windrows of refuse, one can see in the exposed cross sections almost only plastic. But at least Cape Town municipality is turning that to advantage. A local industry has been created. It mines the dump, winnowing all plastics from the refuse and by using heat and pressure, turns it into a form of artificial wood which can be sawn, planed, nailed and painted just like wood and can be used for park benches, picket fences, planters and duck boarding. The residue at the dump is rapidly broken down into first class compost.

There was a lot of talk in the 1980s about biodegradable plastic but there were two things wrong with the concept: one was that the plastic merely broke down into microscopic plastic dust which, in quantity, would not be good for the soil. In any event the breakdown period was very long so one still had the problem of a long-lived litter component. The second drawback was that it was a waste of a product which could be recycled or burned as fuel. A piece of plastic is capable of giving back 25 per cent of the energy that went into it. But there is now a truly degradable plastic being developed by AECI in South Africa. This is a "rubbery" substance produced from a bacteria (Pseudomonas) using molasses as a medium. A special chemical in the plastic triggers off biological degradation once the material is exposed to ultraviolet light from the sun. The substance, Biopol, although still in the development stage, shows great promise as an alternative plastic in the medical field as well as in pharmacology, veterinarian technology and in agriculture. Researcher Liz de Vincentiis described it as a non-toxic product that is compatible with human tissue. It breaks down into PHB, 3-hydroxybutyric acid which is found in significant quantities in mammalian blood so it could be used for artificial skin, bone plates, bone fracture pins and swabs. But it also shows promise in packaging: for instance, it could be coated on to paper and used for wrapping fish and chips or hamburgers, replacing foam plastic which is known to release ozone-destroying CFCs. Dr de Vincentiis says "it breaks down to nothing, or next to nothing." They can be used for babies' nappies, shopping bags and fertiliser and compost bags – just dig them into the ground after use.

In the meantime many environmentalists feel conventional plastic bags should be banned. In Britain, and most European countries, supermarkets do not give out plastic shopping bags but require shoppers to bring their own or buy them. The most popular bag is the string bag. A problem is that carelessly discarded plastic bags kill hundreds of cattle in South Africa every year. Cattle find them in the veld and eat them. This blocks their digestive tract. Fish, wild mammals and birds are also killed by them. Thor Heyerdahl, the ocean expolorer, years ago was appalled at how much floating plastic he saw even in mid-Atlantic and in mid-Pacific thousands of kilometres from land. The seas off Southern Africa have on average 3 500 pieces to the square kilometre. That's just the floating stuff. Nobody has measured that which has sunk.

I have only ever had one "Big Mac" and that was in Anchorage. I ordered it more to see its legendary volume of polystyrene packaging, for I am not particularly fond of hamburgers. McDonalds of Alaska did not let me down: the burger was wrapped up like an old Inuit and placed inside a polystyrene box. In the 1980s, after mounting pressure from environmentalists, McDonald's said polystyrene would be no problem in future because their researchers were into a $1 000 million scheme to recycle the stuff. In the meantime their 8 500 fast food outlets in the US were taking up enormous volumes of landfill sites at great public expense because polystyrene takes centuries to decompose once it is buried. And, of course, as the packaging disintegrates it releases CFCs. By the beginning of 1991 McDonalds was abandoning the use of foam plastic altogether and converting to a thin paper. The paper cannot be recycled but at least it takes up only 10 per cent of the volume of the foam plastic and does not emit CFCs. Two Californian companies, in 1990, moved from using polystyrene foam pellets to using popcorn. At least nobody can argue that that isn't biodegradable.

Plastics manufacturers say that if all plastic packaging were replaced by paper, two things would happen: the volume of packaging would double and the energy consumption of the packaging industry would increase 25 per cent. And, of course, a mind-boggling number of trees would be needed and that means more food-producing land smothered by plantations. Paper packaging is not the ideal route. Interestingly plastic supermarket shopping bags are 71 per cent lighter than in the 1960s and the 2 litre soft drink bottles are down by one-third in 10 years.

There is no easy solution to the plastics question. But one must concede that plastics manufacturers are right: if the public were more sensible and plastic waste could be channelled back to the recyclers, and if people did not litter, plastic would not be a problem. Part of the solution seems to be for the industry to pay higher prices for used plastic collected by informal sector scavengers. Although there is a limit to the number of times plastic can be recycled, the useless residues can, as a final resort, be burned as fuel.

METAL. The tin "can" (can is short for cannister) was invented in 1810 and is one of the great inventions of the Industrial Revolution. In the last decade, because of environmental and economic pressures, cans have been reduced in weight by 44 per cent.

South Africa is probably using around 5 million cans a day and although 46 000 tons of tinplate are annually recycled, this is only one-sixth of the 269 000 tons produced. The industry could use it all if there were an economic way to collect it and get it to the mills. Not that it can go back into making cans but it can go into steel. New steel in South Africa is 17 per cent scrap. In the United States it can be as high as 50 per cent.

Like many other recyclable materials the industry concerned is not paying enough to get its product back – and this questions its sincerity about recycling. Used cans fetch about R25 a ton – and a ton is 25 000 cans. That's 1c for every 10 cans. A barrow load is not going to buy you even a loaf of bread.

In 1990 Pick 'n Pay, one of South Africa's major chain stores, began assembling "one armed bandits" outside its stores into which the public could feed one can at a time, pull a lever to crush them, and, with luck, win a prize. Each machine is capable of swallowing 2 000 cans a day, so theoretically, 2 500 machines countrywide would solve the can problem. If the scheme works it will overcome the big problem of transporting tins to the mills. After all, a truck full of uncrushed cans is really a truck full of fresh air. One would be squandering fuel to save metal. Getting the public to crush its own cans is a stroke of genius.

GLASS. Glass manufacturers claim glass is the most "environmentally friendly" of all packaging. This is partly because the commodity is easily recycled back into bottles but also because there is no production waste. Reject bottles from the assembly line are automatically re-routed back to the production line. Of the 3,7 million glass bottles which daily leave the factories half are returnable according to the industry.

The glass makers claim two thirds of the bottles they make are recycled. (In Europe it is 85 per cent.) One scheme is to place large igloo-shaped containers outside major shopping centres. They are painted green, brown and white for the respective coloured glass. The money paid for broken glass goes to charity. Igloos are said by the packaging industry to have increased the amount of reclaimed glass by 30 per cent. There is a 25 per cent saving in energy when making new bottles from old glass.

PAPER. One-third of South Africa's annual production of 1,9 million tons of paper is recycled. This saves 1,5 million tons of raw materials or, of you like, 23 million trees. That is important more in terms of the amount of land that does not have to be smothered by monotonous and sterilising pine trees. Mondi's "Paper Pick-up" recycling project which involves R5 million worth of vehicles and many new jobs, should boost the proportion of recycled paper by 15 per cent by mid-1992. This would put South Africa on a par with Europe. The United States recycles only 20 per cent, and Australia 22 per cent. Sappi says it is recycling 1 500 tons a day – 45 per cent of production. It estimates recycled paper needs between 30 to 55 per cent less energy to reconstitute than making virgin paper. Manufacturing recycled paper, compared with virgin paper, reduces air pollution by three-quarters, water pollution by a third and reduces pressure on land. The industry has a problem in that pine trees in South Africa grow far more quickly than in the northern hemisphere and, therefore, produce soft, short-fibred wood – unlike northern pine which is slow growing, long-fibred and hard. The latter can be recycled three times and still be used as newsprint. Local newsprint is unsuitable for recycling back into quality printing paper and is mostly only good for cardboard, egg trays and fruit packaging.

A "future shock" signal for the newspaper industry may be

coming from Connecticut whose newsprint manufacturers, including those outside the state but who sell inside, are obliged to include 20 per cent recycled material by 1993 and 90 per cent by 1998.

Despite this the industry could justifiably contend with the glass industry in claiming to be the most environmentally friendly in that at least paper quickly becomes soil. In Scandinavia newsprint is mixed with nutrients and fed to cattle - print and all.

The paper industry is committed to getting high quality waste paper back to the paper mills and commerce in general can do a lot to help. Offices could easily separate clean waste paper from other rubbish and arrange for it to be collected, or arrange for it to be pooled with waste from neighbouring offices. Waste paper fetches between R70 and R450 a ton depending on quality, the average price being R150.

Roodepoort and Randburg householders are being educated into keeping their waste paper, as well as glass, separate from other refuse, a trend now popular in Europe. In Japan some districts are sophisticated enough to separate their waste into seven categories.

RUBBER. The United States discards 240 million vehicle tyres a year. South Africa, with its five million vehicles, would discard only a fraction of that. Nevertheless, in some areas, tyres smother hectares of land and, from time to time, one hears of "accidental" fires which consume huge tyre dumps conveniently making room for more. In some parts of the world quantities of tyres are baled together and sunk off the coast where they soon become encrusted with marine life and form useful habitats for fish. Tyres are cut up into doormats, the Zulu make everlasting sandals from them; some are made into landing mats for aircraft in dusty or marshy places; some are blended with asphalt to make road surfaces (which last twice as long as ordinary asphalt), and some are burned as fuel.

In March 1990 *New Scientist* reported that two research groups in the United States had come up with simple ways to recycle the billions of used tyres now lying around - tyres which used up a third of America's imported oil. John Cue of Chester, near Philadelphia, received a state grant to convert tyres into drainpipes and fencing. In another part of the state, at Allentown, a chemical products firm led by Bernard

Bauman was working on a method which converts old rubber to a polymer composite that can be made into garden hose, gaskets, rollers and even back into tyres. Old tyres can be made into piping at a quarter of the cost of PVC.

Dumping tyres on landfill sites is entirely unsatisfactory. They tend to work their way to the surface but worse than that they form habitats for insects and rats. Once they are well and truly buried they do not compact and trap pockets of gas. In Modesto, California, 5 million tyres are burned each year to produce 14 MW of electricity – enough for 15 000 homes. The process, known as pyrolosis (burning without air) can also use other types of refuse, plastic being especially useful. In Britain 218 000 tons of scrap tyres are dumped – annually – enough to generate R500 million worth of energy. South Africa is probably dumping a third of that figure. It is a problem that we cannot ignore for much longer.

Inexhaustible oil wells?

Brian la Trobe is an industrial chemist, a product of the University of the Witwatersrand, who later became a small town dentist. He settled in Grahamstown and there, apart from fixing teeth, he became a councillor and mayor. As a councillor he worried about the amount of refuse the town's 20 000 people threw away and where on earth the town would find a landfill site where nobody would complain of the smell. Then he began wondering if the smell could somehow be eliminated. One thing led to another and the dentist, in middle age, once again changed career. Today he is an engineer, and an authority on tapping methane gas from refuse and turning it into a petroleum substitute.

In 1986 he and Professor Trevor Letcher, a biochemist of Rhodes University in Grahamstown, combined talents to find a use for the gases which build up in the town's refuse tip. La Trobe was greatly impressed by the volatility of landfill gas when he read that a house, built on a long-forgotten tip in Britain, was blown apart when somebody accidentally ignited methane which had seeped through the floor. The two men obtained a small grant and persuaded the council to dump its daily 80 tons of refuse in a new landfill site in a clay pit. Each day's load was then smothered by a 50 millimetre layer of clay so that it formed a more or less airtight cell. Almost three years later, in April 1989, the council and the press were invited to a braai on the rubbish dump and, feeding the methane gas from the rotting rubbish into a conventional gas cooker, La Trobe cooked a meal of boerewors and steak. The gas was obtained by sinking a perforated pipe into one of the cells where, anaerobically (that's part of the secret – there must be no oxygen), methane had been building up a few metres below ground. It really was almost as simple as that.

Almost, but not quite. In fact the gas is about 50/50 methane (a serious ozone killing gas) and carbon dioxide, the infamous CO_2 which is largely to blame for the greenhouse effect. Fortunately CO_2 is soluble in water and so can be scrubbed out by passing it through water. It then becomes ordinary soda water which can be safely dumped in the nearest stream. There was also the problem of compressing the gas and here La Trobe improvised by using a small motor run on methane from the dump.

There is no such thing as a free lunch, or braai, and La Trobe used the occasion to point out to his colleagues and the assembled newspapermen that waste must not be considered as waste any more. Every ton of suburban refuse, he said, could produce the equivalent of 290 litres of petrol. It roughly translates to one cubic metre of compacted refuse producing the equivalent of one litre of fuel. Thus South Africa is allowing the equivalent of 7 billion litres of fuel to go to waste every year. Theoretically Johannesburg could run all its municipal vehicles off the methane from its municipal landfill.

In 1990 La Trobe was given the go-ahead, though precious little funds, to experimentally fit Cape Town refuse vehicles with gas cylinders to take landfill gas. The idea is to have Cape Town's refuse collecting vehicles coming to the tip to offload, then filling up with gas from the dump, and continuing with their rounds. It would not be particularly novel. In Modesto, California, 200 police cars run on biogas. In Livermore, California municipal trucks and cars run off biogas which, in 1989, cost a third of the price of conventional fuel. In fact, La Trobe told his audience, California is producing 54 MW of power from gas in its dumps – enough to light up a city. A town of 100 000 can produce 5 400 litres of liquid fuel a day. Yet, up to now, the funding agencies remain unexcited about this line of research and development.

A recent development in Johannesburg might change their minds. In 1990 the city's waste management technologists, in conjunction with technolgists from the explosives and fertiliser plant, AECI, announced a breakthrough at Robinson Deep refuse dump just south of the city. Nearly 60 wells were sunk into the tip and, for the first time in South Africa, methane gas was removed on a commercial scale and for the first time in the world it was turned into a chemical feedstock for industry. The gas is piped 17 kilometres to AECI's Klipspruit plant where the carbon dioxide is removed, ammonia and lime are combined with the methane, and cyanide produced. The cyanide is sold to the gold mines which use it to extract gold from ore. The Klipspruit plant had, for 40 years, received its methane from a nearby municipal waste water treatment plant – enough methane, incidentally, to enable the mining industry to extract 9 000 tons of gold over that period worth, in 1990 terms, R310 billion. The Klipspruit sewerage works became obsolete and the methane from Robinson Deep is being used instead.

The extraction of the gas from the dump has another interesting advantage – it will enable the city council to grow vegetation more easily on the dump (methane gas inhibits grass growth) and it will accelerate the rate of biodegradation of the refuse within the landfill, thus allowing it to stabilise more rapidly.

20 The untrod years

> Thou, too, sail on, O Ship of State!
> Sail on, O Union, strong and great!
> Humanity with all its fears,
> With all the hopes of future years,
> Is hanging breathless on thy fate!
>
> — Henry Wadsworth Longfellow

"I have seen the future and it looks just like Rio." With the future of Cape Town, Durban and Johannesburg in mind, I began an article with these words in a hotel room in the Avenida Princesa Isabel just off Rio de Janeiro's Copacabana in the spring of 1988. I was in a rather depressed state at the time, having spent some weeks, on my own, in a country which had known better days. It is difficult being in Rio or Cuiaba, or even in that much-vaunted town planning disaster called Brazilia, without experiencing subliminal nightmare glimpses of a future South Africa dragged down by mediocrity, corruption, low production, urban congestion and the collapse of law and order.

Rio de Janeiro is a beautiful, tropical city where the ultra rich live uneasily with the terminally poor. Its streets are picked over by muggers who might be in the shape of a knifeman or, perhaps, a small gang of kids operating under the direction of a sweet old lady. The police have given up on street crime. In the beautiful hills which rise above the city, concentrations of shacks have been wedged into the clefts – *favelas*, they are called – and they look just like cascades of refuse spilling down the hills. Along the Estrada das Canoas, which winds into the hills, there are palatial mansions, their massive gates guarded by men with automatic rifles, and right up against some of the fortress-like, graffiti-smothered walls, the shacks are so closely packed they look like so much litter blown into drifts.

Is this South Africa's fate? During the time it took to write this book South Africa's growth rate was on a par with Third World African states while Brazil had a growth rate we could only envy – around 5 per cent. Some may argue we are already halfway towards becoming a banana republic. But being halfway there at least means we have a chance of redeeming the situation. We have several advantages over Brazil. South Africa's environment is, generally speaking, far better than any Third World country and the climate is, most of the time, pleasant. Our urbanisation process is much easier to service and, I believe, there is a much better spirit in our populace. We are in danger of sliding into a Third World malaise, but not inevitably. The challenging, but not particularly daunting task is for a concerted national effort in which the privileged make the necessary sacrifices to catch up with the housing backlog, and, of course, the allocation of desperately needed land for housing; to step up the provision of primary health care for all, and schools, and to support small enterprises. Slowly, too slowly, this is beginning.

Gawie Fagan, an outspoken architect and planner from Cape Town, and a member of the Council for the Environment, speaking at Witwatersrand University's Graduate School of Business in 1990, said that South Africa's privileged should stop deluding themselves that South Africa can afford cities that look like Frankfurt, Dallas and Zurich when the country's per capita gross national product was closer to that of Mexico, Brazil and Turkey.

> *This means we have to become accustomed to adapting our lifestyles to urban complexity, intercultural juxtaposition, a situation far closer to that of Rio than to our [white] delusive image of an unrealistic hyper-privileged past incapable of being sustained save through oppressive and unjust measures.*

All the same, I do not see *favelas* spilling down Northcliff Ridge or Kloofnek Drive, but in our headlong rush towards urbanisation we are going to see more and more shanty towns – hopefully more structured, better tolerated and only temporary.

There are signs that South Africa's population is upwardly mobile – to use that delightful piece of 1970s jargon – and not on the way down. Imagine how it could have been had black people had a fair and equitable education system! I believe we can, if we set our minds to it, attain a level of urbanisation more in tune with the First World than the Third. Before this century is through the major cities will be run by black and white with, I imagine, Johannesburg leading the way. If the economy holds and investment flows in, if the health and education services can indeed be jacked up in time, then our crippling birth rate should begin dropping early next century.

The Minister of nothing

The Environment Conservation Act of 1988 has generally been ineffective and can only remain that way under the present constitution because under the constitution no Government department can override another. Some departments are simply not empowered to take the environment into consideration and should they do so they would, technically speaking, be acting unlawfully. The Act does not incorporate a policy but requires the Minister to frame them. For most of its first year the Act not only had no stated policy but it had no regulations at all. It was, said Jan Glazewski of UCT's law department, a gun without bullets. It still has pathetically few teeth and even if the Minister of Environment should get a sudden urge to start framing policies he would first have to obtain the formal agreement of every Government department. It is not a matter of simply consulting each of them, he must actually seek their blessing. It led the former Environment Minister Gert Kotze to comment ruefully: "I am the Minister of damn all!"

The Government of South Africa has, for many years, not been serious about environmental management. To be blunt, most Ministers, and certainly every State President so far, has simply not understood the situation. They have been short-term thinkers, more concerned (until very recently) with winning the next election than with the long-term survival of South Africa.

As I write, the President's Council is collecting evidence so that it can recommend a new approach to environmental management in South Africa. Although the council, as presently constituted, may not last much longer, at least it is doing some useful spade work which will be there for the new style government.

Is there likely to be any better understanding in the "new South Africa" than there is in the present set up? In fact all three main players among the black political and labour fronts have given assurances regarding environmental awareness. The African National Congress, almost from the time its political gag was removed, has given assurances that it recognises the importance of sustaining all that is good and beautiful in South Africa and that it hears what is being said internationally regarding each country's global responsibilities. Inkatha too has long had an environmental ethic and the trade union movement is also taking a closer interest in the environment generally and, very belatedly, it is looking more questioningly at workplace environments.

Max Sisulu, introduced at a workshop at the University of the Witwatersrand on 3 November 1990 as "an environmental spokesman for the ANC", said:

The ANC is committed to conservation and the rational use

> *of our natural resources for the benefit of the present and future generations ... It is also the ANC's position that in the planning and implementing of an economic growth programme a correct strategy is to maintain a healthy balance between economic and social benefits on the one hand, and environmental protection on the other.*

He emphasised three key elements: protection of environment including fauna, flora, rare species, natural resources; development ("engineering works to enhance the environment and the use of natural resources"), and environmental management. He suggested "deterrent surcharges for those concerns whose activities pollute" which would be used "to compensate those communities adversely affected and to pay the cost of rehabilitation." He was in favour of encouraging the search for alternative energy sources (eg: solar). His document was a lengthy one and very comprehensive and maybe idealistic – but it was the first time any major political power in South Africa had spelled out such a hard and fast and comprehensive green manifesto.

I was interested to see how apparently committed he, and his co-presenter, Stan Shangweni (who actually read the document), were to wildlife preservation. Albie Sachs, in an ANC address at Broederstroom in August 1990, had spoken of the need "to make conservation a constitutional principle":

> *It might appear irreverent to speak of the Maluti mountains and the rolling bushveld when blood is being spilt in our roadways; it would seem inappropriate to lament chimney pollution when the air is thick with teargas ... There are strong arguments against putting the theme of environmental rights on the already crowded agenda of struggle.*

But put it he did – in 12 pages of fine type. He championed not "animal rights" or the "right" of nature to exist – "the interests we protect are our own rights to live in a clean and safe world in harmony with nature."

The question is how? How can one reconcile nature conservation, or even scenic preservation and built-heritage preservation when commercial and industrial greed (which is not the prerogative of any one race group) is sometimes so rampant and pitiless? The 1990 inquiry into this question by the President's Council was told by many offering evidence that South Africa needs a statutory environmental agency with an holistic view and Cabinet status – along the lines of the American EPA. Britain, in 1991, moved a step closer to having an EPA when it altered the status of its Inspectorate of Pollution (which monitors and polices air, soil and water) to make it an executive body. The inspectorate was relieved of day-to-day control by the Department of Environment.

South Africa's Council for the Environment, a body of 22 people appointed by the Minister of Environment Affairs because of their special knowledge, has recommended an EPA. It called for a centralised body empowered to formulate policy and to see that it is carried out. It also strongly urged "integrated environmental management" (IEM) which is a relatively new concept. IEM, in a nutshell, entails considering, at the planning stage, all the environmental impacts which are likely to be encountered with a project from the time the excavations begin to the time the structure is dismantled. An EIA (environmental impact analysis), once the holy grail sought by the environmental lobby, is part of the IEM process. An EIA, in itself, is an essential exercise and should long ago have been made compulsory for all major projects. It entails a developer analysing all the possible side effects of his project, good and bad, and then publishing them for public scrutiny before venturing into the final drawings stage. Ideally, an EIA should reveal what alternatives the developer looked at and why he chose the course or site in question. In the case of a highway, for instance, he would have to show what alternative routes were studied and why they were rejected. The public is then able to study the report, or call in its own experts who might well be able to constructively show the developer how he overlooked some vital side effect which can then be addressed.

In 1979 Eric Hall, then city engineer of Johannesburg, pulled together a committee of five (of which I was one) to thrash out guidelines on EIAs which, hopefully, the Government could be persuaded to write into legislation. A member of the committee was Denis Cowen, a former professor of law at Chicago and Cape Town and, at that time, legal adviser to Johannesburg City Council. He suggested that, at first, it would be enough for the Government simply to compel developers to publish an EIA for each major project. Then, if the public felt the developer had not done his homework – let's say he had not addressed the problem of noise pollution – the public would have a legal right to demand he went into this aspect. Should the developer refuse, the public could take him to court for not complying with the law. The court could then force him to do a fuller impact assessment. But once the developer had met this requirement he could then go ahead with the project – even if the public was outraged by its anticipated impacts. We felt it unlikely a developer would go ahead with a project knowing the public was outraged and we also wanted to avoid the situation American environmental legislation had created where, as somebody said, "an old lady in tennis shoes, with nothing to lose, could hold up a crucial project on frivolous grounds". It also seemed prudent not to ask too much of the Government initially. As it was the Government, while, including the principle of EIAs in its White Paper of 1980, stopped short of making them compulsory. The Minister assured me that the Government itself would set an example by doing EIAs on all its projects. It never did. It made some clumsy attempts but it clearly did not understand the concept. It would announce a development and then offer reasons why the site was good and why the project was necessary and what it was doing to save the animals and plants. To this day it has not advanced much beyond that. And there is nobody to see that it does.

An environmental protection agency would be responsible for a dynamic environmental policy embracing the entire environmental spectrum. For example, it would breathe down the Department of Agriculture's neck with respect to soil erosion measures; it would lay down standards for water quality and would ensure the Department of Water Affairs, the Department of National Health and the various regional water authorities and municipalities complied with them; it would be responsible for air quality via the Department of National Health and so on.

The Council for the Environment suggests that an environmental protection agency would delegate such things as land use control and the conservation of nature to the second tier of Government. This is fair enough: it would be a tragedy if bodies such as the Natal Parks Board, which has an international reputation for successful and innovative wildlife conservation, were to lose its autonomy, and land use should always be a regional rather than a national matter.

The EPA (in the view of the Council for the Environment) should also be responsible for guidelines for physical planning; environmental management plans; IEM; utilisation of environmental resources, services such as environmental law and administration, economics and finance; environmental education, research and monitoring.

Back to earth

The bewildering speed of change since the reform process began in South Africa in February 1990 has masked many environmental triumphs. There is now much more public participation in planning at local level, although it is still clumsy (neither side is used to it yet) and there is a strong trend by industry and commerce to at least appear green – and that's always a first step. Many companies are finding, to their dismay, that they cannot kid the public. Environmental education is now part of education policy (although teachers are desperately lacking knowledge) and the media are aiding the learning, or at least the awareness process. Significantly the SABC television programme, 50/50, which began by dealing only with wildlife conservation, now also looks at the built environment and, in 1990, was moved to a prime weekend viewing time. Green pressure groups at the national and local level are springing up, newsletters and good quality magazines are appearing on the broad subject of environment. What is happening in South Africa is a reflection of the worldwide movement towards a gentler approach to development. As the Cold War recedes into history, and as the enormous funds which were being squandered in maintaining a balance of terror become available for more constructive purposes, there is a trend towards wanting to repair the globe.

Personally I feel optimistic about the future on both the planetary scale and as far as our beloved end of Africa is concerned.

I believe the turning point began about 10 years after astronaut Frank Borman wrote the words I have used in my preface. After many years, and many billions of dollars had been spent on exploring space, we began to realise there was only one beautiful and inhabitable planet – our own planet Earth.

To paraphrase Joel Chandler Harris's Uncle Remus: "I journeyed fur, I journeyed fas'; I glad I foun' dis place at las'."

Further Reading

The facts, theories and estimates in this book come from a multitude of sources, many are referred to in the text and will be easy to trace. I have some 2 000 books on environmental concerns and many papers and articles, so to save pages of bibliography it may be more useful for the general reader who wishes to pursue some subject areas further to know that I have leaned heavily on *New Scientist* magazine, which I have filed and annotated since the 1960s, and upon the files of *The Star,* a newspaper which has been telling the story of the growth, development and peculiar problems of South Africa for more than a century. *The Star's* files reflect its intense concern for the environment over the last 20 years.

I cannot recommend *New Scientist* too highly, both for the generalist and the specialist as well as for high schools. It is the liveliest environmental sciences magazine in the world.

I use *Encyclopaedia Britannica* on a day-to-day basis but can also recommend, for quick local reference, the *South African Family Encyclopaedia* (1990) published by Struik.

The following books are recommended:
On **man and his origins** and "environmental culture": all of Robert Ardrey's books including *African Genesis* (Collins, 1961), even though it is somewhat outdated; *The Dragons of Eden* by Carl Sagan (Hodder and Stoughton, 1977); *Primate Evolution* by Glenn C Conroy (Norton, 1990); *Origins* by Richard Leaky (Macdonald and Jane's, 1977); *Southern Land* by A R Wilcox (Purnell, 1976) is good for basic South African material as well as *Footprints* by the same author (Drakensberg, 1988); *Lucy, the Beginnings of Humankind* by Donald Johanson (Simon and Schuster, 1981); Phillip Tobias's article "The Last Million Years in Southern Africa" in *An Illustrated History of South Africa* (Southern Books, 1988) plus many other of his publications (via the Institute for the Study of Man in Africa); Lynn White Jnr's essay in *Pollution and the Death of Man* by Francis A Scheaffer (AAAS, 1970); Chief Seathl's letter of 1855 (which he almost certainly did not write but which

encompasses the ecological emotions of the redman) in *Voices in the Wilderness,* edited by Ian Player (Jonathan Ball, 1979).

On the **atmosphere** (including climate, etc): there are several useful primers such as John Gribbin's *The Hole in the Sky* (Corgi, 1988) and *Hothouse Earth* (Bantam, 1990); there is John Earl's useful little book on South Africa's weather and climate - *The Weather* (Struik, 1990); Earl's geography book (written with others) - *New Window on the World* (Juta, 1989) - is an absolute must for matric teachers involved in teaching broadspectrum enviro/geography. Peter Tyson's book *Climatic Change and Variation in Southern Africa* (Oxford, 1986) is recommended for students.

On **water**: the Department of Water Affairs book entitled *The Management of Water Resources* (Government Printer, 1988) and Douglas Hey's *Water and Wildlife* (Timmins, 1986) are recommended.

Soil: sadly there is not much for the layman.

Wildlife: there are books too numerous to mention here. For a straightforward, quick reference book on mammals in South Africa I use *Maberly's Mammals of Southern Africa* by Richard Goss (Delta, 1986).

Population: Paul Ehrlich's *The Population Bomb* (Ballantine, 1971) is useful in its historical context and his many subsequent books are important, *Extinction* (Gollancz, 1982) is particularly stimulating. **Aids:** the Panos Institute's journal published in London is a vital source, as is André Spier's *Coping with Aids* (Syncom, 1991). *New Scientist* misses very little in the field of Aids on a week to week basis.

Urban development: A quite brilliant and most important book is Kirkpatrick Sale's *Human Scale* (Secker and Warburg, 1980). There is *Defensible Space* by Oscar Newman (Architectural Press, 1972). I use Nigel Mandy's *A City Divided, Johannesburg and Soweto* (Macmillan, 1984) as a frequent reference for urban development in South Africa and can also recommend Richard Tomlinson's *Urbanisation in Post-apartheid South Africa* (Unwin Hyman, 1990). I find *Urban Outlook,* a fortnightly bulletin (New York) essential reading. I especially recommend Jane Jacobs's *The Economy of Cities* (Vintage, 1970) and *The Death and Life of Great American Cities* (Peregrine, 1984), and in fact anything she has written.

On the **South African environment**, the most important

book is *Environmental Concerns in South Africa* by R F Fuggle and M A Rabie (Juta, 1983); then comes *South African Environments into the 21st Century* by Brian Huntley, Roy Siegfried and Clem Sunter (Human and Rousseau, 1989). On the **global environment** most readers will find Anne and Paul Ehrlich's *Earth* (Thames Methuen, 1987) enjoyable. Essential reading is *Our Common Future* by the World Commission on Environment and Development (Oxford, 1987). For the business executive I recommend *Business and the Environment* by Georg Winter (McGraw Hill, 1987). A very important book is Wes Jackson's *Man and the Environment* (William C Brown, 1971) for its brilliant collection of essays and *The Human Impact* by Andrew Goudie (Oxford, 1981).

Last but by no means least, The Worldwatch Institute (1176 Massachusetts Avenue, NW Washington DC, 20036, USA) produces (at a price of $3), a regular and quite comprehensive specialist paper dedicated to a specific environmental issue. For the layman and journalist they are excellent.

Index

Acid   26, 28, 129
Acid rain   36, 37, 38, 129
Acocks, J   181, 182, 187
Addo Elephant National Park   231, 228
Adriatic Sea   144
AECI   61, 64, 110, 131, 238, 306, 313
Aerosols   61, 64, 87, 138
Afforestation   106
African National Congress   223, 317, 318
Agribiz   210, 211
Agriculture   9, 35, 52, 135, 155, 159, 167, 192, 193, 197, 205, 206, 207, 214, 231
AIDS   170, 242-5, 247, 249, 256, 257, 259
Air   15, 16
Air conditioning   42, 64, 69, 70
Air pollution   15-95, 127, 128, 129, 135, 139, 284
Airborne Arctic Stratospheric Expedition   63
Alaskan landbridge   5
Aldicarb   204
Aldrin   202
Alfafa   211
Algae   130, 131, 132, 144
Alimentary tract   80
Aliwal North   190
Aluminium   303
Amanzimtoti   148
Amatole Mountains   173
Amazon   67, 167, 168, 169, 170
American Lung Association   37, 82
Ammonium sulphate   87
Amsterdam   261
Anchovette   137, 142
Anchovy   140, 141
Angola   239
Antarctic   51, 52, 56, 61, 62, 119, 138, 200
Apartheid   291
Ape Man   161
Aral Sea   122
Architecture   69, 269, 275, 276
Arctic   61
Asbestos   44, 45
Ash   32, 34, 72, 87

Asia   159, 251
Association of Scientific and Technical Societies   86
Asthma   82
Aswan Dam   117
Athens   24, 37, 79
Atlantic Ocean   98
Atmosphere   15-95, 127
Atmospheric Pollution Prevention Act   91, 127
Atomic Energy Council   75
Australasia   169
Australia   25, 59, 309

Baboons   161
Baltic   144
Bangladesh   56
baTonga   118
Beaches   148, 232
Begg, G   191
Belgium   141
Benguela Current   98
Benzine Hexachloride (BHC)   204, 206, 207, 208
Berge, C   269, 287
Betty's Bay   50
Bible   11, 12
Bilharzia   118
Binational parks   228
Biodiversity   236, 237
Biomass   71
Biotechnology   249, 250
Bird, Flo   268, 269
Birds   215, 226, 231, 246
Birmingham   81, 88
Birth control   247
Birth rate   248, 251, 316
Birth to 10 programme   18, 34
Bloemfontein   188
Bloemhof Dam   106
Blooms in dams   129
Blue buck   216
Blyde River Canyon   171
Blyvooruitsig   133
Bobbins   139
Boicides   144, 201, 208
Bontebok   240
Bontebok National Park   228
Bophuthatswana   158, 193, 204, 216, 221, 229
Boreholes   111, 133, 134
Botswana   116, 209, 228, 232
Bottles   296, 298, 299, 300, 308
Boy Scouts   272
Braamfontein Spruit   271
Brazil   67, 169, 295, 315

Brazilia   315
Britain   17, 21, 22, 24, 28, 37, 38, 41, 42, 61, 74, 82, 91, 132, 141, 143, 210, 223, 246, 254, 257, 261, 303, 307, 311
British Lung Foundation   37, 82
British Steel   88
Bronchitis   82
Buffalo   232, 241
Buffels River   176, 177
Bullet train   285
Bureau of Ecological Standards (BEST)   196
Bureau of Natural Resources   186
Bush encroachment   162
Bushmen   98
Bushveld   234
Buthelezi, Mangosuthu   193, 194
Butterflies   215, 236

Cadmium   126, 144
Calcutta   132
California   46, 68, 70, 71, 83, 311, 312
Californian Conservation Corps   180
Canada   21, 28, 38, 56, 58, 59, 61, 67, 95, 129, 173, 288
Cancer   21, 42, 65, 82, 125, 289
Cancer Atlas   20
Cans   296, 298, 308
Capco   19, 91, 92
Cape   55, 71, 98, 107, 119, 146, 148, 159, 164, 180, 231, 237, 241
Cape Agulhas   141, 145
Cape hunting dog   215
Cape lion   217
Cape Peninsula   150, 232
Cape Town   27, 32, 56, 68, 148, 163, 243, 274, 275, 280, 306, 312, 315, 316
Car pooling   284
Carbon   26, 53, 67, 94, 139, 294
Carbon dioxide   16, 32, 48, 49, 51, 52, 53, 54, 55, 59, 67, 68, 79, 83, 86, 94, 95, 139, 170, 294, 312, 313
Carbon monoxide   78, 80, 84
CARE   145, 271, 296, 297
Caribbean   257
Carlton Centre   69, 278
Cars   37, 43, 58, 76, 78-84, 148, 264, 265, 266, 277, 279, 280, 282, 283, 284, 286, 287, 288, 290, 291, 312
Carson, R   200, 201, 202
Caspian Sea   122
Cedarberg   163

Central Electricity Generating Board 38, 87, 129
Central nervous system 80
Cereals 249
Chamber of Commerce 278
Chamber of Mines 197, 198
Champagne Castle 192
Chapman's Peak 150
Cheetah 215
Chemical farming 211
Chemical industry 209
Chemicals 43, 57, 86, 144, 201, 202, 206, 207, 208, 211
Chernobyl 74
Children 18, 22, 44, 51, 81, 155, 243, 247, 259, 264
Chile 120, 140
Chimanimani Mountains 231
China 61, 105, 132, 133, 148, 248, 250
China syndrome 73
Chlorinated hydrocarbons 202
Chlorine 61, 62, 64
Chlorofluorocarbons (CFCs) 7, 53, 61-5, 87, 94, 138, 298, 306, 307
Chobe River 115, 116
Cholera 135
Christiana 189
CITES 239
Cities 8, 10, 134, 154, 224, 226, 252, 254, 266, 269, 270, 271, 275, 278, 282, 290, 291, 299, 316
Citrus 132
City centre 275, 279, 280
Civic Spine 280
Civil engineers 235, 267, 289
Clean Community System 295
Clean Water Act (US) 191
Cleopatra's Needle 17
Cloud seeding 134
Coal 23, 24, 27, 30, 32, 37, 39, 40, 41, 51, 58, 68, 70, 71, 74, 75, 78, 83, 112, 122, 197, 282
Coalbrook 74
Coast 3, 217
Coastal development 148, 151
Coastal forest 151
Coastal Management Advisory Programme 151
Cohen, Dr M 224, 226, 241
Colombia 192, 254, 255
Connecticut 310
Conservancies 184, 241
Conservation of Agricultural Resources Act 193
Consol 300

Coolants 64, 73
Copper 21, 126, 235, 301
Coral reefs 139, 147
Cotton 132
Council for the Environment 151, 316, 320
Co-operative instinct 2, 7
Crime 265
Crop rotation 190, 210
Crops 36, 38, 82, 98, 207, 210, 249, 250, 254
CSIR 20, 28, 36, 125
Culling 217, 229
Cyanamid 126
Cyprus 70
Czechoslovakia 18, 19, 29, 38

Dams 68, 102, 107, 117, 186, 206, 271
Dart, R 2
Davie, T B 213
DDT 200, 201, 202, 203, 209, 298
De Beers 72
Deforestation 176
Department of Agriculture 172, 197, 204, 320
Department of Economic Affairs 139
Department of the Environment 151, 171, 172, 224, 226, 234, 239, 241, 319
Department of Forestry 192, 197, 241
Department of Health 20, 21, 28, 30, 33, 92, 93, 126, 289, 320
Department of Transport 78, 235, 280, 288, 290
Department of Water Affairs 106, 108, 111, 118, 120, 122, 126, 128, 320
Desalination 115, 134
Desert Encroachment Committee 188
Desertification 155, 167, 176-97
Deserts 54, 248, 249
Desulphurisation 37, 39, 40
Detergents 127
Detroit 273
Development Bank 257
Diamonds 72, 102, 163
Diazinon 204
Dieldrin 202, 203, 209
Difacane 252
Dinosaurs 238
Docklands 280
Dodo 5

Dolomite 111
Dolphins 144, 147, 215
Drakensberg 25, 68, 100, 111, 191, 192
Drought 108, 109, 110, 111, 112, 115, 116, 131, 134, 185
Dry-cooling 111
Du Pont 87
Du Toits Kloof Pass 235
Durban 56, 75, 124, 126, 148, 255, 280, 315
Dust 25, 34, 93
Duvha 29

Earth Resources Technology Satellite 157, 181
Earthlife Africa 124, 126, 208, 305
Education 173, 190
Egypt 17
Eland 215, 232
Elands River 89, 127
Electricity 32, 33, 71, 112, 311
Electronics 287
Electrostatic precipitators 34
Elephant 147, 213, 214, 215, 216, 222, 232, 239, 241
Eloff Street 276, 278
Emphysema 75
Endangered Wildlife Trust 221, 232, 238
Environmental Conservation Act 150, 151, 287, 356
Environmental education 321
Environmental impact assessments (EIA) 69, 150, 173, 235, 319, 320
Environmental Protection Agency (EPA) 34, 87, 93, 117, 125, 203, 304, 319, 320
Erosion 100, 155, 156, 157, 185, 189
Eskimos 202
Eskom 32, 33, 34, 37, 39, 41, 68, 70, 71, 72, 87, 197, 235, 236, 238
Ethanol 71
Eucalyptus 171, 174, 233
European Community 303, 305
Eutrophication 129, 131, 143, 144
Evaporation 55, 102, 103, 107, 111
Exxon Valdez 145, 146

False Bay 141, 232
Far East 37, 121, 226, 239
Farming 52, 116, 147, 165
Fearnside, Prof P 67, 167, 168
Fenitrothion 204

Fertilizer   38, 87, 132, 143, 186, 194, 210, 211, 249, 313
Finland   38
Fire   161, 162, 163, 164, 169, 172
Fish   65, 118, 122, 127, 130, 132, 139, 146, 148, 237, 307, 310
Fish farming   148
Fish Hoek   141
Fish River   118
Fishing industry   7, 136-48
Flavin, C   57, 58, 94
Flight distance   5
Floods   107, 108, 176, 186
Floral kingdoms   233
Foam plastic   307
Foetal damage   83
Food   51, 172, 191
Food and Agricultural Organisation (FAO)   118, 165, 166, 169
Food wastes   303
Forestry   35, 36, 106, 172, 218, 233
Forests   28, 67, 110, 148, 154, 155, 163, 165, 176, 228
Formaldehyde   43
Foundation for Research Development   92
France   74
Fuggle, Prof R   99, 116, 135, 197
Fungicides   203
Fynbos   148, 228

Gaia   53
Game fishing   232
Game ranching   184
Game reserves   221, 224
Gandoupas   232
Garden of Eden   171
Garland, Dr G   185, 186, 192
Gaza Strip   157
Gencor   45
Genetic engineering   249
Germany   18, 19, 28, 29, 45, 51, 55, 74, 82, 119, 125, 141, 203, 209, 273, 293, 299, 303
Germiston Lake   123
Giraffe   214, 215
Glass   303, 305, 309
Global warming   48
Goddard Institute of Space Studies   48
Gold   41, 64, 121, 124, 133, 163, 198
Graaff-Reinet   177, 181
Grand Apartheid   193
Grande Carajas Development Programme   168
Granite   21

Grasslands   54
Grazing   207
Great Drought   108, 109, 110, 111, 112, 115
Great Lakes   121
Great Plains   105, 213
Green revolution   249
Greenhouse effect   47-59, 65, 72, 76, 79, 94, 251
Greenpeace   126, 203
Greens, The   14
Gribbin, J   48, 53, 55, 62, 65
Grobler, H   241
Grootdraai Dam   108
Ground water   133
GROW   255
Guys Hospital   23

Hair spray   46
Haiti   259
Hammanskraal   126
Hanks, John   240
Hardin, G   6
Hardwoods   67, 170
Harris, W Cornwallis   163, 227
Harrismith   111
Hartebeespoort Dam   72, 102, 116, 130, 218
Hartz River Valley   105
Hawaii   48, 97
Health   18, 19, 20, 21, 23, 24, 25, 29, 34, 42-6, 61, 79, 80, 82, 90, 92, 125, 126, 200, 211, 224, 243, 244, 245, 252, 256, 264, 288, 289, 316
Hendrik Verwoerd Dam   101, 103, 111, 118, 187
Heptachlor   202
Herbicides   173, 203, 208
Heyerdahl, T   137, 307
Highveld   18, 19, 20, 28, 32, 34, 35, 37, 38, 56, 72, 75, 106, 109, 135, 148, 161, 183, 197
Hiking trails   173, 217, 218, 228, 271
Hillbrow   155, 271
Hiroshima   73
HIV   244, 256, 258
Hluhluwe River   234
HL&H Mining Timber   173
Holland   125, 265
Homelands   228
Homo sapiens   3, 5
Hong Kong   305
Hormone herbicide   208
Hottentots Holland   98, 164, 232, 233

Housing   251
Hout Bay   163
Howick Falls   234
Human scale   268, 273
Humidifier fever   43
Hunting   227
Hunting instinct   2, 5, 12
Huntley, B   37, 102, 186, 194, 236, 238, 242, 243, 244, 255
Hydrapulper   302
Hydro power   68
Hydrocarbons   37, 78, 80, 82
Hydrochloroflurocarbons   64
Hydrofluorocarbons   64
Hydrogen sulphide   33, 88
Hydroponics   254
Hydropower   68, 107
Hydro-electric   117
Hydro-electricity   107, 112
Hyena   215
Hysteria   43, 86

Ice age   55, 76, 185
Iceberg   120
Ichthyology, J L B Smith Institute of   215
Imperial Chemical Industries   88
India   61, 94
Indian Ocean   56, 98
Indonesia   169
Indus River Valley   176
Industrial Revolution   52, 65, 261
Industrial waste   125
Industry   14, 18, 28, 29, 30, 32, 37, 49, 54, 59, 67, 73, 74, 75, 79, 88, 90, 91, 92, 93, 105, 106, 125, 126, 127, 144, 145, 146
Influx control   291
Informal public transport   280
Insecticides   200, 203, 204
Insects   200
Integrated Environmental Management (IEM)   198, 319, 321
International law   59
International parks   231, 232
International Union for the Conservation of Nature and Natural Resources (IUCN)   37, 223, 224, 228, 240
Iowa   211
Iron Age   18, 161
Irrigation   97, 105, 106, 119, 121, 132, 133, 249
Iscor   88
Israel   70, 119, 134, 154

Ivory 147, 239

Jackal 215
Jackass penguins 141, 240
Japan 39, 59, 83, 132, 139, 144, 146, 169, 254, 284, 310
Jericho 9, 11, 176
Jewish National Fund 67, 179
Johannesburg 18, 21, 34, 42, 69, 71, 79, 80, 86, 109, 110, 111, 124, 161, 183, 218, 235, 244, 247, 255, 261, 264, 268, 271, 273, 274, 276, 277, 278, 279, 280, 283, 284, 286, 287, 289, 295, 303, 304, 312, 315, 316
Johannesburg Central Business District Association (CBDA) 277, 278, 280
Johannesburg Children's Hospital 81
Johannesburg General Hospital 269
Johannesburg Zoo 155
Jonkershoek 98
Jordan 70
Jozini Dam 118

Kalahari Desert 228, 249
Kalahari Gemsbok National Park 219, 232
Kangwana National Park 229
Kaolin 150
Kariba Dam 102
Karoo 55, 56, 89, 133, 163, 174, 176, 177, 178, 179, 180, 181, 183, 187, 188, 189, 206, 219
Karoo National Park 217, 231
Kauai 97, 98
Kimberley 63, 69
Klip Spruit 272
Klipriviersberg 226
Klipspruit sewage works 313
Knysna 164, 171
Koch, E 44, 124, 203
Koeberg 27, 72, 75, 108
Kori Bustard 215
Kotze, G 141, 150, 151, 317
Krill 137
Kruger National Park 70, 89, 106, 107, 135, 162, 174, 216, 217, 219, 220, 221, 223, 227, 228, 231, 232, 234, 235, 238
Kruger, Paul 226, 227
Kuruman 45
KwaZulu 192, 193, 226, 230, 231, 241

Laingsburg 176
Lake Sibaya 129
Lakes 128, 129
Land Act 196
Land Bank 211
Landfills 53, 132, 311
Latin America 165
Law 46, 59, 91, 135, 142, 146, 147, 165, 288, 294, 295, 315, 319, 320, 321
Lead 21, 80, 81, 90
Leatherback turtle 215
Lebowa 44, 157
Ledger, Dr J 232, 236
Legionaire's disease 43
Lekgetho, J 272
Lesotho 100, 102, 111, 112, 192, 232
Lesotho Highlands Scheme 102, 112, 135
Leukaemia 42, 236
Liebensbergvlei River 112
Limpopo River 115, 231
Linksfield Ridge 235
Lions 215, 217
Litter 266, 295, 296, 297, 308
Livestock 21, 65, 98, 130, 153, 180-1, 184, 187, 194, 195, 196, 210, 235, 307
Locusts 205, 206, 207
Logging 169
London 22, 23, 26, 28, 40, 56, 61, 80, 81, 261, 263, 267, 276, 283, 284, 290, 291
Los Angeles 20, 24, 78
Loskop 218
Lower Sabie River 107, 228
Lowveld 231
Lunos 25, 28, 37, 42, 80, 87, 89

Mafikeng 189
Magaliesberg 183, 204, 218, 226, 300
Maize 37, 56, 155, 186, 193, 197, 211, 250
Makatini Flats 118
Malaria 200
Malawi 298
Maldive Islands 56
Mallows, W 9, 252, 254, 261, 262
Malls 279
Malnutrition 195
Mammals 215, 226, 229
Mandy, N 277, 278, 280
Maputo 231
Marxism 222

Mauna Loa 48
Mauritius 139, 295
Medical Research Council 18, 34, 42, 65, 243, 244
Megalopolises 261
Melanoma 65
Mellanby, K 51, 53, 58
Mercury 126, 144
Mesothelioma 44
Metal 305, 308
Methane 53, 65, 86, 130, 311, 312, 313
Mexico 24, 84, 255
Middelburg 29
Midgley, D 32, 55, 98, 100, 106, 187
Midmar Dam 102
Minamata disease 144, 145
Mine dumps 124, 198
Mine waste 294
Mining 64, 102, 106, 121, 124, 133, 163, 197, 198
Minniapolis 276
Mkuzi Game Reserve 230
Mkuzi River 234
Mkuzi Valley 165
Mmafafe school 44
Moa 5, 153
Mobay Corporation 203
Modder River 100
Modderfontein 131
Mole snakes 237
Mondi 173, 238, 309
Monks Wood Experimental Station 51
Monocultures 210
Montreal 61
Montreal protocol 7, 61
Moshav 180
Mosquitoes 200, 201, 209
Mossel Bay 148
Motorways 81, 224, 235, 287, 288, 289, 290
Mozambique 107, 174, 227, 231, 232

Namaqualand 233
Namib Desert 249
Namibia 72, 98, 139, 232
Narina 228
Nasa 62
Natal 3, 98, 107, 112, 165, 173, 214, 216, 219, 220, 221, 240
Natal Parks Board 192, 216, 229, 230, 240, 241, 320
National Monuments Council 269

Index

National Parks Act 198, 219, 220
National Parks Board 179
National Party 139, 219, 220, 223, 226
National Veld Trust 100, 101, 134, 190
National water grid 111, 112
Natural gas 74
Natural Resources Board 229
Navajo 252
Ndumu Game Reserve 150, 231
New Obsidian 9, 11
New South Africa 223, 317
New York 80, 273
New Zealand 153, 154, 299
Newcastle 23
Newsprint 296, 309, 310
Ngodwana paper mill 89
Nigeria 192
Nile River 105
Nitric acid 37
Nitrogen 16, 48, 131, 186, 211
Nitrogen dioxide 52
Nitrogen fertilizer 207
Nitrogen oxides 37, 78, 82, 83
Nitrous oxide 53, 65
Noise 266, 276, 278, 279, 287-90, 319
Non-government organisation (ngo) 238, 240, 254
North Atlantic 137
North Sea 132
North Sea gas 24
Norway 141
Nuclear power 21, 27, 41, 71, 72, 73, 74, 75, 76
Nuclear waste 76
Nylstroom 20

Oceanographic Research Institute 139
Office parks 286
Ohio 28, 128
Oil 27, 58, 59, 71, 74, 80, 122, 137, 145, 146, 282, 300, 311
Okavango Delta 115, 209, 231, 239
Okavango River 115
Operation Hunger 195
Orange Free State 19, 25, 37, 56, 122
Orange River 98, 100, 101, 102, 109, 111, 112, 118, 141, 187, 190, 219
Orange River Project 103
Otter Trail 217, 228
Overgrazing 157
Overkill 3, 4, 12, 106, 144, 164, 168, 210

Oxygen 48, 61, 127, 139, 170, 294
Ozone 53, 57, 58, 60-5, 82, 138, 306, 312
Ozone holes 57

P K le Roux Dam 117
Pacific islands 154
Pacific Ocean 147, 307
Packaging 64, 296, 298, 307
Packaging industry 238, 296, 298, 307
Palaborwa Mining 234
Palmer, E 163, 164
Palmiet River 68
Panama 168
Panos Institute 195, 259
Paper 303, 309
Paper mill 128
Paper packaging 307
Papua-New Guinea 25
Paris 273, 276
Parktown 264, 268, 286
Parthenon 17, 79
Pedestrians 273, 277, 279
Percy Fitzpatrick Institute for African Ornithology 146
Perlman, I 195, 196
Peru 120, 137, 142, 192
Pesticide 203, 210, 249
Petroglyphs 18
Peurto Rican trench 137
Phalaborwa 21, 22, 23
Phenol compounds 126
Philippines 192
Phosphate 132
Phosphorus 186
Photochemical smog 20, 79, 82
Photosynthesis 138
Pienaars River 125
Pilanesberg National Park 216, 229
Pines 233, 234
Plankton 65, 138, 139, 146, 200, 201
Plants 16, 67, 157, 184, 215, 232, 236, 249
Plastic 64, 146, 147, 296, 301, 303, 305, 306, 308
Platinum 82
Platinum exhaust filters 80, 82
Player, I 11, 230, 231, 238
Pleistocene overkill 4
Plutonium 76
Pneumonia 82
Poisons 209

Poland 18, 29
Polar caps 54, 56, 61
Polluter Pays Principle 127
Polychlorinated biphenyls 144
Polystyrene 64, 307
Pongola Game Reserve 226
Pongola River 118
Population 115, 135, 243-59, 291
Population explosion 246
Port Elizabeth 125, 148
Potassium 186
Power stations 27, 32, 37, 40, 41, 49, 58, 68, 71, 74, 75, 97, 108, 129
Prairies 56, 251
Precambrian Research Unit 72
President's Council 89, 317, 318
Pretoria 23, 42, 69, 79, 84, 133, 163, 261, 268, 275, 287, 303
Primary health care 252, 316
Prince Alfred 227
Proteas 233
Public transport 282, 283, 284, 285, 291
Pulp Wood 67
Pumped storage schemes 69
Pylons 235
Pyramids 18
Pyrolosis 311

Quagga 214, 216, 217
Quelea finch 205

Rabie, A 30, 92, 99, 135, 189, 197, 299
Radiation 75
Radioactive Waste 76
Radioactivity 41, 74, 86
Radon 41, 42
Rain forests 164, 166, 167, 170
Rainfall 97, 98, 134, 153, 157, 188, 193, 271, 294
Ramsar wetlands conservation agreement 114
Ramsgate 149
Rand Airport 79
Rand Carbide 89
Randburg 271, 288, 295, 304, 310
Recycling 120, 294, 299, 304, 308, 309
Refrigerants 138
Refrigerators 64
Religion 12, 13
Reunion 98
Rhine River 119
Rhino 216, 221, 229, 230, 236, 239, 240, 241

Rhino horn   147, 239
Rice   132, 231, 232
Richards Bay Minerals   115, 150, 220, 234
Richlab   40
Richtersveld   219
Rio de Janeiro   282, 315, 316
Rio Tinto Zinc (RTZ)   149, 150, 234
River Rangers   272
River trails   218, 271
Roan antelope   240
Robberg Peninsula   150
Robertson, T C   100, 101, 134, 180, 181, 182, 186, 187, 189, 193, 194, 196
Robinson Deep   303, 305, 313
Rome   37, 79, 261, 269, 273, 276
Roodepoort   310
Rossing   72
Rubber   303, 310, 311
Ruhr Valley   29, 127, 128
Rural Foundation   179
Russia   49, 56, 59, 74, 81, 121, 122, 141, 184, 190

SABC   244, 321
Sabi Sabi   214, 222, 227
Sabie River   227
Sahara Desert   155, 248
Sahel   155, 248
Saldanha Bay   219
Sale, K   209, 210, 267
Salinisation   131
Salt   120, 122
Samancor   90
Sandton   161, 271, 272, 288
Sappi   89, 127, 173, 191
SARCCUS   231
Sardines (pilchard)   3, 139, 140, 141
Sasol   33, 80, 88
Sasolburg   19, 22
Satellite images   158
Saudi Arabia   59, 97
Scandinavia   38, 39, 129, 310
Schon, Peter   170, 173
Schonland Research Centre for Nuclear Sciences   30
Sea   54, 56, 67, 97, 100, 115, 134, 136-51, 307
Seagulls   237
Seals   144, 146, 147, 220
Seathl, Chief   12
Seattle   132, 288
Secunda   33
Security   263, 265, 278, 279

Selenium   38
Seoul   282
Sewage   143, 144, 147
Sewage works   129, 130, 132
Shaka   226
Shell   208
Shellfish   144, 147
Shopping centres   279
Shrew   215
Sick building syndrome   42, 43
Siegfried, R   37, 194, 242, 255
Simonstown   139
Sinkholes   111
Six Day War   157
Skukuza   228
Skyscrapers   266
Sludge   132
Smog   20, 22, 23, 24, 26, 40, 78, 79, 82
Smoke   26, 34, 40, 57, 71, 93, 129
Smokeless fuel   41
Sofala   211
Soil   10, 16, 132, 153-98, 202, 210, 211, 250
Soil Conservation Act   127, 187
Solar power   70
Solar radiation   75
Solid Waste Office   302
Solvents   138
South African Breweries   238
South African Bureau of Standards   126, 135
South African Institute of Ecologists   206
South African Nature Foundation (SANF)   229, 240
South Coast   149, 214
Soweto   18, 20, 34, 39, 40, 45, 110, 247, 262, 263, 272, 273, 282, 283, 291
Soybeans   211
Space   16, 53
Species diversity   224
Sphynx   18
Spier, A   178, 245, 258
Springbok   213
Springs   20
Squatters   251
SS *Knopivic*   137
St Bartholomew's Hospital   23
St Lucia   114, 149, 150, 155, 170, 220, 231, 234, 236
Standerton   37, 108, 121
Statue of Liberty   18
Steady state universe   261
Steel   303, 308

Steppes   213
Sterkfontein Dam   69, 111
Statosphere   62
Streams   271
Streets   264, 265, 271, 273, 275, 276, 277, 279
Suburbia   69, 264, 286, 287, 290
Sugar cane   71, 191, 193, 208
Suikerbosrand   218, 226
Sulphur   28, 29, 30, 35, 36, 38, 39, 128, 129, 294
Sulphur dioxide   26, 28, 30, 32, 33, 37, 38, 41, 48, 82, 86, 87
Sulphuric acid   37
Sundays River   112
Sunflower   197
Sunter, C   37, 194, 242, 255
Supertree   170, 174
Swaziland   229
Switzerland   18, 74, 125, 294
Syncom   178
Syria   155

Taaibos   74
Table Bay   163
Taiwan   40, 132, 139, 146, 220, 305
Taj Mahal   18
Tanzania   195
Tembe National Park   231
Termites   52
Thalidomide   207
Thatch   221
The Star   21, 28, 42, 44, 88, 106, 108, 109, 124, 125, 126, 145, 204, 268, 271, 296, 297
Thor Chemicals   126
Threatened species   240
Three Mile Island   73, 74
Timber   35, 67, 209
Timber industry   170-4
Tobacco smoke   43
Toilets   117
Tokuthion   203
Tokyo   24, 276
Toronto   58, 94, 95, 279
Total dissolved solids   121
Tourism   107, 135, 148, 173, 217, 222, 228, 234, 238
Town planners   267
Townships Board   268, 286
Toxic gases   43
Traffic   79, 264, 265, 273, 275, 279, 280, 282, 283, 284, 287, 290, 291
Tragedy of the commons   6, 120, 137, 156
Transkei   164, 186, 193

Index

Transport 49, 58
Transportation 49
Transvaal 18, 19, 20, 21, 28, 29, 32, 33, 36, 37, 38, 40, 44, 56, 68, 72, 75, 90, 92, 106, 112, 121, 124, 125, 127, 129, 133, 135, 140, 161, 163, 188, 189, 191, 204, 218, 231, 233, 252, 261, 268, 282
Transvaal Chamber of Industries 86
Transvaal Escarpment 98, 107
Transvaal Provincial Council 269
Transvaal Republic 226
Transvaal Rubber Company 234
Tree r ings 99
Trees 36, 66-76, 86, 94, 160-74
Trek netting 141
Tribal customs 12, 222
Trihalomethanes 125
Trout 148
Tsetse fly 209
Tsitsikamma Coastal National Park 171, 228
Tuberculosis 256
Tugela River 33, 100, 107, 111, 114, 191, 192, 194
Tulbagh earthquake 161
Tuna 142
Turkey 8
Turtles 147
Tuva scheme 68
Typhoid 135
Tyres 310
Tyson, P 28, 29, 55, 99, 106
Tyson report 37
Tzaneen 98

Ultraviolet radiation 63, 138
Ultraviolet rays 82
Umfolozi River 226
Umfolozi Valley 230
Umfolozi-Hluhluwe Game Reserve 230
Umlambonja River 191
Underground trains 282
Unesco 156
Union Carbide (US) 89, 90
United Nations 245, 252
United Nations Children's Fund 247
United Nations Environment and Development Congress 59
United Nations Environmental Programme (UNEP) 246
United Nations Environmental Project 84

United Nations International Panel on Climate Change (IPCC) 49
United Nations Population Fund 245
United States 20, 24, 28, 34, 38, 49, 59, 61, 64, 67, 70, 82, 84, 87, 105, 120, 132, 134, 135, 144, 156, 159, 167, 168, 182, 184, 191, 204, 210, 223, 246, 247, 251, 257, 259, 295, 302, 308, 309
United States Agency for International Development 155
United States Lung Associations 84
Uranium 72, 74, 235
Urban areas 226
Urban Foundation 291
Urbanisation 7, 154, 251, 253, 254, 261-92

Vaal Barrage 121, 122, 123, 124
Vaal Dam 69, 102, 108, 112, 124, 133
Vaal River 99, 100, 107, 108, 109, 111, 112, 123, 188, 192
Vaal Triangle 90
Vaalhartz Irrigation Scheme 102, 105, 106
Vaalputs 72, 75, 76
Valindaba 72
Venda 193
Venice 17
Vereeniging 32, 74
Von Schirnding, Dr Y 18, 19, 81
Voyager 1, 16
Vryburg 163, 189
Vulture Study Group 236
Vultures 204, 221, 235

Wafra 145
Walker, C 238
Walker Bay 142
Walvis Bay 140
Waste 76, 121, 125, 128, 131, 144, 147, 294, 295, 302, 305
Waste management 295
Water 16, 53, 54, 68, 69, 96-135, 156, 191, 249
Water Act 92, 126, 127
Water conservation 133
Water control measures 135
Water Research Commission 131, 134
Waterberg 218
Waterval Boven 89
Wattle 173

Wattled crane 240
Webster, I 26, 28, 81
Welkom 20
Western Cape Marine Conservation Society 141
Wetlands 114, 115, 173, 190, 191, 192
Whales 147, 215
Whaling 138
Whange National Park 231, 239
Wheat 132
White River 173
Wild flowers 232
Wildebeest 159, 216, 240
Wilderness 224, 230, 231, 235
Wilderness Education Trust 238
Wilderness Leadership Foundation 238
Wilderness trail 230
Wildlife, variety 214
Wildlife 182, 183, 184, 204, 213, 215, 216, 217, 221, 222, 223, 224, 227, 229, 236, 238, 240, 241
Wildlife Society 165, 218, 221, 241
Wiley, J 139, 140, 142, 150, 151
Wilge River 111, 112
Windmills 71
Witbank 19, 20, 89, 92
Witwatersrand 33, 84, 88, 102, 105, 110, 122, 124, 192, 226, 252, 272
Witwatersrand ridge 133
Witwatersrand System 161
Wolmaransstad 20
Wood 164, 221
Woodburning 71
Woodbush Forest Reserve 98, 171, 172, 234
Woodlots 173
Woonerf 266
Work camps 180
World Bank 250, 282
World Health Organisation (WHO) 65, 84, 124, 125, 126, 201, 204, 245
World War II 2, 73
Worldwatch Institute 41, 51, 55, 57, 70, 78, 105, 120, 121, 132, 139, 143, 146, 250

Xinave 231

Yellowtail 141

Zaire 166, 169, 245
Zaire Forest 163

Zaire River   68, 115
Zambezi   231
Zambezi Basin   229
Zambezi River   98, 115, 116, 135
Zambia   261
Zebra   159, 217, 240
Zero population growth (ZPG)   10, 256, 261
Zimbabwe   157, 159, 182, 195, 239, 245, 298
Zinc   126
Zoning   285
Zulu   194, 310
Zululand   107, 129, 137, 186, 195, 219

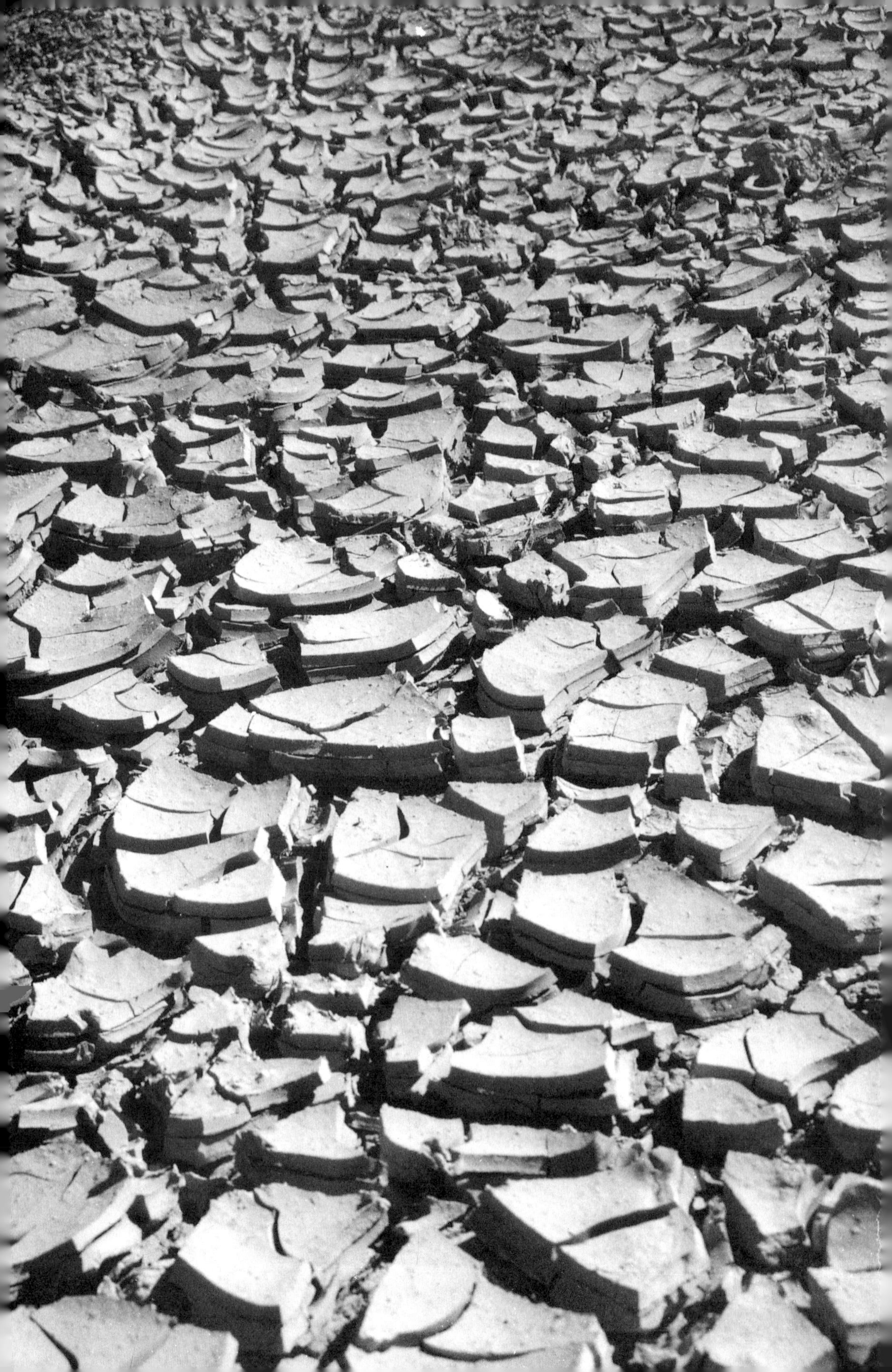